EGALITARIANISM AS A REVOLT AGAINST NATURE AND OTHER ESSAYS

SECOND EDITION

MURRAY N. ROTHBARD

Egalitarianism as a Revolt Against Nature and Other Essays

Second Edition

Murray N. Rothbard

Ludwig von Mises Institute
Auburn, Alabama

CONTENTS

INTRODUCTION TO
THE SECOND EDITION

E*galitarianism as a Revolt Against Nature* displays remarkable organic unity: the book is much more than the sum of its parts. Points made in the various essays included in the book mesh together to form a consistent worldview. The system of thought set forward in these essays, moreover, illuminates both history and the contemporary world.

In the book's initial essay, whose title has been adopted for the whole book, Murray Rothbard raises a basic challenge to schools of economics and politics that dominate the current opinion.[1] Almost everyone assumes that equality is a "good thing": even proponents of the free market like Milton Friedman join this consensus. The dispute between conservatives and radicals centers on the terms of trade between equality and efficiency.

Rothbard utterly rejects the assumption on which this argument turns. Why assume that equality is desirable? It is not enough, he contends, to advocate it as a mere aesthetic preference. Quite the contrary, equalitarians, like everyone else, need rationally to justify their ethical mandates.

But this at once raises a deeper issue. How can ethical premises be justified? How do we get beyond bare appeals to

---

[1]The essay first appeared in *Modern Age*, Fall 1973, pp. 348–57.

moral intuition? Our author answers that correct ethics must be in accord with human nature.

When egalitarianism is measured by this commonsense criterion, the results are devastating. Everywhere in nature we find inequality. Attempts to remake human beings so that everyone fits the same mold lead inevitably to tyranny. "The great fact of individual difference and variability (that is, inequality) is evident from the long record of human experience; hence the general recognition of the antihuman nature of a world of coerced uniformity" (p. 9).

Rothbard broadens and extends his criticism of equality in "Freedom, Inequality, Primitivism, and the Division of Labor."[2] Not only do biology and history make human beings inherently different from one another, but civilization depends on the existence of these differences. A developed economic system has as its linchpin the division of labor; and this, in turn, springs from the fact that human beings vary in their abilities.

Marx spoke of an end to "alienation" caused by the division of labor; but were his fantasies put into effect, civilized life would collapse. Why, then, do many intellectuals claim that the division of labor dehumanizes?

In large part, Rothbard argues, these intellectuals have fallen victim to a myth popular in the Romantic Era. The Romantics conjured up primitive men who, untouched by the division of labor, lived in harmony with nature. Rothbard will have none of this. In a few well-chosen words, he excoriates Karl Polanyi, an influential panegyrist of the primitive: "This worship of the primitive permeates Polanyi's book, which at one point seriously applies the term 'noble savage' to the Kaffirs of South Africa" (p. 323).

---

[2]First published in *Modern Age*, Summer, 1971, pp. 226–45.

In an "Introduction" dated February 1991, to a reprint of "Freedom, Inequality, Primitivism, and the Division of Labor," Rothbard refines his critique even further. He notes, following M.H. Abrams, that the Romantic myth of primitivism rests upon a yet deeper layer of myth. According to the "emanationist" view, which has influenced both neo-Platonism and gnosticism, creation is fundamentally evil. Human beings must be reabsorbed into the primitive oneness of all things. Rothbard sees this strange doctrine as "constituting a heretical and mystical underground in Western thought" (p. 297).

It is clear that Rothbard views Romanticism in decidedly negative terms, at least so far as its impact on politics is concerned. He makes clear the nefarious consequences of Romanticism in "Left and Right: The Prospects for Liberty."[3] The exaltation of the primitive, which characterizes the Romantics, by no means is confined to the Left. Quite the contrary, it underlies apologies for what Rothbard terms the "Old Order" of feudalism and militarism. Both European conservatism and socialism reject the free market. Accordingly, Rothbard argues, a task of lovers of liberty is to oppose both these ideologies.

In doing so, he maintains, libertarianism must adopt a revolutionary strategy. Not for Rothbard is the path of compromise: all statist ideologies must be combatted root-and-branch. He notes that Lord Acton, long before Leon Trotsky, advocated "permanent revolution" (p. 29). Rothbard reiterates his support for revolution in the short essay, "The Meaning of Revolution."[4]

---

[3]This essay originally appeared in *Left and Right*, Spring, 1965, pp. 4–22.

[4]The essay was first published in *The Libertarian Forum*, vol. 1, no. 7, July 1, 1969.

Society, Rothbard has argued, rests on the division of labor. Given the manifest advantages of peaceful cooperation that uses human differences in abilities to the greatest extent possible, what blocks human progress? Why has not history been an uninterrupted march of progress? Rothbard locates the chief obstacle to human betterment in his essay, "The Anatomy of the State." Unlike voluntary exchange, which by its nature benefits those who freely choose to engage in it, the state rests on predation. Following Franz Oppenheimer and Albert J. Nock, Rothbard contends that the state cannot create wealth: it can only take from some and give to others.

But does not this account raise a new problem? Given the manifestly predatory essence of the state, how has it survived? Why have not popular rebellions put an end to the triumphant beast? Our author blames "court intellectuals." Throughout history, a group of the literate elite has always been ready with a facile justification for the depredations of the powers-that-be.

As always in Rothbard, the parts of his thought fit together; and we now return to a theme posed at the beginning of this Introduction. Rothbard attacks egalitarians because they do not have a reasoned defense of their ethical judgments. But is Rothbard himself in a better position? How does he defend his libertarian brand of ethics? Supporters of freedom, he argues, in "Justice and Property Rights," should not rely principally on utilitarian arguments.[5] If they do so, Rothbard avers, they will quickly come to grief. Utilitarians may say that the free market wins out over less efficient rival systems; but a vital part of the case for

---

[5]The essay originally appeared in Samuel Blumenfeld, ed., *Property in a Humane Economy*, Open Court Publishing, 1974, pp. 101–22.

the free market finds no place in the utilitarian system. How are we to justify an initial assignment of property rights? To this, the utilitarians have no reply. In practice, Rothbard claims, they are reduced to defending the *status quo*. Readers of Rothbard's *Ethics of Liberty* will not be surprised to see what our author puts in utilitarianism's place. Only an ethics based on each person's self-ownership, along with the Lockean right to acquire initially unowned property, is adequate to the task of rigorously justifying a free-market order.

Rothbard extends his criticism of utilitarian-style ethics in the brief essay "The Fallacy of the Public Sector."[6] Many economists find justification for the state in "external benefits" that the market cannot adequately manage, but Rothbard at once sees the central fallacy in this class of argument. "[S]uffice it to say here that any argument proclaiming the right and goodness of, say, three neighbors, who yearn to form a string quartet, forcing a fourth neighbor at bayonet point to learn and play the viola, is hardly deserving of sober comment" (p. 166).

If Rothbard is right, we now know the proper way to defend liberty; and we also stand in no doubt as to our main obstacle: the Leviathan state. In "War, Peace, and the State," Rothbard narrows the target, in order to enable defenders of liberty to wage their struggle more effectively.[7] One activity marks the state more than any other as the enemy of liberty, and it is here that supporters of liberty must concentrate their efforts.

The activity, of course, is waging war. Besides the death and destruction directly incident on war, nations engaging in

---

[6]Originally in *New Individualist Review*, Summer, 1961.

[7]The essay first appeared in *The Standard*, April, 1963, pp. 2–5, 15–16.

armed conflict pay a heavy price in liberty. Accordingly, Rothbard calls for nations to engage in a strictly defensive foreign policy. Crusades to "make the world safe for democracy" stimulate our author to vigorous opposition: how can the chief agency of predation, the state, serve as a means to secure freedom?

In "National Liberation," Rothbard refuses to extend his condemnation of war to revolution.[8] Often, revolutions manifest a drive against the state and merit support. He applies his analysis to Ireland in the 1960s, with the results that deserve careful attention today.

Unfortunately for the cause of liberty, political philosophers have not rushed to embrace Rothbard's revolutionary challenge to the foundations of their discipline. One of the characteristic objections mainstream theorists have to natural-rights libertarianism goes like this: "Even if one concedes that self-ownership applies to rational adults, what is to be done with children? Surely the rights of these dependent human beings, and our duties toward them, cannot be encompassed within the confines of Rothbard's framework." Our author was well aware of this objection, and in "Kid Lib," he offers a cogent response.[9] He sensitively balances the rights of children, which increase as they become capable of exercising self-ownership, with the powers of parents to set rules for those living in their home, and supported by them.

We are, it must be admitted, a long way from the day when the conclusions of "Kid Lib" can be fully applied to current legal systems. But Rothbard was no spinner of idle

---

[8]*Libertarian Forum*, vol. 1, no. 11, September 1, 1969.

[9]The article first appeared in *Outlook*, December, 1972, pp. 8–10.

utopian fantasies: he always had in mind what can be done immediately to achieve his libertarian goals. In "Conservation in the Free Market" he shows that conservationists who are rationally inclined ought to rely on the market rather than the state.[10] Regrettably, many in the environmentalist movement have radical goals, inconsistent with the continuation of human life on earth. But those who do not should find Rothbard's case that, e.g., the market best conserves forests, of pressing interest.

Indeed, Rothbard continually alternated between elaborations of principle and applications to particular issues. In "The Great Women's Liberation Issue: Setting it Straight," Rothbard applies a principle to which we have already made frequent reference.[11] People differ in their abilities, a fact, Rothbard has abundantly shown, that egalitarians neglect to their peril. But do not men and women also differ in their abilities? The unisex dreams of radical feminists contravene nature and must be rejected.

Rothbard's own stance on the women's movement characteristically stresses freedom. "I do not go so far as the extreme male 'sexists' who contend that women should confine themselves to the home and children and that any search for alternative careers is unnatural. On the other hand, I do not see much more support for the opposite contention that domestic-type women are violating their natures" (p. 187).

Rothbard, like Nock, could speak of "our enemy the state." But it does not follow that he viewed all anarchists with sympathy. Quite the contrary, in "Anarcho-Communism"

---

[10]From *The Individualist*, February, 1970.

[11]From *The Individualist*, May, 1970.

Rothbard makes evident his distaste for anarchists who seek to combine opposition to the state with communism.[12] Often the advocates of this position straightforwardly embrace irrationalism. Norman O. Brown, e.g., thought that socialists should, in the face of Mises's proof that a socialist system cannot rationally calculate, abandon calculation.

Our author viewed with much greater tolerance lapses committed by the great individualist anarchists, Lysander Spooner and Benjamin Tucker. In "The Spooner–Tucker Doctrine: An Economist's View," he gently but firmly criticizes the monetary fallacies of these individualist pioneers.[13]

If Rothbard improved on Spooner and Tucker, his success in large part stemmed from his deft combination of individualist anarchism with Austrian economics. And of course Rothbard's knowledge of the Austrian School stemmed from his careful study of Ludwig von Mises's works, and his attendance at Mises's seminar at New York University. In "Ludwig von Mises and the Paradigm for Our Age," Rothbard pays generous tribute to his teacher.[14]

After a hard-hitting summary of Mises's main contributions to economics, Rothbard comments that "Mises, almost singlehandedly, has offered us the correct paradigm for economic theory for social science, and for the economy itself, and it is high time that this paradigm be embraced, in all of its parts" (p. 276).

Like his Marxist adversaries, Rothbard stressed the unity of theory and practice: philosophy is a guide to action. In

---

[12]*Libertarian Forum*, vol. 2, no. 1, January 1, 1970.

[13]*A Way Out*, May–July, 1965.

[14]*Modern Age*, Fall, 1971, pp. 370–79.

"Why Be Libertarian?" he asks the most basic question of all.[15] Why should libertarian theorizing matter to us? Why care about liberty? The answer cannot be found, he contends, in the narrow pursuit of individual advantage. Only the love of justice suffices. In that love of justice Rothbard was unmatched.

David Gordon
2000

---

[15]*Left and Right*, vol. 2, no. 3, Autumn, 1966.

INTRODUCTION TO THE FIRST EDITION

Probably the most common question that has been hurled at me—in some exasperation—over the years is: "Why don't you stick to economics?" For different reasons, this question has been thrown at me by fellow economists and by political thinkers and activists of many different persuasions: Conservatives, Liberals, and Libertarians who have disagreed with me over political doctrine and are annoyed that an economist should venture "outside of his discipline."

Among economists, such a question is a sad reflection of the hyperspecialization among intellectuals of the present age. I think it manifestly true that very few of even the most dedicated economic technicians began their interest in economics because they were fascinated by cost curves, indifference classes, and the rest of the paraphernalia of modern economic theory. Almost to a man, they became interested in economics because they were interested in social and political problems and because they realized that the really hard political problems cannot be solved without an understanding of economics. After all, if they were really interested mainly in equations and tangencies on graphs, they would have become professional mathematicians and not have devoted their energies to an economic theory that is, at best, a third-rate application of mathematics. Unfortunately, what usually happens to these people is that as they learn the often xvi   *Egalitarianism as a Revolt Against Nature and Other Essays*

imposing structure and apparatus of economic theory, they become so fascinated by the minutiae of technique that they lose sight of the political and social problems that sparked their interest in the first place. This fascination is also reinforced by the economic structure of the economics profession (and all other academic professions) itself: namely, that prestige, rewards, and brownie points are garnered not by pondering the larger problems but by sticking to one's narrow last and becoming a leading expert on a picayune technical problem.

Among some economists, this syndrome has been carried so far that they scorn any attention to politico-economic problems as a demeaning and unclean impurity, even when such attention is given by economists who have made their mark in the world of specialized technique. And even among those economists who do deal with political problems, any consideration devoted to such larger extra-economic matters as property rights, the nature of government, or the importance of justice is scorned as hopelessly "metaphysical" and beyond the pale.

It is no accident, however, that the economists of this century of the broadest vision and the keenest insight, men such as Ludwig von Mises, Frank H. Knight, and F.A. Hayek, came early to the conclusion that mastery of pure economic theory was not enough, and that it was vital to explore related and fundamental problems of philosophy, political theory, and history. In particular, they realized that it was possible and crucially important to construct a broader systematic theory encompassing human action as a whole, in which economics could take its place as a consistent but subsidiary part.

In my own particular case, the major focus of my interest and my writings over the last three decades has been a part of this broader approach—libertarianism—the discipline of liberty. For I have come to believe that libertarianism is indeed a discipline, a "science," if you will, of its own, even though it has been only barely developed over the generations. Libertarianism is a new and emerging discipline which touches closely on many other areas of the study of human action: economics, philosophy, political theory, history, even—and not least—biology. For all of these provide in varying ways the groundwork, the elaboration, and the application of libertarianism. Some day, perhaps, liberty and "libertarian studies" will be recognized as an independent, though related, part of the academic curriculum.

This present volume is a collection of essays on liberty, on the groundwork, nature, and applications of the "science" of libertarianism. Some of them have been unpublished until now; most of the others appeared in fugitive publications that are now defunct.

The title essay was delivered at a conference on human differentiation held by the Institute for Humane Studies at Gstaad, Switzerland, in the summer of 1972. A fundamental reason and grounding for liberty are the ineluctable facts of human biology; in particular, the fact that each individual is a unique person, in many ways different from all others. If individual diversity were not the universal rule, then the argument for liberty would be weak indeed. For if individuals were as interchangeable as ants, why should anyone worry about maximizing the opportunity for every person to develop his mind and his faculties and his personality to the fullest extent possible? The title essay locates the prime horror of socialism as the egalitarian attempt to stamp out diversity among individuals and groups. In short, it reflects the grounding of libertarianism in individualism and individual diversity.

"Left and Right: The Prospects for Liberty" is an ideological manifesto for libertarianism, placing the current movement and ideology in a world-historical context and perspective, and analyzing our relation to "left," "right," and in between, to socialism and to conservatism. It also presents the basic reasons for the growth of statism in the modern world and the case for fundamental long-run optimism on the future prospects for liberty.

"The Anatomy of the State" presents the libertarian case for the State as the age-old enemy of liberty, an analysis of how the State arises, and how it perpetuates itself through an alliance with "Court Intellectuals" who propagate the apologetics for despotism and State rule. Also included is a critique of various arguments for State rule and for the supposed solution of a Constitution to bind the State down.

"Justice and Property Rights" is an unpublished paper delivered at a conference on property rights held by the Institute for Humane Studies in January 1973. It presents the philosophic groundwork for the libertarian axiom of nonaggression against person and property, and adumbrates a theory of justice in property rights; that is, which asserted property rights are truly to be supported and which are not.

"War, Peace, and the State" specifically applies the libertarian axiom of nonaggression to an area where most Libertarians have been weakest: war and foreign policy. Given the unfortunate existence of States, how can their nonintervention abroad as well as at home best be secured?

"The Fallacy of the Public Sector" analyzes the fallacy of economists placing government operations as part of legitimate and productive activity and criticizes the two major arguments of even the most free-market oriented of economists for government intervention: "collective goods" and "neighborhood effects."

"Kid Lib" and "Women's Lib" apply the libertarian creed to various areas of assertedly needed "liberation." To what extent have women or children been "oppressed," and what does a rigorous application of the libertarian creed have to say about it? In particular, how can the concept of property rights and self-ownership be applied to children? At what stage in their development should they be considered as having full rights?

"Conservation and the Free Market" applies free-market economics and property rights to the area of the most recent hullaballoo by Leftists and opponents of a free society: the whole area of ecology and pollution. Can a free market and free society work in this area, or is comprehensive State planning needed to solve these broad interpersonal problems?

The next four essays take concepts that are propounded by various brands of Leftists and analyze their merits and demerits. "The Meaning of Revolution" discusses what "revolution" really is and to what extent Libertarians may be considered as "revolutionaries." "National Liberation" explains how this concept can be interpreted as a libertarian movement from below, against continuing imperial aggression by other nations. "Anarcho-Communism" is a critique of the self-contradictory movement for libertarian collectivism which took hold among some Libertarians in the late 1960s. "The Spooner–Tucker Doctrine" is a critique of the nineteenth-century individualist anarchist creed from the point of view of a laissez-faire economist—with the differences found in the Spooner–Tucker ignorance of the politics and economics of money, their refusal to recognize the legitimacy of land rent, and their failure to see that private juries must adopt an objective code of libertarian law in order to make consistent or libertarian decisions.

"Ludwig von Mises and the Paradigm for Our Age" is my tribute to the economic genius of Mises and his courageous battle for laissez-faire, but it is also something else: a philosophico–sociological explanation of why Misesian economics has been neglected in the modern world, using Thomas Kuhn's famous "paradigm" theory in the history of science.

Finally, the concluding essay is a cry from the heart on the basic reason why a person should be a Libertarian: not as an intellectual parlor game, not from the utilitarian weighing of costs and benefits, and not because there will be X percent more bathtubs produced in the free society. The basic reason for one's libertarianism should be a passion for justice, for sweeping away as quickly as possible the tyranny, the thievery, the mass murder, and enslavement, which statism has, for too long, imposed upon mankind. It is only such a concern for justice that can inspire the Libertarian to try to abolish, as quickly as he can (and far from the Marxian sense), the exploitation of man by man.

Murray N. Rothbard
1974

FOREWORD TO THE 1974 EDITION BY R.A. CHILDS, JR.

Historians and anthologists of anarchist thought, in comparing the great libertarian classics with other schools of political philosophy, have always been eager to mention the fact that no anarchist theorist has ever been on the level of a Marx or Hegel. What they have meant by this fact is easy to pin down: traditionally, anarchist philosophers have not been system-builders and have not been on as profound a level in analyzing ideas and institutions as have the great ideologists. Marx is mentioned most frequently, perhaps, as a contrast, because Marx was equally competent in philosophy, economics, and history. Furthermore, Marx took a great variety of strands of thought prevalent in the mid-nineteenth century and unified them into a mighty system of socialism. Marx, moreover, was the father of a powerful ideological movement which has had a profound historical impact. And, whatever one may think of the fact, it is true that compared with Marx, all of the anarchist theorists can be considered superficial. Not that Warren, Tucker, Spooner, Stirner, Bakunin, Kropotkin, and Tolstoy, just to mention a few of the most famous anarchists, were in any way ignorant. Few theorists of any camp, for instance, are as rigorous, passionate, and systematic as Lysander Spooner. And few considered as many issues and events as Tucker. Bakunin, too, was the founder of a movement which, for a time at least, rivalled that of Marx. But after all of this is said, it remains to be faced: no anarchist theorist has reached the stature, intellectually speaking, of the great political philosophers in Western Civilization.

Until now, that is. For within the last few years, libertarians have seen the initial signs of widespread recognition of the youngest of the libertarian "superstars": Murray N. Rothbard. Still in his mid-40s, Rothbard's writings have begun to see the light of day in the *New York Times, Intellectual Digest,* and many other prominent publications—left, right, and center. He has appeared on numerous radio and television shows, including the *Today Show,* and his ideas have been debated widely throughout the country. He is stirring up more and more admirers with the publication of his latest book, *For A New Liberty.* While Rothbard has yet to have the impact of Rand, Friedman, or Hayek, his influence is rapidly growing.

But the most significant things to be said about Rothbard are intellectual. For in Rothbard we have one of the only explicit system-builders writing today. He has already published three volumes of a treatise on economic principles, namely the two volumes of his *Man, Economy, and State* and its sequel, *Power and Market.* Numerous works on economic history have been published, and with the publication of *For A New Liberty,* there is the first book-length statement of his political philosophy. Moreover, the best is yet to come. Rothbard is working to complete his book on the ethics of liberty and to bring the first several volumes of his multi-volume history of the United States to publication in the near future. This last involves one of the most ambitious undertakings of any contemporary historian.

But if Rothbard's intellectual scope and prolific nature come as surprises to some, others have been eagerly following his writings for several years. For scattered throughout dozens of journals and magazines are literally scores of articles on everything under the sun, from the methodology of the social sciences to detailed researches into the nature of World War I collectivism, from the philosophy of ownership to the nature and fallacies of egalitarianism. For some time now, the Rothbard boom has been proceeding apace, yet relatively few of his pathbreaking essays have been seen outside of obscure journals. Few people understand the Rothbardian ideology in its full context.

It is our purpose, in publishing this little book of some of Rothbard's greatest essays so closely on the heels of the publication of *For A New Liberty*, to pick up where that book left off. Thus here is Murray N. Rothbard, system-builder. To students of anarchist thought there is something else present here: the first anarchist social philosopher who not only is on the level of Marx in terms of scope and originality, but who is a libertarian as well. For Murray N. Rothbard was one of the first truly free-market anarchists, and the only one so far to put forward an original system of ideology. Whether one agrees with Rothbard or not, his ideas are both original in important ways and also significant.

The contents of this book are from a wide variety of sources: "Egalitarianism as a Revolt Against Nature" was first delivered before an international symposium on human inequality and is being reprinted from the Fall, 1973, number of *Modern Age*. "Left and Right: The Prospects for Liberty," is reprinted from the famous first issue of *Left and Right*. "Justice and Property Rights" is drawn from yet another symposium. The remainder of the essays are drawn from the "little" magazines, from *The Individualist, Outlook, Modern Age, The Standard, Rampart Journal, New Individualist Review, Left and Right,* and *The Libertarian Forum*.

All of these essays can speak for themselves, and it is not necessary to introduce them individually. They deal with some of the most significant issues of our time: with war, peace, human inequality, justice in property rights, the rights of children, national liberation, and many others.

It would be nearly arbitrary to pick out a few as being most important, but in my view, the essay "Left and Right: The Prospects for Liberty" is one of the most important essays ever penned. Not only is it a virtuoso piece of the highest order, but also the level of integration is simply astonishing. Here, in just a few short pages, Rothbard presents the closest thing in print to a true libertarian manifesto comparable to *The Communist Manifesto*.

Here is the entire libertarian worldview, the unique way of viewing history and world affairs that even now few libertarians fully grasp. In fact, I do not recall anything in the literature of political thought fully comparable to this essay. If nothing else, it is so tightly integrated and condensed that Rothbard has packed more information here than most authors do in all of the books that they might publish over the course of a lifetime. It is in this essay that Rothbard outlines what can only be regarded as the culmination of the entire worldview of both the Enlightenment and of the entire natural-rights, natural-law classical liberal tradition. But the reader can discover this for himself.

No collection of essays can fully represent the nature of an ideology as comprehensive as that of Murray Rothbard, and this book is no different. But it is our hope that this book will help add fuel to the growing interest in Rothbard's thought and writings, and help to stimulate the publication of many of the remainder of his essays in book form.

For until Rothbard's work is carefully studied by every advocate of liberty, the value of his contributions to the libertarian system cannot be fully appreciated and, moreover, the unity and true historical context of libertarianism will not even be fully grasped. It is in order to help achieve this end that we are making this book available at the present time. If it helps to stimulate consideration and discussion of this remarkable man's ideology, our end will have been achieved.

R.A. Childs, Jr.
Los Angeles, California
January, 1974

1
EGALITARIANISM AS A REVOLT AGAINST NATURE

F or well over a century, the Left has generally been conceded to have morality, justice, and "idealism" on its
side; the Conservative opposition to the Left has largely
been confined to the "impracticality" of its ideals. A common
view, for example, is that socialism is splendid "in theory,"
but that it cannot "work" in practical life. What the Conservatives failed to see is that while short-run gains can indeed be
made by appealing to the impracticality of radical departures
from the *status quo*, that by conceding the ethical and the
"ideal" to the Left they were doomed to long-run defeat. For
if one side is granted ethics and the "ideal" from the start, then
that side will be able to effect gradual but sure changes in its
own direction; and as these changes accumulate, the stigma of
"impracticality" becomes less and less directly relevant. The
Conservative opposition, having staked its all on the seemingly
firm ground of the "practical" (that is, the *status quo*) is doomed
to lose as the *status quo* moves further in the left direction. The
fact that the unreconstructed Stalinists are universally considered to be the "Conservatives" in the Soviet Union is a happy
logical joke upon conservatism; for in Russia the unrepentant
statists are indeed the repositories of at least a superficial
"practicality" and of a clinging to the existing *status quo*.

1

Never has the virus of "practicality" been more wide-spread than in the United States, for Americans consider themselves a "practical" people, and hence, the opposition to the Left, while originally stronger than elsewhere, has been perhaps the least firm at its foundation. It is now the advocates of the free market and the free society who have to meet the common charge of "impracticality."

In no area has the Left been granted justice and morality as extensively and almost universally as in its espousal of massive equality. It is rare indeed in the United States to find anyone, especially any intellectual, challenging the beauty and goodness of the egalitarian ideal. So committed is everyone to this ideal that "impracticality"—that is, the weakening of economic incentives—has been virtually the only criticism against even the most bizarre egalitarian programs. The inexorable march of egalitarianism is indication enough of the impossibility of avoiding ethical commitments; the fiercely "practical" Americans, in attempting to avoid ethical doctrines, cannot help setting forth such doctrines, but they can now only do so in unconscious, *ad hoc*, and unsystematic fashion. Keynes's famous insight that "practical men, who believe themselves to be quite exempt from any intellectual influences, are usually the slaves of some defunct economist"—is true all the more of ethical judgments and ethical theory.[1]

The unquestioned ethical status of "equality" may be seen in the common practice of economists. Economists are often caught in a value-judgment bind—eager to make political pronouncements. How can they do so while remaining "scientific" and value-free? In the area of egalitarianism, they

---

[1]John Maynard Keynes, *The General Theory of Employment, Interest, and Money* (New York: Harcourt, Brace, 1936), p. 383.

have been able to make a flat value judgment on behalf of
equality with remarkable impunity. Sometimes this judgment
has been frankly personal; at other times, the economist has
pretended to be the surrogate of "society" in the course of
making its value judgment. The result, however, is the same.
Consider, for example, the late Henry C. Simons. After properly criticizing various "scientific" arguments for progressive
taxation, he came out flatly for progression as follows:

> The case for drastic progression in taxation must be rested
> on the case against inequality—on the ethical or aesthetic
> judgment that the prevailing distribution of wealth and
> income reveals a degree (and/or kind) of inequality which is
> distinctly evil or unlovely.[2]

Another typical tactic may be culled from a standard text on
public finance. According to Professor John F. Due,

> [t]he strongest argument for progression is the fact that
> the consensus of opinion in society today regards pro-
> gression as necessary for equity. This is, in turn, based on
> the principle that the pattern of income distribution,
> before taxes, involves excessive inequality.

The latter "can be condemned on the basis of inherent
unfairness in terms of the standards accepted by society."[3]

Whether the economist boldly advances his own value
judgments or whether he presumes to reflect the values of
"society," his immunity from criticism has been remarkable
nonetheless. While candor in proclaiming one's values may
be admirable, it is surely not enough; in the quest for truth it

---

[2]Henry C. Simons, *Personal Income Taxation* (1938), pp. 18–19, quoted
in Walter J. Blum and Harry Kalven, Jr., *The Uneasy Case for Progressive
Taxation* (Chicago: University of Chicago Press, 1953), p. 72.

[3]John F. Due, *Government Finance* (Homewood, Ill.: Richard D. Irwin,
1954), pp. 128–29.

is scarcely sufficient to proclaim one's value judgments as if they must be accepted as tablets from above that are not themselves subject to intellectual criticism and evaluation. Is there no requirement that these value judgments be in some sense valid, meaningful, cogent, *true?* To raise such considerations, of course, is to flout the modern canons of pure *wertfreiheit* in social science from Max Weber onward, as well as the still older philosophic tradition of the stern separation of "fact and value," but perhaps it is high time to raise such fundamental questions. Suppose, for example, that Professor Simons's ethical or aesthetic judgment was not on behalf of equality but of a very different social ideal. Suppose, for example, he had been in favor of the murder of all short people, of all adults under five feet, six inches in height. And suppose he had then written: "The case for the liquidation of all short people must be rested on the case against the existence of short people—on the ethical or aesthetic judgment that the prevailing number of short adults is distinctly evil or unlovely." One wonders if the reception accorded to Professor Simons's remarks by his fellow economists or social scientists would have been quite the same. Or, we can ponder Professor Due writing similarly on behalf of the "opinion of society today" in the Germany of the 1930s with regard to the social treatment of Jews. The point is that in all these cases the logical status of Simons's or Due's remarks would have been precisely the same, even though their reception by the American intellectual community would have been strikingly different.

My point so far has been twofold: (1) that it is not enough for an intellectual or social scientist to proclaim his value judgments—that these judgments must be rationally defensible and must be demonstrable to be valid, cogent, and correct: in short, that they must no longer be treated as above intellectual criticism; and (2) that the goal of equality has for too long been treated uncritically and axiomatically as the ethical ideal. Thus, economists in favor of egalitarian programs have typically counterbalanced their uncriticized "ideal" against possible disincentive effects on economic productivity; but rarely has the ideal itself been questioned.[4]

Let us proceed, then, to a critique of the egalitarian ideal itself—should equality be granted its current status as an unquestioned ethical ideal? In the first place, we must challenge the very idea of a radical separation between something that is "true in theory" but "not valid in practice." If a theory is correct, then it *does* work in practice; if it does not work in practice, then it is a bad theory. The common separation between theory and practice is an artificial and fallacious one. But this is true in ethics as well as anything else. If an ethical ideal is inherently "impractical," that is, if it *cannot* work in practice, then it is a poor ideal and should be discarded forthwith. To put it more precisely, if an ethical goal violates the nature of man and/or the universe and, therefore, *cannot* work in practice, then it is a bad ideal and should be dismissed as a goal. If the goal itself violates the nature of man, then it is also a poor idea to work in the direction of that goal.

Suppose, for example, that it has come to be adopted as a universal ethical goal that all men be able to fly by flapping

---

[4]Thus:

> A third line of objection to progression, and undoubtedly the one which has received the most attention, is that it lessens the economic productivity of the society. Virtually everyone who has advocated progression in an income tax has recognized this as a counterbalancing consideration. (Blum and Kalven, *The Uneasy Case for Progressive Taxation*, p. 21)

The "ideal" vs. the "practical" once again!

their arms. Let us assume that "pro-flappers" have been generally conceded the beauty and goodness of their goal, but have been criticized as "impractical." But the result is unending social misery as society tries continually to move in the direction of arm-flying, and the preachers of arm-flapping make everyone's lives miserable for being either lax or sinful enough not to live up to the common ideal. The proper critique here is to challenge the "ideal" goal itself; to point out that the goal itself is impossible in view of the physical nature of man and the universe; and, therefore, to free mankind from its enslavement to an inherently impossible and, hence, evil goal. But this liberation could never occur so long as the anti-armfliers continued to be solely in the realm of the "practical" and to concede ethics and "idealism" to the high priests of arm-flying. The challenge must take place at the core—at the presumed ethical superiority of a nonsensical goal. The same, I hold, is true of the egalitarian ideal, except that its social consequences are far more pernicious than an endless quest for man's flying unaided. For the condition of equality would wreak far more damage upon mankind.

What, in fact, is "equality"? The term has been much invoked but little analyzed. A and B are "equal" if they are identical to each other with respect to a given attribute. Thus, if Smith and Jones are both exactly six feet in height, then they may be said to be "equal" in height. If two sticks are identical in length, then their lengths are "equal," etc. There is one and only one way, then, in which any two people can really be "equal" in the fullest sense: they must be identical in all of their attributes. This means, of course, that equality of *all* men—the egalitarian ideal—can only be achieved if all men are precisely uniform, precisely identical with respect to all of their attributes. The egalitarian world would necessarily be a world of horror fiction—a world of faceless and identical creatures, devoid of all individuality, variety, or special creativity.

Indeed, it is precisely in horror fiction where the logical implications of an egalitarian world have been fully drawn. Professor Schoeck has resurrected for us the depiction of such a world in the British anti-Utopian novel *Facial Justice*, by L.P. Hartley, in which envy is institutionalized by the State's making sure that all girls' faces are equally pretty, with medical operations being performed on both beautiful and ugly girls to bring all of their faces up or down to the general common denominator.[5] A short story by Kurt Vonnegut provides an even more comprehensive description of a fully egalitarian society. Thus, Vonnegut begins his story, "Harrison Bergeron":

> The year was 2081, and everybody was finally equal. They weren't only equal before God and the law. They were equal every which way. Nobody was smarter than anybody else. Nobody was better looking than anybody else. Nobody was stronger or quicker than anybody else. All this equality was due to the 211th, 212th, and 213th Amendments to the Constitution, and to the unceasing vigilance of agents of the United States Handicapper General.

The "handicapping" worked partly as follows:

> Hazel had a perfectly average intelligence, which meant she couldn't think about anything except in short bursts. And George, while his intelligence was way above normal, had a little mental handicap radio in his ear. He was required by law to wear it at all times. It was tuned to a government transmitter. Every twenty seconds or so, the transmitter would send out some sharp noise to keep people like George from taking unfair advantage of their brains.[6]

The horror we all instinctively feel at these stories is the intuitive recognition that men are *not* uniform, that the

---

[5] Helmut Schoeck, *Envy* (New York: Harcourt, Brace, and World, 1970), pp. 149–55.

[6] Kurt Vonnegut, Jr., "Harrison Bergeron," in *Welcome to the Monkey House* (New York: Dell, 1970), p. 7.

species, mankind, is uniquely characterized by a high degree of variety, diversity, differentiation; in short, inequality. An egalitarian society can only hope to achieve its goals by totalitarian methods of coercion; and, even here, we all believe and hope the human spirit of individual man will rise up and thwart any such attempts to achieve an ant-heap world. In short, the portrayal of an egalitarian society is horror fiction because, when the implications of such a world are fully spelled out, we recognize that such a world and such attempts are profoundly antihuman; being antihuman in the deepest sense, the egalitarian goal is, therefore, evil and any attempts in the direction of such a goal must be considered evil as well.

The great fact of individual difference and variability (that is, inequality) is evident from the long record of human experience; hence, the general recognition of the antihuman nature of a world of coerced uniformity. Socially and economically, this variability manifests itself in the universal division of labor, and in the "Iron Law of Oligarchy"—the insight that, in every organization or activity, a few (generally the most able and/or the most interested) will end up as leaders, with the mass of the membership filling the ranks of the followers. In both cases, the same phenomenon is at work— outstanding success or leadership in any given activity is attained by what Jefferson called a "natural aristocracy"— those who are best attuned to that activity.

The age-old record of inequality seems to indicate that this variability and diversity is rooted in the biological nature of man. But it is precisely such a conclusion about biology and human nature that is the most galling of all possible irritants to our egalitarians. Even egalitarians would be hard put to deny the historical record, but their answer is that "culture" has been to blame; and since they obviously hold that culture is a pure act of the will, then the goal of changing the culture and inculcating society with equality seems to be attainable. In this area, the egalitarians slough off any pretense to scientific caution; they are scarcely content with acknowledging biology and culture as mutually interacting influences. Biology must be read out of court quickly and totally.

Let us ponder an example that is deliberately semi-frivolous. Suppose that we observe our culture and find a common dictum to be: "Redheads are excitable." Here is a judgment of inequality, a conclusion that redheads as a group tend to differ from the nonredhead population. Suppose, then, that egalitarian sociologists investigate the problem, and they find that redheads do, indeed, tend to be more excitable than nonredheads by a statistically significant amount. Instead of admitting the possibility of some sort of biological difference, the egalitarian will quickly add that the "culture" is responsible for the phenomenon: the generally accepted "stereotype" that redheads are excitable had been instilled into every redheaded child from an early age, and he or she has simply been internalizing these judgments and acting in the way society was expecting him to act. Redheads, in brief, had been "brainwashed" by the predominant nonredhead culture.

While not denying the possibility of such a process occurring, this common complaint seems decidedly unlikely on rational analysis. For the egalitarian culture-bugaboo implicitly assumes that the "culture" arrives and accumulates haphazardly, with no reference to social facts. The idea that "redheads are excitable" did not originate out of the thin air or as a divine commandment; how, then, did the idea come into being and gain general currency? One favorite egalitarian device is to attribute all such group-identifying statements to obscure psychological drives. The public had a psychological need to accuse *some* social group of excitability, and redheads were fastened on as scapegoats. But why were redheads singled out? Why not blondes or brunettes? The horrible suspicion begins to loom that perhaps redheads were singled out because they *were* and are indeed more excitable and that, therefore, society's "stereotype" is simply a general insight into the facts of reality. Certainly this explanation accounts for more of the data and the processes at work and is a much simpler explanation besides. Regarded objectively, it seems to be a far more sensible explanation than the idea of the culture as an arbitrary and *ad hoc* bogeyman. If so, then we might conclude that redheads are biologically more excitable and that propaganda beamed at redheads by egalitarians urging them to be less excitable is an attempt to induce redheads to violate their nature; therefore, it is this latter propaganda that may more accurately be called "brainwashing."

This is not to say, of course, that society can never make a mistake and that its judgments of group-identity are always rooted in fact. But it seems to me that the burden of proof is far more on the egalitarians than on their supposedly "unenlightened" opponents.

Since egalitarians begin with the *a priori* axiom that all people, and hence all groups of peoples, are uniform and equal, it then follows for them that any and all group differences in status, prestige, or authority in society *must* be the result of unjust "oppression" and irrational "discrimination." Statistical proof of the "oppression" of redheads would proceed in a manner all too familiar in American political life; it might be shown, for example, that the median redhead income is lower than nonredheaded income, and further that the proportion of redheaded business executives, university professors, or congressmen is below their quotal representation in the population. The most recent and conspicuous manifestation of this sort of quotal thinking was in the

McGovern movement at the 1972 Democratic Convention. A few groups are singled out as having been "oppressed" by virtue of delegates to previous conventions falling below their quotal proportion of the population as a whole. In particular, women, youth, blacks, Chicanos (or the so-called Third World) were designated as having been oppressed; as a result, the Democratic Party, under the guidance of egalitarian-quota thinking, overrode the choices of the voters in order to compel their due quotal representation of these particular groups.

In some cases, the badge of "oppression" was an almost ludicrous construction. That youths of 18 to 25 years of age had been "underrepresented" could easily have been placed in proper perspective by a *reductio ad absurdum*, surely some impassioned McGovernite reformer could have risen to point out the grievous "underrepresentation" of five-year olds at the convention and to urge that the five-year-old bloc receive its immediate due. It is only commonsense biological and social insight to realize that youths win their way into society through a process of apprenticeship; youths know less and have less experience than mature adults, and so it should be clear why they tend to have less status and authority than their elders. But to accept this would be to cast the egalitarian creed into some substantial doubt; further, it would fly into the face of the youth-worship that has long been a grave problem of American culture. And so young people have been duly designated as an "oppressed class," and the coercing of their population quota is conceived as only just reparation for their previously exploited condition.[7]

---

[7]Egalitarians have, among their other activities, been busily at work "correcting" the English language. The use of the word "girl," for example, is now held to grievously demean and degrade female youth and to

Women are another recently discovered "oppressed class," and the fact that political delegates have habitually been far more than 50 percent male is now held to be an evident sign of their oppression. Delegates to political conventions come from the ranks of party activists, and since women have not been nearly as politically active as men, their numbers have understandably been low. But, faced with this argument, the widening forces of "women's liberation" in America again revert to the talismanic argument about "brainwashing" by our "culture." For the women's liberationists can hardly deny the fact that every culture and civilization in history, from the simplest to the most complex, has been dominated by males. (In desperation, the liberationists have lately been countering with fantasies about the mighty Amazonian empire.) Their reply, once again, is that from time immemorial a male-dominated culture has brainwashed oppressed females to confine themselves to nurture, home, and the domestic hearth. The task of the liberationists is to effect a revolution in the female condition by sheer will, by the "raising of consciousness." If most women continue to cleave to domestic concerns, this only reveals the "false consciousness" that must be extirpated.

Of course, one neglected reply is that if, indeed, men have succeeded in dominating every culture, then this in itself is a demonstration of male "superiority"; for if all genders are equal, how is it that male domination emerged in every case? But apart from this question, biology itself is being angrily denied and cast aside. The cry is that there are no, can be no, must be no biological differences between the sexes; all historical or current differences must be due to cultural brainwashing. In his brilliant refutation of the women's liberationist

---

imply their natural subservience to adults. As a result, Left egalitarians now refer to girls of virtually any age as "women," and we may confidently look forward to reading about the activities of "a five-year-old woman."

Kate Millett, Irving Howe outlines several important biological differences between the sexes, differences important enough to have lasting social effects. They are: (1) "the distinctive female experience of maternity" including what the anthropologist Malinowski calls an "intimate and integral connection with the child . . . associated with physiological effects and strong emotions"; (2) "the hormonic components of our bodies as these vary not only between the sexes but at different ages within the sexes"; (3) "the varying possibilities for work created by varying amounts of musculature and physical controls"; and (4) "the psychological consequences of different sexual postures and possibilities," in particular the "fundamental distinction between the active and passive sexual roles" as biologically determined in men and women respectively.[8]

Howe goes on to cite the admission by Dr. Eleanor Maccoby in her study of female intelligence that

> it is quite possible that there are genetic factors that differentiate the two sexes and bear upon their intellectual performance. . . . For example, there is good reason to believe that boys are innately more aggressive than girls—and I mean aggressive in the broader sense, not just as it implies fighting, but as it implies dominance and initiative as well—and if this quality is one which underlies the later growth of analytic thinking, then boys have an advantage which girls . . . will find difficult to overcome.

Dr. Maccoby adds that "if you try to divide child training among males and females, we might find out that females need to do it and males don't."[9]

---

[8]Irving Howe, "The Middle-Class Mind of Kate Millett," *Harper's* (December, 1970): 125–26.

[9]Ibid., p. 126.

The sociologist Arnold W. Green points to the repeated emergence of what the egalitarians denounce as "stereotyped sex roles" even in communities originally dedicated to absolute equality. Thus, he cites the record of the Israeli kibbutzim:

> The phenomenon is worldwide: women are concentrated in fields which require, singly or in combination, housewifely skills, patience and routine, manual dexterity, sex appeal, contact with children. The generalization holds for the Israeli kibbutz, with its established ideal of sexual equality. A "regression" to a separation of "women's work" from "men's work" occurred in the division of labor, to a state of affairs which parallels that elsewhere. The kibbutz is dominated by males and traditional male attitudes, on balance to the content of both sexes.[10]

Irving Howe unerringly perceives that at the root of the women's liberation movement is resentment against the very existence of women as a distinctive entity:

> For what seems to trouble Miss Millett isn't merely the injustices women have suffered or the discriminations to which they continue to be subject. What troubles her most of all . . . is the sheer existence of women. Miss Millett dislikes the psychobiological distinctiveness of women, and she will go no further than to recognize— what choice is there, alas?—the inescapable differences of anatomy. She hates the perverse refusal of most women to recognize the magnitude of their humiliation, the shameful dependence they show in regard to (not very independent) men, the maddening pleasures they even take in cooking dinners for the "master group" and wiping the noses of their snotty brats. Raging against

---

[10]Arnold W. Green, *Sociology* (6th ed., New York: McGraw-Hill, 1972), p. 305. Green cites the study by A.I. Rabin, "The Sexes: Ideology and Reality in the Israeli Kibbutz," in G.H. Seward and R.G. Williamson, eds., *Sex Roles in Changing Society* (New York: Random House, 1970), pp. 285–307.

> the notion that such roles and attitudes are biologically
> determined, since the very thought of the biological
> seems to her a way of forever reducing women to sub-
> ordinate status, she nevertheless attributes to "culture"
> so staggering a range of customs, outrages, and evils
> that this culture comes to seem a force more immovable
> and ominous than biology itself.[11]

In a perceptive critique of the women's liberation movement, Joan Didion perceives its root to be a rebellion not
only against biology but also against the "very organization
of nature" itself:

> If the necessity for conventional reproduction of the
> species seemed unfair to women, then let us transcend,
> via technology, "the very organization of nature," the
> oppression, as Shulamith Firestone saw it, "that goes
> back through recorded history to the animal kingdom
> itself." *I accept the Universe*, Margaret Fuller had finally
> allowed: Shulamith Firestone did not.[12]

To which one is tempted to paraphrase Carlyle's admonition:
"Egad, madam, you'd better."

Another widening rebellion against biological sex norms,
as well as against natural diversity, has been the recently
growing call for bisexuality by Left intellectuals. The avoidance of "rigid, stereotyped" heterosexuality and the adoption
of indiscriminate bisexuality is supposed to expand consciousness, to eliminate "artificial" distinctions between the
sexes and to make all persons simply and unisexually
"human." Once again, brainwashing by a dominant culture (in
this case, heterosexual) has supposedly oppressed a homosexual

---

[11]Howe, "The Middle-Class Mind of Kate Millett," p. 124.

[12]Joan Didion, "The Women's Movement," New York *Times Review
of Books* (July 30, 1972), p. 1.

minority and blocked off the uniformity and equality inherent
in bisexuality. For then every individual could reach his or her
fullest "humanity" in the "polymorphous perversity" so dear to
the hearts of such leading New Left social philosophers as
Norman O. Brown and Herbert Marcuse.

That biology stands like a rock in the face of egalitarian
fantasies has been made increasingly clear in recent years.
The researches of biochemist Roger J. Williams have repeat-
edly emphasized the great range of individual diversity
throughout the entire human organism. Thus:

> Individuals differ from each other even in the minutest
> details of anatomy and body chemistry and physics; finger
> and toe prints; microscopic texture of hair; hair pattern on
> the body, ridges and "moons" on the finger and toenails;
> thickness of skin, its color, its tendency to blister; distribu-
> tion of nerve endings on the surface of the body; size and
> shape of ears, of ear canals, or semi-circular canals; length
> of fingers; character of brain waves (tiny electrical impulses
> given off by the brain); exact number of muscles in the
> body; heart action; strength of blood vessels; blood groups;
> rate of clotting of blood—and so on almost *ad infinitum*.
>
> We now know a great deal about how inheritance works
> and how it is not only possible but certain that every human
> being possesses by inheritance an exceedingly complex
> mosaic, composed of thousands of items, which is distinc-
> tive for him alone.[13]

The genetic basis for inequality of intelligence has also
become increasingly evident, despite the emotional abuse
heaped upon such studies by fellow scientists as well as the
lay public. Studies of identical twins raised in contrasting
environments have been among the ways that this conclusion

---

[13]Roger J. Williams, *Free and Unequal* (Austin: University of Texas
Press, 1953), pp. 17, 23. See also by Williams *Biochemical Individuality*
(New York: John Wiley, 1963) and *You are Extraordinary* (New York: Ran-
dom House, 1967).

has been reached; and Professor Richard Herrnstein has recently estimated that 80 percent of the variability in human intelligence is genetic in origin. Herrnstein concludes that any political attempts to provide environmental equality for all citizens will only intensify the degree of socioeconomic differences caused by genetic variability.[14]

The egalitarian revolt against biological reality, as significant as it is, is only a subset of a deeper revolt: against the ontological structure of reality itself, against the "very organization of nature"; against the universe as such. At the heart of the egalitarian left is the pathological belief that there is no structure of reality; that all the world is a *tabula rasa* that can be changed at any moment in any desired direction by the mere exercise of human will—in short, that reality can be instantly transformed by the mere wish or whim of human beings. Surely this sort of infantile thinking is at the heart of Herbert Marcuse's passionate call for the comprehensive negation of the existing structure of reality and for its transformation into what he divines to be its true potential.

Nowhere is the Left Wing attack on ontological reality more apparent than in the Utopian dreams of what the future socialist society will look like. In the socialist future of Charles Fourier, according to Ludwig von Mises:

> all harmful beasts will have disappeared, and in their places will be animals which will assist man in his labors—or even do his work for him. An antibeaver will see to the fishing; an antiwhale will move sailing ships in a calm; an antihippopotamus will tow the river boats. Instead of the lion there will be an antilion, a steed of wonderful swiftness, upon whose back the rider will sit

---

[14]Richard Herrnstein, "IQ," *Atlantic Monthly* (September, 1971).

> as comfortably as in a well-sprung carriage. "It will be a
> pleasure to live in a world with such servants."[15]

Furthermore, according to Fourier, the very oceans would
contain lemonade rather than salt water.[16]

Similarly absurd fantasies are at the root of the Marxian
utopia of communism. Freed from the supposed confines of
specialization and the division of labor (the heart of any production above the most primitive level and hence of any civilized society), each person in the communist utopia would
fully develop all of his powers in every direction.[17] As Engels
wrote in his *Anti-Dühring*, communism would give "each
individual the opportunity to develop and exercise all his faculties, physical and mental, in all directions."[18] And Lenin
looked forward in 1920 to the "abolition of the division of
labor among people . . . the education, schooling, and training of people with *an all-around development* and *an all-around
training*, people *able to do everything*. Communism is marching and must march toward this goal, and *will reach it*."[19]

In his trenchant critique of the communist vision, Alexander Gray charges:

---

[15]Ludwig von Mises, *Socialism: An Economic and Sociological Analysis*
(New Haven, Conn.: Yale University Press, 1951), pp. 163–64.

[16]Ludwig von Mises, *Human Action* (New Haven, Conn.: Yale University Press, 1949), p. 71. Mises cites the first and fourth volumes of
Fourier's *Oeuvres Complètes*.

[17]For more on the communist utopia and the division of labor, see
Murray N. Rothbard, *Freedom, Inequality, Primitivism, and the Division of
Labor* (chap. 16, present volume).

[18]Quoted in Alexander Gray, *The Socialist Tradition* (London: Longmans, Green, 1947), p. 328.

[19]Italics are Lenin's. V.I. Lenin, *Left-Wing Communism: An Infantile
Disorder* (New York: International Publishers, 1940), p. 34.

> That each individual should have the opportunity of developing all his faculties, physical and mental, in all directions, is a dream which will cheer the vision only of the simple-minded, oblivious of the restrictions imposed by the narrow limits of human life. For life is a series of acts of choice, and each choice is at the same time a renunciation.
>
> Even the inhabitant of Engels's future fairyland will have to decide sooner or later whether he wishes to be Archbishop of Canterbury or First Sea Lord, whether he should seek to excel as a violinist or as a pugilist, whether he should elect to know all about Chinese literature or about the hidden pages in the life of a mackerel.[20]

Of course one way to try to resolve this dilemma is to fantasize that the New Communist Man of the future will be a superman, superhuman in his abilities to transcend nature. William Godwin thought that, once private property was abolished, man would become immortal. The Marxist theoretician Karl Kautsky asserted that in the future communist society, "a new type of man will arise . . . a superman . . . an exalted man." And Leon Trotsky prophesied that under communism:

> man will become incomparably stronger, wiser, finer. His body more harmonious, his movements more rhythmical, his voice more musical. . . . The human average will rise to the level of an Aristotle, a Goethe, a Marx. Above these other heights new peaks will arise.[21]

We began by considering the common view that the egalitarians, despite a modicum of impracticality, have ethics and moral idealism on their side. We end with the conclusion that egalitarians, however intelligent as individuals, deny the very basis of human intelligence and of human reason: the identification of the ontological structure of reality, of the laws of

---

[20]Gray, *The Socialist Tradition*, p. 328.

[21]Quoted in Mises, *Socialism: An Economic and Sociological Analysis*, p. 164.

human nature, and the universe. In so doing, the egalitarians are acting as terribly spoiled children, denying the structure of reality on behalf of the rapid materialization of their own absurd fantasies. Not only spoiled but also highly dangerous; for the power of ideas is such that the egalitarians have a fair chance of destroying the very universe that they wish to deny and transcend, and to bring that universe crashing around all of our ears. Since their methodology and their goals deny the very structure of humanity and of the universe, the egalitarians are profoundly antihuman; and, therefore, their ideology and their activities may be set down as profoundly evil as well. Egalitarians do *not* have ethics on their side unless one can maintain that the destruction of civilization, and even of the human race itself, may be crowned with the laurel wreath of a high and laudable morality.

2
LEFT AND RIGHT: THE PROSPECTS FOR LIBERTY

The Conservative has long been marked, whether he knows it or not, by long-run pessimism: by the belief that the long-run trend, and therefore time itself, is against him. Hence, the inevitable trend runs toward left-wing statism at home and communism abroad. It is this long-run despair that accounts for the Conservative's rather bizarre short-run optimism, for since the long run is given up as hopeless, the Conservative feels that his only hope of success rests in the current moment. In foreign affairs, this point of view leads the Conservative to call for desperate showdowns with communism, for he feels that the longer he waits the worse things will ineluctably become; at home, it leads him to total concentration on the very next election, where he is always hoping for victory and never achieving it. The quintessence of the practical man, and beset by long-run despair, the Conservative refuses to think or plan beyond the election of the day.

Pessimism, however, both short-run *and* long-run, is precisely what the prognosis of conservatism deserves, for conservatism is a dying remnant of the *ancien régime* of the preindustrial era, and, as such, it *has* no future. In its contemporary American form, the recent Conservative revival embodied the death throes of an ineluctably moribund, fundamentalist, rural, small-town, white Anglo-Saxon America. What, however, of the prospects for *liberty?* For too many libertarians mistakenly link the prognosis for liberty with that of the seemingly stronger and supposedly allied Conservative movement; this linkage makes the characteristic long-run pessimism of the modern Libertarian easy to understand. But this chapter contends that, while the short-run prospects for liberty at home and abroad may seem dim, the proper attitude for the Libertarian to take is that of unquenchable long-run optimism.

The case for this assertion rests on a certain view of history which holds, first, that before the eighteenth century in Western Europe there existed (and still continues to exist outside the West) an identifiable Old Order. Whether the Old Order took the form of feudalism or Oriental despotism, it was marked by tyranny, exploitation, stagnation, fixed caste, and hopelessness and starvation for the bulk of the population. In sum, life was "nasty, brutish, and short"; here was Maine's "society of status" and Spencer's "military society." The ruling classes, or castes, governed by conquest and by getting the masses to believe in the alleged divine *imprimatur* to their rule.

The Old Order was, and still remains, the great and mighty enemy of liberty; and it was particularly mighty in the past because there was then no inevitability about *its* overthrow. When we consider that basically the Old Order had existed since the dawn of history, in all civilizations, we can appreciate even more the glory and the magnitude of the triumph of the liberal revolution of and around the eighteenth century.

Part of the dimensions of this struggle has been obscured by a great myth of the history of Western Europe implanted by antiliberal German historians of the late nineteenth century.

The myth held that the growth of absolute monarchies and of mercantilism in the early modern era was necessary for the development of capitalism, since these served to liberate the merchants and the people from local feudal restrictions. In actuality, this was not at all the case; the king and his nation–State served rather as a super-feudal overlord reimposing and reinforcing feudalism just as it was being dissolved by the peaceful growth of the market economy. The king superimposed his own restrictions and monopoly privileges onto those of the feudal regime. The absolute monarchs were the Old Order writ large and made even more despotic than before. Capitalism, indeed, flourished earliest and most actively precisely in those areas where the central State was weak or nonexistent: the Italian cities, the Hanseatic League, the confederation of seventeenth-century Holland. Finally, the Old Order was overthrown or severely shaken in its grip in two ways. One was by industry and the market expanding through the interstices of the feudal order (for example, industry in England developing in the countryside beyond the grip of feudal, State and guild restrictions). More important was a series of cataclysmic revolutions that blasted loose the Old Order and the old ruling classes: the English Revolutions of the seventeenth century, the American Revolution, and the French Revolution, all of which were necessary for the ushering in of the Industrial Revolution and of at least partial victories for individual liberty, laissez-faire, separation of church and state, and international peace. The society of status gave way, at least partially, to the "society of contract"; the military society gave way partially to the "industrial society." The mass of the population now achieved a mobility of labor and place, and accelerating expansion of their living standards, for which they had scarcely dared to hope. Liberalism had indeed brought to the Western world not only liberty, the prospect of peace, and the rising living standards of an industrial society, but above all, perhaps, it brought hope, a hope in ever-greater progress that lifted the mass of mankind out of its age-old sinkhole of stagnation and despair.

Soon there developed in Western Europe two great political ideologies, centered around this new revolutionary phenomenon: one was liberalism, the party of hope, of radicalism, of liberty, of the Industrial Revolution, of progress, of humanity; the other was conservatism, the party of reaction, the party that longed to restore the hierarchy, statism, theocracy, serfdom, and class exploitation of the Old Order. Since liberalism admittedly had reason on its side, the Conservatives darkened the ideological atmosphere with obscurantist calls for romanticism, tradition, theocracy, and irrationalism. Political ideologies were polarized, with liberalism on the extreme "left," and conservatism on the extreme "right," of the ideological spectrum. That genuine liberalism was essentially radical and revolutionary was brilliantly perceived, in the twilight of its impact, by the great Lord Acton (one of the few figures in the history of thought who, charmingly, grew *more* radical as he grew older). Acton wrote that "Liberalism wishes for what ought to be, irrespective of what is." In working out this view, incidentally, it was Acton, not Trotsky, who first arrived at the concept of the "permanent revolution." As Gertrude Himmelfarb wrote in her excellent study of Acton:

> . . . his philosophy develop(ed) to the point where the future was seen as the avowed enemy of the past, and where the past was allowed no authority except as it happened to conform to morality. To take seriously this Liberal theory of history, to give precedence to "what ought to be" over "what is," was, he admitted, virtually to install a "revolution in permanence."
>
> The "revolution in permanence," as Acton hinted in the inaugural lecture and admitted frankly in his notes, was the culmination of his philosophy of history and theory of

politics. . . . This idea of conscience, that men carry about
with them the knowledge of good and evil, is the very root
of revolution, for it destroys the sanctity of the past. . . .
"Liberalism is essentially revolutionary," Acton observed.
"Facts must yield to ideas. Peaceably and patiently if possible. Violently if not."[1]

The Liberal, wrote Acton, far surpassed the Whig:

The Whig governed by compromise. The Liberal begins
the reign of ideas. . . . One is practical, gradual, ready for
compromise. The other works out a principle philosophically. One is a policy aiming at a philosophy. The other is a
philosophy seeking a policy.[2]

What happened to liberalism? Why then did it decline
during the nineteenth century? This question has been pon-
dered many times, but perhaps the basic reason was an inner
rot within the vitals of liberalism itself. For, with the partial
success of the Liberal Revolution in the West, the Liberals
increasingly abandoned their radical fervor and, therefore,
their liberal goals, to rest content with a mere defense of the
uninspiring and defective *status quo*. Two philosophical roots
of this decay may be discerned. First is the abandonment of
natural rights and "higher law" theory for utilitarianism, for
only forms of natural or higher law theory can provide a radical base outside the existing system from which to challenge
the *status quo*; and only such theory furnishes a sense of necessary immediacy to the libertarian struggle by focusing on
the necessity of bringing existing criminal rulers to the bar of
justice. Utilitarians, on the other hand, in abandoning justice
for expediency, also abandon immediacy for quiet stagnation

---

[1]Gertrude Himmelfarb, *Lord Acton* (Chicago: University of Chicago
Press, 1962), pp. 204–05.

[2]Ibid., p. 209.

and inevitably end up as objective apologists for the existing order.

The second great philosophical influence on the decline of liberalism was evolutionism, or Social Darwinism, which put the finishing touches to liberalism as a radical force in society. For the Social Darwinist erroneously saw history and society through the peaceful, rose-colored glasses of infinitely slow, infinitely gradual social evolution. Ignoring the prime fact that no ruling caste in history has ever voluntarily surrendered its power, and that, therefore, liberalism had to break through by means of a series of revolutions, the Social Darwinists looked forward peacefully and cheerfully to thousands of years of infinitely gradual evolution to the next supposedly inevitable stage of individualism.

An interesting illustration of a thinker who embodies within himself the decline of liberalism in the nineteenth century is Herbert Spencer. Spencer began as a magnificently radical liberal, indeed virtually a pure libertarian. But, as the virus of sociology and Social Darwinism took over in his soul, Spencer abandoned libertarianism as a dynamic historical movement, although at first without abandoning it in pure theory. In short, while looking forward to an eventual ideal of pure liberty, Spencer began to see its victory as inevitable, but only after millennia of gradual evolution, and thus, in actual fact, Spencer abandoned liberalism as a fighting, radical creed and confined his liberalism in practice to a weary, rearguard action against the growing collectivism of the late nineteenth century. Interestingly enough, Spencer's tired shift "rightward" in strategy soon became a shift rightward in theory as well, so that Spencer abandoned pure liberty even in theory, for example, in repudiating his famous chapter in *Social Statics*, "The Right to Ignore the State."

In England, the classical liberals began their shift from radicalism to quasi-conservatism in the early nineteenth century; a touchstone of this shift was the general British liberal attitude toward the national liberation struggle in Ireland. This struggle was twofold: against British political imperialism and against feudal landlordism which had been imposed by that imperialism. By their Tory blindness toward the Irish drive for national independence, and especially for peasant property against feudal oppression, the British Liberals (including Spencer) symbolized their effective abandonment of genuine liberalism, which had been virtually born in a struggle against the feudal land system. Only in the United States, the great home of radical liberalism (where feudalism had never been able to take root outside the South), did natural rights and higher-law theory, and consequent radical liberal movements, continue in prominence until the mid-nineteenth century. In their different ways, the Jacksonian and Abolitionist movements were the last powerful radical libertarian movements in American life.[3]

Thus, with liberalism abandoned from within, there was no longer a party of hope in the Western world, no longer a "Left" movement to lead a struggle against the state and against the unbreached remainder of the Old Order. Into this gap, into this void created by the drying up of radical liberalism, there stepped a new movement: socialism. Libertarians of the present day are accustomed to think of socialism as the polar opposite of the libertarian creed. But this is a grave mistake, responsible for a severe ideological disorientation of libertarians in the present world. As we have seen, conservatism

[3]Carl Becker, *The Declaration of Independence* (New York: Vintage Books, 1958), chap. 6.

was the polar opposite of liberty; and socialism, while to the "left" of conservatism, was essentially a confused, middle-of-the-road movement. It was, and still is, middle-of-the-road because it tries to achieve liberal *ends* by the use of conservative *means*.

In short, Russell Kirk, who claims that socialism was the heir of classical liberalism, and Ronald Hamowy, who sees socialism as the heir of conservatism, are both right; for the question is on what aspect of this confused centrist movement we happen to be focusing. Socialism, like liberalism and against conservatism, accepted the industrial system and the liberal *goals* of freedom, reason, mobility, progress, higher living standards for the masses, and an end to theocracy and war; but it tried to achieve these ends by the use of incompatible, conservative means: statism, central planning, communitarianism, etc. Or rather, to be more precise, there were from the beginning two different strands within socialism: one was the right-wing, authoritarian strand, from Saint-Simon down, which glorified statism, hierarchy, and collectivism and which was thus a projection of conservatism trying to accept and dominate the new industrial civilization. The other was the left-wing, relatively libertarian strand, exemplified in their different ways by Marx and Bakunin, revolutionary and far more interested in achieving the libertarian goals of liberalism and socialism; but especially the smashing of the state apparatus to achieve the "withering away of the State" and the "end of the exploitation of man by man." Interestingly enough, the very Marxian phrase, the "replacement of the government by *men* by the administration of things," can be traced, by a circuitous route, from the great French radical laissez-faire liberals of the early nineteenth century, Charles Comte (no relation to Auguste Comte) and Charles Dunoyer. And so, too, may the concept of the "class struggle"; except that for Dunoyer and Comte the inherently antithetical classes were not businessmen ver-sus workers, but the producers in society (including free businessmen, workers, peasants, etc.) versus the exploiting classes constituting, and privileged by, the State apparatus.[4] Saint-Simon at one time in his confused and chaotic life was close to Comte and Dunoyer and picked up his class analysis from them, in the process characteristically getting the whole thing balled up and converting businessmen on the market, *as well as* feudal landlords and others of the State privileged, into "exploiters." Marx and Bakunin picked this up from the Saint-Simonians, and the result gravely misled the whole left-socialist movement; for, then, *in addition to* smashing the repressive State, it became supposedly necessary to smash private capitalist ownership of the means of production. Rejecting private property, especially of capital, the left socialists were then trapped in a crucial inner contradiction: if the State is to disappear after the revolution (immediately for Bakunin, gradually "withering" for Marx), then how is the "collective" to run its property without becoming an enor-mous State itself in fact, even if not in name? This was a con-tradiction which neither the Marxists nor the Bakuninists were ever able to resolve.

Having replaced radical liberalism as the party of the "left," socialism, by the turn of the twentieth century, fell

---

[4]The information about Comte and Dunoyer, as well, indeed, as the entire analysis of the ideological spectrum, I owe to Mr. Leonard P. Lig-gio. For an emphasis on the positive and dynamic aspect of the Utopian drive, much traduced in our time, see Alan Milchman, "The Social and Political Philosophy of Jean-Jacques Rousseau: Utopia and Ideology," *The November Review* (November, 1964): 3–10. Also cf. Jurgen Ruhle, "The Philosopher of Hope: Ernst Bloch," in Leopold Labedz, ed., *Revi-sionism* (New York: Praeger, 1962), pp. 166–78.

prey to this inner contradiction. Most socialists (Fabians, Lassalleans, even Marxists) turned sharply rightward, completely abandoned the old libertarian goals and ideals of revolution and the withering away of the State and became cozy conservatives permanently reconciled to the State, the *status quo*, and the whole apparatus of neomercantilism, State monopoly capitalism, imperialism, and war that was rapidly being established and riveted on European society at the turn of the twentieth century. For conservatism, too, had reformed and regrouped to try to cope with a modern industrial system and had become a refurbished mercantilism, a regime of statism, marked by State monopoly privilege, in direct and indirect forms, to favored capitalists and to quasi-feudal landlords. The affinity between right socialism and the new conservatism became very close, the former advocating similar policies but with a demagogic populist veneer. Thus, the other side of the coin of imperialism was "social imperialism," which Joseph Schumpeter trenchantly defined as "an imperialism in which the entrepreneurs and other elements woo the workers by means of social welfare concessions which appear to depend on the success of export monopolism."[5]

Historians have long recognized the affinity, and the welding together, of right-wing socialism with conservatism in Italy and Germany, where the fusion was embodied first in Bismarckism and then in fascism and national socialism—the

-----

[5]Joseph A. Schumpeter, *Imperialism and Social Classes* (New York: Meridian Books, 1955), p. 175. Schumpeter, incidentally, realized that, far from being an inherent stage of capitalism, modern imperialism was a throwback to the precapitalist imperialism of earlier ages, but with a minority of privileged capitalists now joined to the feudal and military castes in promoting imperialist aggression.

latter fulfilling the Conservative program of nationalism, imperialism, militarism, theocracy, and a right-wing collectivism that retained and even cemented the rule of the old privileged classes. But only recently have historians begun to realize that a similar pattern occurred in England and the United States. Thus, Bernard Semmel, in his brilliant history of the social-imperialist movement in England at the turn of the twentieth century, shows how the Fabian Society welcomed the rise of the imperialists in England.[6] When, in the mid-1890s, the Liberal Party in England split into the radicals on the left and the liberal-imperialists on the right, Beatrice Webb, co-leader of the Fabians, denounced the radicals as "laissez-faire and anti-imperialists," while hailing the latter as "collectivists and imperialists." An official Fabian manifesto, *Fabianism and the Empire* (1900), drawn up by George Bernard Shaw (who was later, with perfect consistency, to praise the domestic policies of Stalin *and* Mussolini *and* Sir Oswald Mosley), lauded imperialism and attacked the radicals, who "still cling to the fixed-frontier ideals of individualist republicanism (and) noninterference." In contrast, "a Great Power . . . must govern (a world empire) in the interests of civilization as a whole." After this, the Fabians collaborated closely with Tories and liberal-imperialists. Indeed, in late 1902, Sidney and Beatrice Webb established a small, secret group of brain-trusters, called The Coefficients; as one of the leading members of this club, the Tory imperialist, Leopold S. Amery, revealingly wrote:

> Sidney and Beatrice Webb were much more concerned with getting their ideas of the welfare state put into practice by anyone who might be prepared to help, even on the most

---

[6]Bernard Semmel, *Imperialism and Social Reform: English Social-Imperial Thought, 1895–1914* (Cambridge, Mass.: Harvard University Press, 1960).

> modest scale, than with the early triumph of an avowedly
> Socialist Party. . . . There was, after all, nothing so very
> unnatural, as [Joseph] Chamberlain's own career had
> shown, in a combination of Imperialism in external affairs
> with municipal socialism or semi-socialism at home.[7]

Other members of The Coefficients, who, as Amery wrote, were to function as "Brain Trusts or General Staff" for the movement, were: the liberal-imperialist Richard B. Haldane; the geopolitician Halford J. Mackinder; the Imperialist and Germanophobe Leopold Maxse, publisher of the *National Review*; the Tory socialist and imperialist Viscount Milner; the naval imperialist Carlyon Bellairs; the famous journalist J.L. Garvin; Bernard Shaw; Sir Clinton Dawkins, partner of the Morgan Bank; and Sir Edward Grey, who, at a meeting of the club first adumbrated the policy of Entente with France and Russia that was to eventuate in World War I.[8]

The famous betrayal during World War I of the old ideals of revolutionary pacifism by the European Socialists, and even by the Marxists, should have come as no surprise; that each Socialist Party supported its "own" national government in the war (with the honorable exception of Eugene Victor Debs's Socialist Party in the United States) was the final embodiment of the collapse of the classic Socialist Left. From then on, Socialists and quasi-Socialists joined Conservatives in a basic amalgam, accepting the state and the mixed economy (= neo-mercantilism = the welfare state = interventionism = state monopoly capitalism, merely synonyms for the same essential

---

[7]Leopold S. Amery, *My Political Life* (1953). Quoted in Semmel, *Imperialism and Social Reform*, pp. 74–75.

[8]The point, of course, is not that these men were products of some "Fabian conspiracy," but, on the contrary, that Fabianism, by the turn of the century, was socialism so conservatized as to be closely aligned with the other dominant neo-Conservative trends in British political life.

reality). It was in reaction to this collapse that Lenin broke out of the Second International to reestablish classic revolutionary Marxism in a revival of left socialism.

In fact, Lenin, almost without knowing it, accomplished *more* than this. It is common knowledge that "purifying" movements, eager to return to a classic purity shorn of recent corruptions, generally purify further than what had held true among the original classic sources. There were, indeed, marked "conservative" strains in the writings of Marx and Engels themselves which often justified the State, Western imperialism, and aggressive nationalism, and it was these *motifs*, in the ambivalent views of the masters on this subject, that provided the fodder for the later shift of the majority Marxists into the "social imperialist" camp.[9] Lenin's camp turned more "left" than had Marx and Engels themselves. Lenin had a decidedly more revolutionary stance toward the State and consistently defended and supported movements of national liberation against imperialism. The Leninist shift was more "leftist" in other important senses as well. For while Marx had centered his attack on market capitalism *per se*, the major focus of Lenin's concerns was on what he con-ceived to be the highest stages of capitalism: imperialism and monopoly. Hence Lenin's focus, centering as it did *in practice* on State monopoly and imperialism rather than on laissez-faire capitalism, was in that way far more congenial to the Libertarian than that of Karl Marx.

Fascism and Nazism were the local culmination in domestic affairs of the modern drift toward right-wing collectivism. It has become customary among libertarians, as indeed among

---

[9]Thus, see Horace O. Davis, "Nations, Colonies, and Social Classes: The Position of Marx and Engels," *Science and Society* (Winter, 1965): 26–43.

the Establishment of the West, to regard fascism and communism as fundamentally identical. But while both systems were indubitably collectivist, they differed greatly in their socioeconomic content. Communism was a genuine revolutionary movement that ruthlessly displaced and overthrew the old ruling elites, while fascism, on the contrary, cemented into power the old ruling classes. Hence, fascism was a counterrevolutionary movement that froze a set of monopoly privileges upon society; in short, fascism was the apotheosis of modern State monopoly capitalism.[10] Here was the reason

---

[10]See the penetrating article by Alexander J. Groth, "The 'Isms' in Totalitarianism," *American Political Science Review* (December, 1964): 888–901. Groth writes:

> The Communists . . . have generally undertaken measures directly and indirectly uprooting existing socioeconomic elites: the landed nobility, business, large sections of the middle class and the peasantry, as well as the bureaucratic elites, the military, the civil service, the judiciary, and the diplomatic corps. . . . Second, in every instance of Communist seizure of power there has been a significant ideological–propagandistic commitment toward a proletarian or workers' state . . . [which] has been accompanied by opportunities for upward social mobility for the economically lowest classes, in terms of education and employment, which invariably have considerably exceeded the opportunities available under previous regimes. Finally, in every case, the Communists have attempted to change basically the character of the economic systems which fell under their say, typically from an agrarian to an industrial economy. . . .
>
> Fascism (both in the German and Italian versions) . . . was socioeconomically a counter-revolutionary movement. . . . It certainly did not dispossess or annihilate existent socioeconomic elites. . . . Quite the contrary, Fascism did not arrest the trend toward monopolistic private concentrations in business but instead augmented this tendency. . . .
>
> Undoubtedly, the Fascist economic system was not a free-market economy, and hence not "capitalist" if one wishes to restrict

that fascism proved so attractive (which communism, of course, never did) to big business interests in the West—openly and unabashedly so in the 1920s and early 1930s.[11]

We are now in a position to apply our analysis to the American scene. Here we encounter a contrasting myth about recent American history which has been propagated by current conservatives and adopted by most American libertarians. The myth goes approximately as follows: America was, more or less, a haven of laissez-faire until the New Deal; then Roosevelt, influenced by Felix Frankfurter, the Intercollegiate Socialist Society, and other "Fabian" and communist "conspirators," engineered a revolution which set America on the path to socialism, and further on beyond the horizon, to communism. The present-day libertarian who adopts this or a similar view of the American experience, tends to think of himself as an "extreme right-winger"; slightly to the left of him, then, stands the conservative, to the left of that the middle-of-the-road, and then leftward to socialism and communism. Hence, the enormous temptation for some

---

the use of this term to a laissez-faire system. But did it not operate . . . to preserve in being and maintain the material rewards of, the existing socioeconomic elites?

[11] For examples of the attractions of fascist and right-wing collectivist ideas and plans for American big businessmen in this era, see Murray N. Rothbard, *America's Great Depression* (Auburn, Ala.: Mises Institute, 2000). Also cf. Gaetano Salvemini and George LaPiana, *What to Do With Italy* (New York: Duell, Sloan, and Pearce, 1943), pp. 65ff.

Of the fascist economy, Salvemini perceptively wrote: In actual fact, it is the State, that is, the taxpayer who has become responsible to private enterprise. In Fascist Italy the State pays for the blunders of private enterprise. . . . Profit is private and individual. Loss is public and social. Gaetano Salvemini, *Under the Axe of Fascism* (London: Victor Gollancz, 1936), p. 416.

libertarians to red-bait; for, since they see America as drifting inexorably leftward to socialism and, therefore, to communism, the great temptation is for them to overlook the intermediary stages and tar all of their opposition with the hated Red brush.

One would think that the "right-wing Libertarian" would quickly be able to see some drastic flaws in this conception. For one thing, the income tax amendment, which he deplores as the beginning of socialism in America, was put through Congress in 1909 by an overwhelming majority of both parties. To look at this event as a sharp leftward move toward socialism would require treating President William Howard Taft, who put through the Sixteenth Amendment, as a Leftist, and surely few would have the temerity to do that. Indeed, the New Deal was not a *revolution* in any sense; its entire collectivist program was anticipated: proximately by Herbert Hoover during the depression, and, beyond that, by the war-collectivism and central planning that governed America during World War I. Every element in the New Deal program: central planning, creation of a network of compulsory cartels for industry and agriculture, inflation and credit expansion, artificial raising of wage rates and promotion of unions within the overall monopoly structure, government regulation and ownership, all this had been anticipated and adumbrated during the previous two decades.[12] And this program, with its privileging of various big business interests at the top of the collectivist heap, was in no sense reminiscent of socialism or leftism; there was nothing smacking of the egalitarian or the proletarian here. No, the kinship of this burgeoning collectivism was not at all

---

[12]Thus, see Rothbard, passim.

with socialism–communism but with fascism, or socialism-of-the-right, a kinship which many big businessmen of the twenties expressed openly in their yearning for abandonment of a quasi-laissez-faire system for a collectivism which they could control. And, surely, William Howard Taft, Woodrow Wilson, and Herbert Clark Hoover make far more recognizable figures as proto-Fascists than they do as crypto-communists.

The essence of the New Deal was seen, far more clearly than in the Conservative mythology, by the Leninist movement in the early 1930s; that is, until the mid-thirties, when the exigencies of Soviet foreign relations caused a sharp shift of the world communist line to "Popular Front" approval of the New Deal. Thus, in 1934, the British Leninist theoretician R. Palme Dutt published a brief but scathing analysis of the New Deal as "social fascism"—as the reality of fascism cloaked with a thin veneer of populist demagogy. No Conservative opponent has ever delivered a more vigorous or trenchant denunciation of the New Deal. The Roosevelt policy, wrote Dutt, was to "move to a form of dictatorship of a war-type"; the essential policies were to impose a State monopoly capitalism through the NRA, to subsidize business, banking, and agriculture through inflation and the partial expropriation of the mass of the people through lower real-wage rates and to the regulation and exploitation of labor by means of government-fixed wages and compulsory arbitration. When the New Deal, wrote Dutt, is stripped of its "social-reformist 'progressive' camouflage," "the reality of the new Fascist type of system of concentrated State capitalism and industrial servitude remains," including an implicit "advance to war." Dutt effectively concluded with a quote from an editor of the highly respected *Current History Magazine*:

> The new America [the editor had written in mid-1933] will not be capitalist in the old sense, nor will it be socialist. If

at the moment the trend is towards fascism, it will be an
American fascism, embodying the experience, the tradi-
tions, and the hopes of a great middle-class nation.[13]

Thus, the New Deal was not a qualitative break from the
American past; on the contrary, it was merely a quantitative
extension of the web of State privilege that had been proposed and acted upon before: in Hoover's administration, in
the war collectivism of World War I, and in the Progressive
Era. The most thorough exposition of the origins of State
monopoly capitalism, or what he calls "political capitalism,"
in the United States is found in the brilliant work of Dr.
Gabriel Kolko. In *The Triumph of Conservatism*, Kolko traces
the origins of political capitalism in the "reforms" of the Progressive Era. Orthodox historians have always treated the
Progressive period (roughly 1900–1916) as a time when free-
market capitalism was becoming increasingly "monopolis-
tic"; in reaction to this reign of monopoly and big business,
so the story runs, altruistic intellectuals and far-seeing politicians turned to intervention by the government to reform
and to regulate these evils. Kolko's great work demonstrates
that the reality was almost precisely the opposite of this
myth. Despite the wave of mergers and trusts formed around
the turn of the century, Kolko reveals, the forces of competition on the free market rapidly vitiated and dissolved these
attempts at stabilizing and perpetuating the economic power
of big business interests. It was precisely in reaction to their
impending defeat at the hands of the competitive storms of
the market that big business turned, increasingly after the
1900s, to the federal government for aid and protection. In
short, the intervention by the federal government was

---

[13]R. Palme Dutt, *Fascism and Social Revolution* (New York: International Publishers, 1934), pp. 247–51.

designed, not to curb big business monopoly for the sake of the public weal, but to create monopolies that big business (as well as trade associations of smaller business) had not been able to establish amidst the competitive gales of the free market. Both left and right have been persistently misled by the notion that intervention by the government is *ipso facto* leftish and antibusiness. Hence the mythology of the New-Fair Deal-as-Red that is endemic on the right. Both the big businessmen, led by the Morgan interests, and Professor Kolko, almost uniquely in the academic world, have realized that monopoly privilege can only be created by the State and not as a result of free-market operations.

Thus, Kolko shows that, beginning with Theodore Roosevelt's New Nationalism and culminating in Wilson's New Freedom, in industry after industry, for example, insurance, banking, meat, exports and business generally, regulations that present-day rightists think of as "socialistic" were not only uniformly hailed, but conceived and brought about by big businessmen. This was a conscious effort to fasten upon the economy a cement of subsidy, stabilization, and monopoly privilege. A typical view was that of Andrew Carnegie; deeply concerned about competition in the steel industry, which neither the formation of U.S. Steel nor the famous "Gary Dinners" sponsored by that Morgan company could dampen, Carnegie declared in 1908 that "it always comes back to me that government control, and that alone, will properly solve the problem." There is nothing alarming about government regulation *per se*, announced Carnegie, "capital is perfectly safe in the gas company, although it is under court control. So will all capital be, although under government control."[14]

---

[14]See Gabriel Kolko, *The Triumph of Conservativm: A Reinterpretation of American History, 1900–1916* (Glencoe, Ill.: The Free Press,

The Progressive Party, Kolko shows, was basically a Morgan-created party to reelect Roosevelt and punish President Taft, who had been overzealous in prosecuting Morgan enterprises, the leftish social workers often unwittingly provided a demagogic veneer for a conservative–statist movement. Wilson's New Freedom, culminating in the creation of the Federal Trade Commission, far from being considered dangerously socialistic by big business, was welcomed enthusiastically as putting their long-cherished program of support, privilege, and regulation of competition into effect (and Wilson's war collectivism was welcomed even more exuberantly). Edward N. Hurley, chairman of the Federal Trade Commission and formerly president of the Illinois Manufacturers Association, happily announced in late 1915, that the Federal Trade Commission was designed "to do for general business" what the ICC had been eagerly doing for the railroads and shippers, what the Federal Reserve was doing for the nation's bankers, and what the Department of Agriculture was accomplishing for the farmers.[15] As would happen more dramatically in European fascism, each economic interest group was being cartelized and monopolized and fitted into its privileged niche in a hierarchically-ordered socioeconomic

----

1963), pp. 173 and passim. For an example of the way in which Kolko has already begun to influence American historiography, see David T. Gilchrist and W. David Lewis, eds., *Economic Change in the Civil War Era* (Greenville, Del.: Eleutherian Mills–Hagley Foundation, 1965), p. 115. Kolko's complementary and confirmatory work on railroads, *Railroads and Regulation, 1877–1916* (Princeton, N.J.: Princeton University Press, 1965) comes too late to be considered here. A brief treatment of the monopolizing role of the ICC for the railroad industry may be found in Christopher D. Stone, "ICC: Some Reminiscences on the Future of American Transportation," *New Individualist Review* (Spring, 1963): 3–15.

[15] Kolko, *The Triumph of Conservatism*, p. 274.

structure. Particularly influential were the views of Arthur Jerome Eddy, an eminent corporation lawyer who specialized in forming trade associations and who helped to father the Federal Trade Commission. In his *magnum opus* fiercely denouncing competition in business and calling for governmentally-controlled and protected industrial "cooperation," Eddy trumpeted that "Competition is War, and 'War is Hell'."[16]

What of the intellectuals of the Progressive period, damned by the present-day Right as "socialistic"? Socialistic in a sense they were, but what *kind* of "socialism"? The conservative state socialism of Bismarck's Germany, the prototype for so much of modern European—and American— political forms, and under which the bulk of American intellectuals of the late nineteenth century received their higher education. As Kolko puts it:

> The conservatism of the contemporary intellectuals . . . the idealization of the state by Lester Ward, Richard T. Ely, or Simon N. Patten . . . was also the result of the peculiar training of many of the American academics of this period. At the end of the nineteenth century the primary influence in American academic social and economic theory was exerted by the universities. The Bismarckian idealization of the state, with its centralized welfare functions . . . was suitably revised by the thousands of key academics who studied in German universities in the 1880s and 1890s.[17]

The ideal of the leading ultraconservative German professors, moreover, who were also called "socialists of the chair,"

---

[16]Arthur Jerome Eddy, *The New Competition: An Examination of the Conditions Underlying the Radical Change that is Taking Place in the Commercial and Industrial World—The Change from a Competitive to a Cooperative Basis* (7th ed., Chicago: A.C. McClurg, 1920).

[17]Kolko, *The Triumph of Conservatism*, p. 214.

was consciously to form themselves into the "intellectual bodyguard of the House of Hohenzollern"—and that they surely were.

As an exemplar of the Progressive intellectual, Kolko aptly cites Herbert Croly, editor of the Morgan-financed *New Republic*. Systematizing Theodore Roosevelt's New Nationalism, Croly hailed this new Hamiltonianism as a system for collectivist federal control and integration of society into a hierarchical structure. Looking forward from the Progressive Era, Gabriel Kolko concludes that:

> a synthesis of business and politics on the federal level was created during the war, in various administrative and emergency agencies, that continued throughout the following decade. Indeed, the war period represents the triumph of business in the most emphatic manner possible . . . big business gained total support from the various regulatory agencies and the Executive. It was during the war that effective, working oligopoly and price and market agreements became operational in the dominant sectors of the American economy. The rapid diffusion of power in the economy and relatively easy entry virtually ceased. Despite the cessation of important new legislative enactments, the unity of business and the federal government continued throughout the 1920s and thereafter, using the foundations laid in the Progressive Era to stabilize and consolidate conditions within various industries. . . . The principle of utilizing the federal government to stabilize the economy, established in the context of modern industrialism during the Progressive Era, became the basis of political capitalism in its many later ramifications.
>
> In this sense progressivism did not die in the 1920s, but became a part of the basic fabric of American society.[18]

Thus the New Deal. After a bit of leftish wavering in the middle of the late thirties, the Roosevelt administration recemented its alliance with big business in the national defense

---

[18]Ibid., pp. 286–87.

and war contract economy that began in 1940. This is an economy and a polity that has been ruling America ever since, embodied in the permanent war economy, the full-fledged State monopoly capitalism and neomercantilism, the military–industrial complex of the present era. The essential features of American society have not changed since it was thoroughly militarized and politicized in World War II—except that the trends intensify, and even in everyday life men have been increasingly molded into conforming *organization men* serving the State and its military–industrial complex. William H. Whyte, Jr., in his justly famous book, *The Organization Man*, made clear that this molding took place amidst the adoption by business of the collectivist views of "enlightened" sociologists and other social engineers. It is also clear that this harmony of views is not simply the result of naïveté by big businessmen—not when such "naïveté" coincides with the requirements of compressing the worker and manager into the mold of willing servitor in the great bureaucracy of the military–industrial machine. And, under the guise of "democracy," education has become mere mass drilling in the techniques of adjustment to the task of becoming a cog in the vast bureaucratic machine.

Meanwhile, the Republicans and Democrats remain as bipartisan in forming and supporting this establishment as they were in the first two decades of the twentieth century. "Me-tooism"—bipartisan support of the *status quo* that underlies the superficial differences between the parties—did not begin in 1940.

How did the corporal's guard of remaining libertarians react to these shifts of the ideological spectrum in America? An instructive answer may be found by looking at the career of one of the great libertarians of twentieth-century America— Albert Jay Nock. In the 1920s, when Nock had formulated his radical libertarian philosophy, he was universally regarded as a member of the extreme Left, and he so regarded himself as well. It is always the tendency, in ideological and political life, to center one's attention on the main enemy of the day, and the main enemy of that day was the conservative statism of the Coolidge-Hoover administration; it was natural, therefore, for Nock, his friend and fellow-libertarian H.L. Mencken and other radicals to join quasi-Socialists in battle against the common foe. When the New Deal succeeded Hoover, on the other hand, the milk-and-water socialists and vaguely leftish Interventionists hopped on the New Deal bandwagon; on the Left only the Libertarians such as Nock and Mencken and the Leninists (before the Popular Front period) realized that Roosevelt was only a continuation of Hoover in other rhetoric. It was perfectly natural for the radicals to form a united front against Roosevelt with the older Hoover and Al Smith conservatives who either believed Roosevelt had gone too far or disliked his flamboyant populistic rhetoric. But the problem was that Nock and his fellow radicals, at first properly scornful of their newfound allies, soon began to accept them and even don cheerfully the formerly despised label of "Conservative." With the rank-and-file radicals, this shift took place, as have so many transformations of ideology in history, unwittingly and in default of proper ideological leadership; for Nock, and to some extent for Mencken, on the other hand, the problem cut far deeper.

For there had always been one grave flaw in the brilliant and finely-honed libertarian doctrine hammered out in their very different ways by Nock and Mencken; both had long adopted the great error of pessimism. Both saw no hope for the human race ever adopting the system of liberty; despairing of the radical doctrine of liberty ever being applied in practice, each in his own personal way retreated from the responsibility of ideological leadership, Mencken joyously and hedonically, Nock haughtily and secretively. Despite the massive contribution of both men to the cause of liberty, therefore, neither could ever become the conscious leader of a libertarian movement, for neither could ever envision the party of liberty as the party of hope, the party of revolution, or *a fortiori*, the party of secular messianism. The error of pessimism is the first step down the slippery slope that leads to conservatism; and hence it was all too easy for the pessimistic radical Nock, even though still basically a Libertarian, to accept the conservative label and even come to croak the old platitude that there is an *a priori* presumption against any social change.

It is fascinating that Albert Jay Nock thus followed the ideological path of his beloved spiritual ancestor Herbert Spencer, both began as pure radical Libertarians, both quickly abandoned radical or revolutionary tactics as embodied in the will to put their theories into practice through mass action, and both eventually glided from Tory tactics to at least a partial toryism of content.

And so the Libertarians, especially in their sense of where they stood in the ideological spectrum, fused with the older Conservatives who were forced to adopt libertarian phraseology (but with no real libertarian content) in opposing a Roosevelt administration that had become too collectivistic for them, either in content or in rhetoric. World War II reinforced and cemented this alliance; for, in contrast to all the previous American wars of the century, the pro-peace and "isolationist" forces were all identified, by their enemies and subsequently by themselves, as men of the "Right." By the end of World War II, it was second nature for libertarians to consider themselves at an "extreme right-wing" pole with the Conservatives immediately to the left of them; and hence the great error of the spectrum that persists to this day. In particular, the modern libertarians forgot or never realized that opposition to war and militarism had always been a "left-wing" tradition which had included Libertarians; and hence when the historical aberration of the New Deal period corrected itself and the "right-wing" was once again the great partisan of total war, the Libertarians were unprepared to understand what was happening and tailed along in the wake of their supposed conservative "allies." The liberals had completely lost their old ideological markings and guidelines.

Given a proper reorientation of the ideological spectrum, what then would be the prospects for liberty? It is no wonder that the contemporary Libertarian, seeing the world going socialistic and communistic, and believing himself virtually isolated and cut off from any prospect of united mass action, tends to be steeped in long-run pessimism. But the scene immediately brightens when we realize that that indispensable requisite of modern civilization—the overthrow of the Old Order—was accomplished by mass libertarian action erupting in such great revolutions of the West as the French and American Revolutions, and bringing about the glories of the Industrial Revolution and the advances of liberty, mobility, and rising living standards that we still retain today. Despite the reactionary swings backward to statism, the modern world stands towering above the world of the past. When we consider also that, in one form or another, the Old Order of despotism, feudalism, theocracy, and militarism dominated every human civilization until the West of the eighteenth century, optimism over what man has and can achieve must mount still higher.

It might be retorted, however, that this bleak historical record of despotism and stagnation only reinforces pessimism, for it shows the persistence and durability of the Old

Order and the seeming frailty and evanescence of the New—
especially in view of the retrogression of the past century. But
such superficial analysis neglects the great change that
occurred with the revolution of the New Order, a change
that is clearly irreversible. For the Old Order was able to
persist in its slave system for centuries precisely because it
awoke no expectations and no hopes in the minds of the sub-
merged masses; their lot was to live and eke out their brutish
subsistence in slavery while obeying unquestioningly the
commands of their divinely appointed rulers. But the liberal
revolution implanted indelibly in the minds of the masses—
not only in the West but in the still feudally-dominated undeveloped world—the burning desire for liberty, for land to the
peasantry, for peace between the nations, and, perhaps above
all, for the mobility and rising standards of living that can only
be brought to them by an industrial civilization. The masses
will never again accept the mindless serfdom of the Old
Order; and given these demands that have been awakened by
liberalism and the Industrial Revolution, long-run victory for
liberty is inevitable.

For only liberty, only a free market, can organize and
maintain an industrial system, and the more that population
expands and explodes, the more necessary is the unfettered
working of such an industrial economy. Laissez-faire and the
free market become more and more evidently necessary as an
industrial system develops; radical deviations cause breakdowns and economic crises. This crisis of statism becomes
particularly dramatic and acute in a fully socialist society; and
hence the inevitable breakdown of statism has first become
strikingly apparent in the countries of the socialist (that is,
communist) camp. For socialism confronts its inner contradiction most starkly. Desperately, it tries to fulfill its proclaimed goals of industrial growth, higher standards of living
for the masses, and eventual withering away of the State and

is increasingly unable to do so with its collectivist means.
Hence the inevitable breakdown of socialism. This progressive breakdown of socialist planning was at first partially
obscured. For, in every instance, the Leninists took power
not in a developed capitalist country as Marx had wrongly
predicted, but in a country suffering from the oppression of
feudalism. Second, the Communists did not attempt to impose
socialism upon the economy for many years after taking
power; in Soviet Russia until Stalin's forced collectivization
of the early 1930s reversed the wisdom of Lenin's New Economic Policy, which Lenin's favorite theoretician, Bukharin,
would have extended onward towards a free market. Even the
supposedly rabid Communist leaders of China did not
impose a socialist economy on that country until the late
1950s. In every case, growing industrialization has imposed a
series of economic breakdowns so severe that the communist
countries, against their ideological principles, have had to
retreat step by step from central planning and return to various degrees and forms of a free market. The Liberman Plan
for the Soviet Union has gained a great deal of publicity; but
the inevitable process of desocialization has proceeded much
further in Poland, Hungary, and Czechoslovakia. Most
advanced of all is Yugoslavia, which, freed from Stalinist
rigidity earlier than its fellows, in only a dozen years has de-
socialized so fast and so far that its economy is now hardly
more socialistic than that of France. The fact that people calling themselves "communists" are still governing the country is
irrelevant to the basic social and economic facts. Central planning in Yugoslavia has virtually disappeared. The private sector not only predominates in agriculture but is even strong in
industry, and the public sector itself has been so radically
decentralized and placed under free pricing, profit-and-loss
tests and a cooperative worker–ownership of each plant that
true socialism hardly exists any longer. Only the final step of
converting workers' syndical control to individual shares of

ownership remains on the path toward outright capitalism. Communist China and the able Marxist theoreticians of *Monthly Review* have clearly discerned the situation and have raised the alarm that Yugoslavia is no longer a socialist country.

One would think that free-market economists would hail the confirmation and increasing relevance of the notable insight of Professor Ludwig von Mises a half-century ago: that socialist states, being necessarily devoid of a genuine price system, could not calculate economically and, therefore, could not plan their economies with any success. Indeed, one follower of Mises, in effect, predicted this process of desocialization in a novel some years ago. Yet neither this author nor other free-market economists have given the slightest indication of even recognizing, let alone saluting, this process in the communist countries—perhaps because their almost hysterical view of the alleged threat of communism prevents them from acknowledging any dissolution in the supposed monolith of menace.[19]

Communist countries, therefore, are increasingly and ineradicably forced to desocialize and will, therefore, eventually reach the free market. The state of the undeveloped countries is also cause for sustained libertarian optimism. For

---

[19]One happy exception is William D. Grampp, "New Directions in the Communist Economics," *Business Horizons* (Fall, 1963): 29–36. Grampp writes:

> Hayek said that centralized planning will lead to serfdom. It follows that a decrease in the economic authority of the State should lead away from serfdom. The Communist countries may show that to be true. It would be a withering away of the state the Marxists have not counted on nor has it been anticipated by those who agree with Hayek. (p. 35)

The novel in question is Henry Hazlitt, *The Great Idea* (New York: Appleton-Century-Crofts, 1951).

all over the world, the peoples of the undeveloped nations are engaged in revolution to throw off their feudal Old Order. It is true that the United States is doing its mightiest to suppress the very revolutionary process that once brought it and Western Europe out of the shackles of the Old Order; but it is increasingly clear that even overwhelming armed might cannot suppress the desire of the masses to break through into the modern world.

We are left with the United States and the countries of Western Europe. Here, the case for optimism is less clear, for the quasi-collectivist system does not present as stark a crisis of self-contradiction as does socialism. And yet, here, too, economic crisis looms in the future and gnaws away at the complacency of the Keynesian economic managers: creeping inflation, reflected in the aggravating balance-of-payments breakdown of the once almighty dollar; creeping secular unemployment brought about by minimum wage scales; and the deeper and long-run accumulation of the uneconomic distortions of the permanent war economy. Moreover, potential crises in the United States are not merely economic; there is a burgeoning and inspiring moral ferment among the youth of America against the fetters of centralized bureaucracy, of mass education in uniformity, and of brutality and oppression exercised by the minions of the State.

Furthermore, the maintenance of a substantial degree of free speech and democratic forms facilitates, at least in the short run, the possible growth of a libertarian movement. The United States is also fortunate in possessing, even if half-forgotten beneath the statist and tyrannical overlay of the last half-century, a great tradition of libertarian thought and action. The very fact that much of this heritage is still reflected in popular rhetoric, even though stripped of its significance in practice, provides a substantial ideological groundwork for a future party of liberty.

What the Marxists would call the "objective conditions" for the triumph of liberty exist, then, everywhere in the world and more so than in any past age; for everywhere the masses have opted for higher living standards and the promise of freedom and everywhere the various regimes of statism and collectivism cannot fulfill these goals. What is needed, then, is simply the "subjective conditions" for victory; that is, a growing body of informed libertarians who will spread the message to the peoples of the world that liberty and the purely free market provide the way out of their problems and crises. Liberty cannot be fully achieved unless libertarians exist in number to guide the peoples to the proper path. But perhaps the greatest stumbling block to the creation of such a movement is the despair and pessimism typical of the Libertarian in today's world. Much of that pessimism is due to his misreading of history and his thinking of himself and his handful of confreres as irredeemably isolated from the masses and, therefore, from the winds of history. Hence he becomes a lone critic of historical events rather than a person who considers himself as part of a potential movement which can and will make history. The modern Libertarian has forgotten that the Liberal of the seventeenth and eighteenth centuries faced odds much more overwhelming than those which face the Liberal of today; for in that era before the Industrial Revolution, the victory of liberalism was far from inevitable. And yet the liberalism of that day was not content to remain a gloomy little sect; instead, it unified theory and action. Liberalism grew and developed as an ideology and, leading and guiding the masses, made the revolution which changed the fate of the world. By its monumental breakthrough, this revolution of the eighteenth century transformed history from a chronicle of stagnation and despotism to an ongoing movement advancing toward a veritable secular utopia of liberty and rationality and abundance. The Old Order is dead or moribund; and the reactionary attempts to run a modern society and economy by various throwbacks to the Old Order are doomed to total failure. The Liberals of the past have left to modern Libertarians a glorious heritage, not only of ideology but of victories against far more devastating odds. The Liberals of the past have also left a heritage of the proper strategy and tactics for libertarians to follow, not only by leading rather than remaining aloof from the masses, but also by not falling prey to short-run optimism. For short-run optimism, being unrealistic, leads straightway to disillusion and then to long-run pessimism; just as, on the other side of the coin, long-run pessimism leads to exclusive and self-defeating concentration on immediate and short-run issues. Short-run optimism stems, for one thing, from a naive and simplistic view of strategy: that liberty will win merely by educating more intellectuals, who in turn will educate opinion-molders, who in turn will convince the masses, after which the State will somehow fold its tent and silently steal away. Matters are not that easy. For libertarians face not only a problem of education but also a problem of power, and it is a law of history that a ruling caste has never voluntarily given up its power.

But the problem of power is, certainly in the United States, far in the future. For the Libertarian, the main task of the present epoch is to cast off his needless and debilitating pessimism, to set his sights on long-run victory and to set out on the road to its attainment. To do this, he must, perhaps first of all, drastically realign his mistaken view of the ideological spectrum; he must discover who his friends and natural allies are, and above all perhaps, who his enemies are. Armed with this knowledge, let him proceed in the spirit of radical long-run optimism that one of the great figures in the history of libertarian thought, Randolph Bourne, correctly identified as the spirit of youth. Let Bourne's stirring words serve also as the guidepost for the spirit of liberty:

[Y]outh is the incarnation of reason pitted against the rigidity of tradition; youth puts the remorseless questions to everything that is old and established—Why? What is this thing good for? And when it gets the mumbled, evasive answers of the defenders it applies its own fresh, clean spirit of reason to institutions, customs and ideas and finding them stupid, inane or poisonous, turns instinctively to overthrow them and build in their place the things with which its visions teem. . . .

Youth is the leaven that keeps all these questioning, testing attitudes fermenting in the world. If it were not for this troublesome activity of youth, with its hatred of sophisms and glosses, its insistence on things as they are, society would die from sheer decay. It is the policy of the older generation as it gets adjusted to the world to hide away the unpleasant things where it can, or preserve a conspiracy of silence and an elaborate pretense that they do not exist. But meanwhile the sores go on festering just the same. Youth is the drastic antiseptic. . . . It drags skeletons from closets and insists that they be explained. No wonder the older generation fears and distrusts the younger. Youth is the avenging Nemesis on its trail. . . .

Our elders are always optimistic in their views of the present, pessimistic in their views of the future; youth is pessimistic toward the present and gloriously hopeful for the future. And it is this hope which is the lever of progress—one might say, the only lever of progress. . . .

The secret of life is then that this fine youthful spirit shall never be lost. Out of the turbulence of youth should come this fine precipitate—a sane, strong, aggressive spirit of daring and doing. It must be a flexible, growing spirit, with a hospitality to new ideas and a keen insight into experience. To keep one's reactions warm and true is to have found the secret of perpetual youth, and perpetual youth is salvation.[20]

---

[20]Randolph Bourne, "Youth," *The Atlantic Monthly* (April, 1912); reprinted in Lillian Schlissel, ed., *The World of Randolph Bourne* (New York: E.P. Dutton, 1965), pp. 9–11, 15.

3
THE ANATOMY
OF THE STATE

WHAT THE STATE IS NOT

The State is almost universally considered an institution of social service. Some theorists venerate the State as the apotheosis of society; others regard it as an amiable, though often inefficient, organization for achieving social ends; but almost all regard it as a necessary means for achieving the goals of mankind, a means to be ranged against the "private sector" and often winning in this competition of resources. With the rise of democracy, the identification of the State with society has been redoubled, until it is common to hear sentiments expressed which violate virtually every tenet of reason and common sense such as, "we are the government." The useful collective term "we" has enabled an ideological camouflage to be thrown over the reality of political life. If "we are the government," then anything a government does to an individual is not only just and untyrannical, but also "voluntary" on the part of the individual concerned. If the government has incurred a huge public debt which must be paid by taxing one group for the benefit of another, this reality of burden is obscured by saying that "we owe it to ourselves"; if the government conscripts a man, or throws him into jail for dissident opinion, then he is "doing it to himself" and, therefore, nothing untoward has occurred. Under this reasoning, any Jews murdered by the Nazi government were *not* murdered; instead, they must have "committed suicide," since they *were* the government (which was democratically chosen), and, therefore, anything the government did to them was voluntary on their part. One would not think it necessary to belabor this point, and yet the overwhelming bulk of the people hold this fallacy to a greater or lesser degree.

We must, therefore, emphasize that "we" are *not* the government; the government is *not* "us." The government does not in any accurate sense "represent" the majority of the people.[1] But, even if it did, even if 70 percent of the people decided to murder the remaining 30 percent, this would still be murder and would not be voluntary suicide on the part of the slaughtered minority.[2] No organicist metaphor, no irrelevant bromide that "we are all part of one another," must be permitted to obscure this basic fact.

If, then, the State is not "us," if it is not "the human family" getting together to decide mutual problems, if it is not a

---

[1]We cannot, in this chapter, develop the many problems and fallacies of "democracy." Suffice it to say here that an individual's true agent or "representative" is always subject to that individual's orders, can be dismissed at any time and cannot act contrary to the interests or wishes of his principal. Clearly, the "representative" in a democracy can never fulfill such agency functions, the only ones consonant with a libertarian society.

[2]Social democrats often retort that democracy—majority choice of rulers—logically implies that the majority must leave certain freedoms to the minority, for the minority might one day become the majority. Apart from other flaws, this argument obviously does not hold where the minority *cannot* become the majority, for example, when the minority is of a different racial or ethnic group from the majority.

lodge meeting or country club, what is it? Briefly, the State is that organization in society which attempts to maintain a monopoly of the use of force and violence in a given territorial area; in particular, it is the only organization in society that obtains its revenue not by voluntary contribution or payment for services rendered but by coercion. While other individuals or institutions obtain their income by production of goods and services and by the peaceful and voluntary sale of these goods and services to others, the State obtains its revenue by the use of compulsion; that is, by the use and the threat of the jailhouse and the bayonet.[3] Having used force and violence to obtain its revenue, the State generally goes on to regulate and dictate the other actions of its individual subjects. One would think that simple observation of all States through history and over the globe would be proof enough of this assertion; but the miasma of myth has lain so long over State activity that elaboration is necessary.

WHAT THE STATE IS

Man is born naked into the world, and needing to use his mind to learn how to take the resources given him by nature,

---

[3]Joseph A. Schumpeter, *Capitalism, Socialism, and Democracy* (New York: Harper and Bros., 1942), p. 198.

> The friction or antagonism between the private and the public sphere was intensified from the first by the fact that . . . the State has been living on a revenue which was being produced in the private sphere for private purposes and had to be deflected from these purposes by political force. The theory which construes taxes on the analogy of club dues or of the purchase of the service of, say, a doctor only proves how far removed this part of the social sciences is from scientific habits of mind.

Also see Murray N. Rothbard, "The Fallacy of the 'Public Sector,'" *New Individualist Review* (Summer, 1961): 3ff.

and to transform them (for example, by investment in "capital") into shapes and forms and places where the resources can be used for the satisfaction of his wants and the advancement of his standard of living. The only way by which man can do this is by the use of his mind and energy to transform resources ("production") and to exchange these products for products created by others. Man has found that, through the process of voluntary, mutual exchange, the productivity and hence the living standards of all participants in exchange may increase enormously. The only "natural" course for man to survive and to attain wealth, therefore, is by using his mind and energy to engage in the production-and-exchange process. He does this, first, by finding natural resources, and then by transforming them (by "mixing his labor" with them, as Locke puts it), to make them his individual *property*, and then by exchanging this property for the similarly obtained property of others. The social path dictated by the requirements of man's nature, therefore, is the path of "property rights" and the "free market" of gift or exchange of such rights. Through this path, men have learned how to avoid the "jungle" methods of fighting over scarce resources so that A can only acquire them at the expense of B and, instead, to multiply those resources enormously in peaceful and harmonious production and exchange.

The great German sociologist Franz Oppenheimer pointed out that there are two mutually exclusive ways of acquiring wealth; one, the above way of production and exchange, he called the "economic means." The other way is simpler in that it does not require productivity; it is the way of seizure of another's goods or services by the use of force and violence. This is the method of one-sided confiscation, of theft of the property of others. This is the method which Oppenheimer termed "the political means" to wealth. It should be clear that the peaceful use of reason and energy in production is the "natural" path for man: the means for his survival and prosperity on this earth. It should be equally clear that the coercive, exploitative means is contrary to natural law; it is parasitic, for instead of adding to production, it subtracts from it. The "political means" siphons production off to a parasitic and destructive individual or group; and this siphoning not only subtracts from the number producing, but also lowers the producer's incentive to produce beyond his own subsistence. In the long run, the robber destroys his own subsistence by dwindling or eliminating the source of his own supply. But not only that; even in the short-run, the predator is acting contrary to his own true nature as a man.

We are now in a position to answer more fully the question: what is the *State*? The State, in the words of Oppenheimer, is the "organization of the political means"; it is the systematization of the predatory process over a given territory.[4] For crime, at best, is sporadic and uncertain; the parasitism is ephemeral, and the coercive, parasitic lifeline may be cut off at any time by the resistance of the victims. The State provides a legal, orderly, systematic channel for the predation

---

[4]Franz Oppenheimer, *The State* (New York: Vanguard Press, 1926) pp. 24–27:

> There are two fundamentally opposed means whereby man, requiring sustenance, is impelled to obtain the necessary means for satisfying his desires. These are work and robbery, one's own labor and the forcible appropriation of the labor of others. . . . I propose in the following discussion to call one's own labor and the equivalent exchange of one's own labor for the labor of others, the "economic means" for the satisfaction of needs while the unrequited appropriation of the labor of others will be called the "political means". . . . The State is an organization of the political means. No State, therefore, can come into being until the economic means has created a definite number of objects for the satisfaction of needs, which objects may be taken away or appropriated by warlike robbery.

of private property; it renders certain, secure, and relatively "peaceful" the lifeline of the parasitic caste in society.[5] Since production must always precede predation, the free market is anterior to the State. The State has never been created by a "social contract"; it has always been born in conquest and exploitation. The classic paradigm was a conquering tribe pausing in its time-honored method of looting and murdering a conquered tribe, to realize that the time-span of plunder would be longer and more secure, and the situation more pleasant, if the conquered tribe were allowed to live and produce, with the conquerors settling among them as rulers exacting a steady annual tribute.[6] One method of the birth of

---

[5]Albert Jay Nock wrote vividly that

> the State claims and exercises the monopoly of crime. . . . It forbids private murder, but itself organizes murder on a colossal scale. It punishes private theft, but itself lays unscrupulous hands on anything it wants, whether the property of citizen or of alien.

Nock, *On Doing the Right Thing, and Other Essays* (New York: Harper and Bros., 1929), p. 143; quoted in Jack Schwartzman, "Albert Jay Nock—A Superfluous Man," *Faith and Freedom* (December, 1953): 11.

[6]Oppenheimer, *The State*, p. 15:

> What, then, is the State as a sociological concept? The State, completely in its genesis . . . is a social institution, forced by a victorious group of men on a defeated group, with the sole purpose of regulating the dominion of the victorious group of men on a defeated group, and securing itself against revolt from within and attacks from abroad. Teleologically, this dominion had no other purpose than the economic exploitation of the vanquished by the victors.

And de Jouvenel has written: "the State is in essence the result of the successes achieved by a band of brigands who superimpose themselves on small, distinct societies." Bertrand de Jouvenel, *On Power* (New York: Viking Press, 1949), pp. 100–01.

a State may be illustrated as follows: in the hills of southern "Ruritania," a bandit group manages to obtain physical control over the territory, and finally the bandit chieftain proclaims himself "King of the sovereign and independent government of South Ruritania"; and, if he and his men have the force to maintain this rule for a while, lo and behold! a new State has joined the "family of nations," and the former bandit leaders have been transformed into the lawful nobility of the realm.

How the State Preserves Itself

Once a State has been established, the problem of the ruling group or "caste" is how to maintain their rule.[7] While force is their *modus operandi*, their basic and long-run problem is ideological. For in order to continue in office, *any* government (not simply a "democratic" government) must have the support of the majority of its subjects. This support, it must be noted, need not be active enthusiasm; it may well be passive resignation as if to an inevitable law of nature. But support in the sense of acceptance of some sort it must be; else the minority of State rulers would eventually be outweighed by the active resistance of the majority of the public. Since predation must be supported out of the surplus of production, it is necessarily true that the class constituting the State—the full-time bureaucracy (and nobility)—must be a rather small minority in the land, although it may, of course, purchase allies among important groups in the population. Therefore, the chief task of the rulers is always to

---

[7]On the crucial distinction between "caste," a group with privileges or burdens coercively granted or imposed by the State and the Marxian concept of "class" in society, see Ludwig von Mises, *Theory and History* (New Haven, Conn.: Yale University Press, 1957), pp. 112ff.

secure the active or resigned acceptance of the majority of the citizens.[8,9]

Of course, one method of securing support is through the creation of vested economic interests. Therefore, the King alone cannot rule; he must have a sizable group of followers who enjoy the prerequisites of rule, for example, the members of the State apparatus, such as the full-time bureaucracy or the established nobility.[10] But this still secures only a minority of eager supporters, and even the essential purchasing of support by subsidies and other grants of privilege still does not obtain the consent of the majority. For this essential acceptance, the majority must be persuaded by *ideology* that their government is good, wise and, at least, inevitable, and certainly better than other conceivable alternatives. Promoting

---

[8]Such acceptance does not, of course, imply that the State rule has become "voluntary"; for even if the majority support be active and eager, this support is not unanimous by every individual.

[9]That every government, no matter how "dictatorial" over individuals, must secure such support has been demonstrated by such acute political theorists as Étienne de la Boétie, David Hume, and Ludwig von Mises. Thus, cf. David Hume, "Of the First Principles of Government," in *Essays, Literary, Moral and Political* (London: Ward, Locke, and Taylor, n.d.), p. 23; Étienne de la Boétie, *Anti-Dictator* (New York: Columbia University Press, 1942), pp. 8–9; Ludwig von Mises, *Human Action* (Auburn, Ala.: Mises Institute, 1998), pp. 188ff. For more on the contribution to the analysis of the State by la Boétie, see Oscar Jaszi and John D. Lewis, *Against the Tyrant* (Glencoe, Ill.: The Free Press, 1957), pp. 55–57.

[10]La Boétie, *Anti-Dictator*, pp. 43–44.

> Whenever a ruler makes himself dictator . . . all those who are corrupted by burning ambition or extraordinary avarice, these gather around him and support him in order to have a share in the booty and to constitute themselves petty chiefs under the big tyrant.

this ideology among the people is the vital social task of the "intellectuals." For the masses of men do not create their own ideas, or indeed think through these ideas independently; they follow passively the ideas adopted and disseminated by the body of intellectuals. The intellectuals are, therefore, the "opinion-molders" in society. And since it is precisely a molding of opinion that the State most desperately needs, the basis for age-old alliance between the State and the intellectuals becomes clear.

It is evident that the State needs the intellectuals; it is not so evident why intellectuals need the State. Put simply, we may state that the intellectual's livelihood in the free market is never too secure; for the intellectual must depend on the values and choices of the masses of his fellow men, and it is precisely characteristic of the masses that they are generally uninterested in intellectual matters. The State, on the other hand, is willing to offer the intellectuals a secure and permanent berth in the State apparatus; and thus a secure income and the panoply of prestige. For the intellectuals will be handsomely rewarded for the important function they perform for the State rulers, of which group they now become a part.[11]

The alliance between the State and the intellectuals was symbolized in the eager desire of professors at the University

---

[11]This by no means implies that all intellectuals ally themselves with the State. On aspects of the alliance of intellectuals and the State, cf. Bertrand de Jouvenel, "The Attitude of the Intellectuals to the Market Society," *The Owl* (January, 1951): 19–27; idem, "The Treatment of Capitalism by Continental Intellectuals," in F.A. Hayek, ed., *Capitalism and the Historians* (Chicago: University of Chicago Press, 1954), pp. 93–123; reprinted in George B. de Huszar, *The Intellectuals* (Glencoe, Ill.: The Free Press, 1960), pp. 385–99; and Schumpeter, *Imperialism and Social Classes* (New York: Meridian Books, 1975), pp. 143–55.

of Berlin in the nineteenth century to form the "intellectual
bodyguard of the House of Hohenzollern." In the present
day, let us note the revealing comment of an eminent Marxist scholar concerning Professor Wittfogel's critical study of
ancient Oriental despotism: "The civilization which Professor Wittfogel is so bitterly attacking was one which could
make poets and scholars into officials."[12] Of innumerable
examples, we may cite the recent development of the "science" of strategy, in the service of the government's main vio-
lence-wielding arm, the military.[13] A venerable institution,
furthermore, is the official or "court" historian, dedicated to
purveying the rulers' views of their own and their predeces-
sors' actions.[14]

---

[12]Joseph Needham, "Review of Karl A. Wittfogel, *Oriental
Despotism,*" *Science and Society* (1958): 65. Needham also writes that "the
successive [Chinese] emperors were served in all ages by a great company of profoundly humane and disinterested scholars," p. 61. Wittfogel
notes the Confucian doctrine that the glory of the ruling class rested on
its gentleman scholar-bureaucrat officials, destined to be professional
rulers dictating to the mass of the populace. Karl A. Wittfogel, *Oriental
Despotism* (New Haven, Conn.: Yale University Press, 1957), pp. 320–21
and passim. For an attitude contrasting to Needham's, cf. John Lukacs,
"Intellectual Class or Intellectual Profession?" in de Huszar, *The
Intellectuals*, pp. 521–22.

[13]Jeanne Ribs, "The War Plotters," *Liberation* (August, 1961): 13.
"[s]trategists insist that their occupation deserves the 'dignity of the academic counterpart of the military profession.'" Also see Marcus Raskin,
"The Megadeath Intellectuals," *New York Review of Books* (November 14,
1963): 6–7.

[14]Thus the historian Conyers Read, in his presidential address, advocated the suppression of historical fact in the service of "democratic" and
national values. Read proclaimed that "total war, whether it is hot or cold,
enlists everyone and calls upon everyone to play his part. The historian is
not freer from this obligation than the physicist." Read, "The Social
Responsibilities of the Historian," *American Historical Review* (1951):

Many and varied have been the arguments by which the State and its intellectuals have induced their subjects to support their rule. Basically, the strands of argument may be summed up as follows: (a) the State rulers are great and wise men (they "rule by divine right," they are the "aristocracy" of men, they are the "scientific experts"), much greater and wiser than the good but rather simple subjects, and (b) rule by the extent government is inevitable, absolutely necessary, and far better, than the indescribable evils that would ensue upon its downfall. The union of Church and State was one of the oldest and most successful of these ideological devices. The ruler was either anointed by God or, in the case of the absolute rule of many Oriental despotisms, was himself God; hence, any resistance to his rule would be blasphemy. The States' priestcraft performed the basic intellectual function of obtaining popular support and even worship for the rulers.[15]

Another successful device was to instill fear of any alternative systems of rule or nonrule. The present rulers, it was maintained, supply to the citizens an essential service for which they should be most grateful: protection against sporadic criminals and marauders. For the State, to preserve its own monopoly of predation, did indeed see to it that private and unsystematic crime was kept to a minimum; the State has

---

283ff. For a critique of Read and other aspects of court history, see Howard K. Beale, "The Professional Historian: His Theory and Practice," *The Pacific Historical Review* (August, 1953): 227–55. Also cf. Herbert Butterfield, "Official History: Its Pitfalls and Criteria," *History and Human Relations* (New York: Macmillan, 1952), pp. 182–224; and Harry Elmer Barnes, *The Court Historians Versus Revisionism* (n.d.), pp. 2ff.

[15]Cf. Wittfogel, *Oriental Despotism*, pp. 87–100. On the contrasting roles of religion *vis-á-vis* the State in ancient China and Japan, see Norman Jacobs, *The Origin of Modern Capitalism and Eastern Asia* (Hong Kong: Hong Kong University Press, 1958), pp. 161–94.

always been jealous of its own preserve. Especially has the State been successful in recent centuries in instilling fear of *other* State rulers. Since the land area of the globe has been parceled out among particular States, one of the basic doctrines of the State was to identify itself with the territory it governed. Since most men tend to love their homeland, the identification of that land and its people with the State was a means of making natural patriotism work to the State's advantage. If "Ruritania" was being attacked by "Walldavia," the first task of the State and its intellectuals was to convince the people of Ruritania that the attack was really upon *them* and not simply upon the ruling caste. In this way, a war between *rulers* was converted into a war between *peoples*, with each people coming to the defense of its rulers in the erroneous belief that the rulers were defending *them*. This device of "nationalism" has only been successful, in Western civilization, in recent centuries; it was not too long ago that the mass of subjects regarded wars as irrelevant battles between various sets of nobles.

Many and subtle are the ideological weapons that the State has wielded through the centuries. One excellent weapon has been tradition. The longer that the rule of a State has been able to preserve itself, the more powerful this weapon; for then, the X Dynasty or the Y State has the seeming weight of centuries of tradition behind it.[16] Worship of

---

[16]de Jouvenel, *On Power*, p. 22:

> The essential reason for obedience is that it has become a habit of the species. . . . Power is for us a fact of nature. From the earliest days of recorded history it has always presided over human destinies . . . the authorities which ruled [societies] in former times did not disappear without bequeathing to their successors their privilege nor without leaving in men's minds imprints which are cumulative in

one's ancestors, then, becomes a none too subtle means of worship of one's ancient rulers. The greatest danger to the State is independent intellectual criticism; there is no better way to stifle that criticism than to attack any isolated voice, any raiser of new doubts, as a profane violator of the wisdom of his ancestors. Another potent ideological force is to deprecate the *individual* and exalt the collectivity of society. For since any given rule implies majority acceptance, any ideological danger to that rule can only start from one or a few independently-thinking individuals. The new idea, much less the new *critical* idea, needs to begin as a small minority opinion; therefore, the State must nip the view in the bud by ridiculing any view that defies the opinions of the mass. "Listen only to your brothers" or "adjust to society" thus become ideological weapons for crushing individual dissent.[17] By such measures, the masses will never learn of the nonexistence of their Emperor's clothes.[18] It is also important for the State to make its rule seem inevitable; even if its reign is

---

their effect. The succession of governments which, in the course of centuries, rule the same society may be looked on as one underlying government which takes on continuous accretions.

[17]On such uses of the religion of China, see Norman Jacobs, passim.

[18]H.L. Mencken, *A Mencken Chrestomathy* (New York: Knopf, 1949), p. 145:

All [government] can see in an original idea is potential change, and hence an invasion of its prerogatives. The most dangerous man, to any government, is the man who is able to think things out for himself, without regard to the prevailing superstitions and taboos. Almost inevitably he comes to the conclusion that the government he lives under is dishonest, insane and intolerable, and so, if he is romantic, he tries to change it. And even if he is not romantic personally he is very apt to spread discontent among those who are.

disliked, it will then be met with passive resignation, as witness the familiar coupling of "death and taxes." One method is to induce historiographical determinism, as opposed to individual freedom of will. If the X Dynasty rules us, this is because the Inexorable Laws of History (or the Divine Will, or the Absolute, or the Material Productive Forces) have so decreed and nothing any puny individuals may do can change this inevitable decree. It is also important for the State to inculcate in its subjects an aversion to any "conspiracy theory of history;" for a search for "conspiracies" means a search for motives and an attribution of responsibility for historical misdeeds. If, however, any tyranny imposed by the State, or venality, or aggressive war, was caused *not* by the State rulers but by mysterious and arcane "social forces," or by the imperfect state of the world or, if in some way, *everyone* was responsible ("We Are All Murderers," proclaims one slogan), then there is no point to the people becoming indignant or rising up against such misdeeds. Furthermore, an attack on "conspiracy theories" means that the subjects will become more gullible in believing the "general welfare" reasons that are always put forth by the State for engaging in any of its despotic actions. A "conspiracy theory" can unsettle the system by causing the public to doubt the State's ideological propaganda.

Another tried and true method for bending subjects to the State's will is inducing guilt. Any increase in private well-being can be attacked as "unconscionable greed," "materialism," or "excessive affluence," profit-making can be attacked as "exploitation" and "usury," mutually beneficial exchanges denounced as "selfishness," and somehow with the conclusion always being drawn that more resources should be siphoned from the private to the "public sector." The induced guilt makes the public more ready to do just that. For while individual persons tend to indulge in "selfish greed," the failure of the State's rulers to engage in exchanges is supposed to signify *their* devotion to higher and nobler causes—parasitic predation being apparently morally and esthetically lofty as compared to peaceful and productive work.

In the present more secular age, the divine right of the State has been supplemented by the invocation of a new god, Science. State rule is now proclaimed as being ultrascientific, as constituting planning by experts. But while "reason" is invoked more than in previous centuries, this is not the true reason of the individual and his exercise of free will; it is still collectivist and determinist, still implying holistic aggregates and coercive manipulation of passive subjects by their rulers.

The increasing use of scientific jargon has permitted the State's intellectuals to weave obscurantist apologia for State rule that would have only met with derision by the populace of a simpler age. A robber who justified his theft by saying that he really helped his victims, by his spending giving a boost to retail trade, would find few converts; but when this theory is clothed in Keynesian equations and impressive references to the "multiplier effect," it unfortunately carries more conviction. And so the assault on common sense proceeds, each age performing the task in its own ways.

Thus, ideological support being vital to the State, it must unceasingly try to impress the public with its "legitimacy," to distinguish its activities from those of mere brigands. The unremitting determination of its assaults on common sense is no accident, for as Mencken vividly maintained:

> The average man, whatever his errors otherwise, at least sees clearly that government is something lying outside him and outside the generality of his fellow men—that it is a separate, independent, and hostile power, only partly under his control, and capable of doing him great harm. Is it a fact of no significance that robbing the government is everywhere

regarded as a crime of less magnitude than robbing an individual, or even a corporation? ... What lies behind all this, I believe, is a deep sense of the fundamental antagonism between the government and the people it governs. It is apprehended, not as a committee of citizens chosen to carry on the communal business of the whole population, but as a separate and autonomous corporation, mainly devoted to exploiting the population for the benefit of its own members. ... When a private citizen is robbed, a worthy man is deprived of the fruits of his industry and thrift; when the government is robbed, the worst that happens is that certain rogues and loafers have less money to play with than they had before. The notion that they have earned that money is never entertained; to most sensible men it would seem ludicrous.[19]

HOW THE STATE TRANSCENDS ITS LIMITS

As Bertrand de Jouvenel has sagely pointed out, through the centuries men have formed concepts designed to check and limit the exercise of State rule; and, one after another, the State, using its intellectual allies, has been able to transform these concepts into intellectual rubber stamps of legitimacy and virtue to attach to its decrees and actions. Originally, in Western Europe, the concept of divine sovereignty held that the kings may rule only according to divine law; the kings turned the concept into a rubber stamp of divine approval for any of the kings' actions. The concept of parliamentary democracy began as a popular check upon absolute monarchical rule; it ended with parliament being the essential part of the State and its every act totally sovereign. As de Jouvenel concludes:

Many writers on theories of sovereignty have worked out one . . . of these restrictive devices. But in the end every single such theory has, sooner or later, lost its original

---

[19]Ibid., pp. 146–47.

> purpose, and come to act merely as a springboard to Power,
> by providing it with the powerful aid of an invisible sover-
> eign with whom it could in time successfully identify
> itself.[20]

Similarly with more specific doctrines: the "natural rights" of the individual enshrined in John Locke and the Bill of Rights, became a statist "right to a job"; utilitarianism turned from arguments for liberty to arguments against resisting the State's invasions of liberty, etc.

Certainly the most ambitious attempt to impose limits on the State has been the Bill of Rights and other restrictive parts of the American Constitution, in which written limits on government became the fundamental law to be interpreted by a judiciary supposedly independent of the other branches of government. All Americans are familiar with the process by which the construction of limits in the Constitution has been inexorably broadened over the last century. But few have been as keen as Professor Charles Black to see that the State has, in the process, largely transformed judicial review itself from a limiting device to yet another instrument for furnishing ideological legitimacy to the government's actions. For if a judicial decree of "unconstitutional" is a mighty check to government power, an implicit or explicit verdict of "constitutional" is a mighty weapon for fostering public acceptance of ever-greater government power.

Professor Black begins his analysis by pointing out the crucial necessity of "legitimacy" for any government to endure, this legitimation signifying basic majority acceptance of the government and its actions.[21] Acceptance of legitimacy

---

[20]de Jouvenel, *On Power*, pp. 27ff.

[21]Charles L. Black. Jr., *The People and the Court* (New York: Macmillan, 1960), pp. 35ff.

becomes a particular problem in a country such as the United States, where "substantive limitations are built into the theory on which the government rests." What is needed, adds Black, is a means by which the government can assure the public that its increasing powers are, indeed, "constitutional." And this, he concludes, has been the major historic function of judicial review.

Let Black illustrate the problem:

> The supreme risk [to the government] is that of disaffection and a feeling of outrage widely disseminated throughout the population, and loss of moral authority by the government as such, however long it may be propped up by force or inertia or the lack of an appealing and immediately available alternative. Almost everybody living under a government of limited powers, must sooner or later be subjected to some governmental action which as a matter of private opinion he regards as outside the power of government or positively forbidden to government. A man is drafted, though he finds nothing in the Constitution about being drafted. . . . A farmer is told how much wheat he can raise; he believes, and he discovers that some respectable lawyers believe with him, that the government has no more right to tell him how much wheat he can grow than it has to tell his daughter whom she can marry. A man goes to the federal penitentiary for saying what he wants to, and he paces his cell reciting . . . "Congress shall make no laws abridging the freedom of speech.". . . . A businessman is told what he can ask, and must ask, for buttermilk.
>
> The danger is real enough that each of these people (and who is not of their number?) will confront the concept of governmental limitation with the reality (as he sees it) of the flagrant overstepping of actual limits, and draw the obvious conclusion as to the status of his government with respect to legitimacy.[22]

This danger is averted by the State's propounding the doctrine that one agency must have the ultimate decision on

---

[22]Ibid., pp. 42–43.

constitutionality and that this agency, in the last analysis, must be *part of* the federal government.[23] For while the seeming independence of the federal judiciary has played a vital part in making its actions virtual Holy Writ for the bulk of the people, it is also and ever true that the judiciary is part and parcel of the government apparatus and appointed by the executive and legislative branches. Black admits that this means that the State has set itself up as a judge in its own cause, thus violating a basic juridical principle for aiming at just decisions. He brusquely denies the possibility of any alternative.[24]

Black adds:

> The problem, then, is to devise such governmental means of deciding as will [hopefully] reduce to a tolerable minimum

---

[23]Ibid., p. 52:

> The prime and most necessary function of the [Supreme] Court has been that of validation, not that of invalidation. What a government of limited powers needs, at the beginning and forever, is some means of satisfying the people that it has taken all steps humanly possible to stay within its powers. This is the condition of its legitimacy, and its legitimacy, in the long run, is the condition of its life. And the Court, through its history, has acted as the legitimation of the government.

[24]To Black, this "solution," while paradoxical, is blithely self-evident:

> the final power of the State . . . must stop where the law stops it. And who shall set the limit, and who shall enforce the stopping, against the mightiest power? Why, the State itself, of course, through its judges and its laws. Who controls the temperate? Who teaches the wise? (Ibid., pp. 32–33)

And:

> Where the questions concern governmental power in a sovereign nation, it is not possible to select an umpire who is outside government. Every national government, so long as

the intensity of the objection that government is judge in its
own cause. Having done this, you can only hope that this
objection, *though theoretically still tenable* [italics mine], will
practically lose enough of its force that the legitimating
work of the deciding institution can win acceptance.[25]

In the last analysis, Black finds the achievement of justice
and legitimacy from the State's perpetual judging of its own
cause as "something of a miracle."[26]

Applying his thesis to the famous conflict between the
Supreme Court and the New Deal, Professor Black keenly
chides his fellow pro-New Deal colleagues for their short-
sightedness in denouncing judicial obstruction:

[t]he standard version of the story of the New Deal and the
Court, though accurate in its way, displaces the emphasis. . . .
It concentrates on the difficulties; it almost forgets how the
whole thing turned out. The upshot of the matter was [and
this is what I like to emphasize] that after some twenty-four
months of balking . . . the Supreme Court, without a single
change in the law of its composition, or, indeed, in its actual

---

it is a government, must have the final say on its own power.
(Ibid., pp. 48–49)

[25]Ibid., p. 49.

[26]This ascription of the miraculous to government is reminiscent of
James Burnham's justification of government by mysticism and irra-
tionality:

In ancient times, before the illusions of science had cor-
rupted traditional wisdom, the founders of cities were known
to be gods or demigods. . . . Neither the source nor the justification of government can be put in wholly rational terms
. . . why should I accept the hereditary or democratic or any
other principle of legitimacy? Why should a principle justify
the rule of that man over me? . . . I accept the principle, well
. . . because I do, because that is the way it is and has been.

James Burnham, *Congress and the American Tradition* (Chicago: Regnery,
1959), pp. 3–8. But what if one does not accept the principle? What will
"the way" be then?

manning, *placed the affirmative stamp of legitimacy on the New Deal, and on the whole new conception of government in America.*[27]

In this way, the Supreme Court was able to put the quietus on the large body of Americans who had had strong constitutional objections to the New Deal:

> Of course, not everyone was satisfied. The Bonnie Prince Charlie of constitutionally commanded laissez-faire still stirs the hearts of a few zealots in the Highlands of choleric unreality. But there is no longer any significant or dangerous public doubt as to the constitutional power of Congress to deal as it does with the national economy. . . .
>
> We had no means, other than the Supreme Court, for imparting legitimacy to the New Deal.[28]

As Black recognizes, one major political theorist who recognized—and largely in advance—the glaring loophole in a constitutional limit on government of placing the ultimate interpreting power in the Supreme Court was John C. Calhoun. Calhoun was not content with the "miracle," but instead proceeded to a profound analysis of the constitutional problem. In his *Disquisition*, Calhoun demonstrated the inherent tendency of the State to break through the limits of such a constitution:

> A written constitution certainly has many and considerable advantages, but it is a great mistake to suppose that the mere insertion of provisions to restrict and limit the power of the government, *without investing those for whose protection they are inserted with the means of enforcing their observance* [my italics] will be sufficient to prevent the major and dominant party from abusing its powers. Being the party in possession of the government, they will, from the same constitution of man which makes government necessary to protect society, be in favor of the powers granted by the constitution and opposed to the restrictions intended to limit them. . . .

----

[27]Black, *The People and the Court*, p. 64.

[28]Ibid., p. 65.

The minor or weaker party, on the contrary, would take the opposite direction and regard them [the restrictions] as essential to their protection against the dominant party. . . . But where there are no means by which they could compel the major party to observe the restrictions, the only resort left them would be a strict construction of the constitution. . . . To this the major party would oppose a liberal construction. . . . It would be construction against construction—the one to contract and the other to enlarge the powers of the government to the utmost. But of what possible avail could the strict construction of the minor party be, against the liberal construction of the major, when the one would have all the power of the government to carry its construction into effect and the other be deprived of all means of enforcing its construction? In a contest so unequal, the result would not be doubtful. The party in favor of the restrictions would be overpowered. . . . The end of the contest would be the subversion of the constitution . . . the restrictions would ultimately be annulled and the government be converted into one of unlimited powers.[29]

One of the few political scientists who appreciated Calhoun's analysis of the Constitution was Professor J. Allen Smith. Smith noted that the Constitution was designed with checks and balances to limit any one governmental power and yet had then developed a Supreme Court with the monopoly of ultimate interpreting power. If the Federal Government was created to check invasions of individual liberty by the separate states, who was to check the Federal power? Smith maintained that implicit in the check-and-balance idea of the Constitution was the concomitant view that no one branch of government may be conceded the ultimate power of interpretation: "It was assumed by the people that

[29]John C. Calhoun, *A Disquisition on Government* (New York: Liberal Arts Press, 1953), pp. 25–27. Also cf. Murray N. Rothbard, "Conservatism and Freedom: A Libertarian Comment," *Modern Age* (Spring, 1961): 219.

the new government could not be permitted to determine the limits of its own authority, since this would make it, and not the Constitution, supreme."[30]

The solution advanced by Calhoun (and seconded, in this century, by such writers as Smith) was, of course, the famous doctrine of the "concurrent majority." If any substantial minority interest in the country, specifically a State Government, believed that the Federal Government was exceeding its powers and encroaching on that minority, the minority would have the right to veto this exercise of power as unconstitutional. Applied to State Governments, this theory implied the right of "nullification" of a Federal law or ruling within a state's jurisdiction.

In theory, the ensuing constitutional system would assure that the Federal Government check any state invasion of individual rights, while the states would check excessive Federal power over the individual. And yet, while limitations would undoubtedly be more effective than at present, there are many difficulties and problems in the Calhoun solution. If, indeed, a subordinate interest should rightfully have a veto over matters concerning it, then why stop with the states? Why not place veto power in counties, cities, wards? Furthermore,

---

[30]J. Allen Smith, *The Growth and Decadence of Constitutional Government* (New York: Henry Holt, 1930), p. 88. Smith added:

> It was obvious that where a provision of the Constitution was designed to limit the powers of a governmental organ, it could be effectively nullified if its interpretation and enforcement were left to the authorities as it was designed to restrain. Clearly, common sense required that no organ of the government should be able to determine its own powers.

Clearly, common sense and "miracles" dictate very different views of government (p. 87).

interests are not only sectional, they are also occupational, social, etc. What of bakers or taxi drivers or any other occupation? Should *they* not be permitted a veto power over their own lives? This brings us to the important point that the nullification theory confines its checks to *agencies of government* itself. Let us not forget that federal and state governments, and their respective branches, are still states, are still guided by their own state interests rather than by the interests of the private citizens. What is to prevent the Calhoun system from working in reverse, with states tyrannizing over *their* citizens and only vetoing the federal government when it tries to intervene to *stop* that state tyranny? Or for states to acquiesce in federal tyranny? What is to prevent federal and state governments from forming mutually profitable alliances for the joint exploitation of the citizenry? And even if the private occupational groupings were to be given some form of "functional" representation in government, what is to prevent them from using the State to gain subsidies and other special privileges for themselves or from imposing compulsory cartels on their own members?

In short, Calhoun does not push his pathbreaking theory on concurrence far enough: he does not push it down to the *individual* himself. If the individual, after all, is the one whose rights are to be protected, then a consistent theory of concurrence would imply veto power by every individual; that is, some form of "unanimity principle." When Calhoun wrote that it should be "impossible to put or to keep it [the government] in action without the concurrent consent of all," he was, perhaps unwittingly, implying just such a conclusion.[31] But such speculation begins to take us away from our subject,

---

[31]Calhoun, *A Disquisition on Government*, pp. 20–21.

for down this path lie political systems which could hardly be called "States" at all.[32] For one thing, just as the right of nullification for a state logically implies its right of *secession*, so a right of individual nullification would imply the right of any individual to "secede" from the State under which he lives.[33]

Thus, the State has invariably shown a striking talent for the expansion of its powers beyond any limits that might be imposed upon it. Since the State necessarily lives by the compulsory confiscation of private capital, and since its expansion necessarily involves ever-greater incursions on private individuals and private enterprise, we must assert that the State is profoundly and inherently *anti*capitalist. In a sense, our position is the reverse of the Marxist dictum that the State is the "executive committee" of the ruling class in the present day, supposedly the capitalists. Instead, the State—the organization of the political means—constitutes, and is the source of, the "ruling class" (rather, ruling *caste*), and is in permanent opposition to *genuinely* private capital. We may, therefore, say with de Jouvenel:

> Only those who know nothing of any time but their own, who are completely in the dark as to the manner of Power's behaving through thousands of years, would

---

[32]In recent years, the unanimity principle has experienced a highly diluted revival, particularly in the writings of Professor James Buchanan. Injecting unanimity into the present situation, however, and applying it only to *changes* in the *status quo* and not to existing laws, can only result in another transformation of a limiting concept into a rubber stamp for the State. If the unanimity principle is to be applied only to *changes* in laws and edicts, the nature of the initial "point of origin" then makes all the difference. Cf. James Buchanan and Gordon Tullock, *The Calculus of Consent* (Ann Arbor: University of Michigan Press, 1962), passim.

[33]Cf. Herbert Spencer, "The Right to Ignore the State," in *Social Statics* (New York: D. Appleton, 1890), pp. 229–39.

regard these proceedings [nationalization, the income
tax, etc.] as the fruit of a particular set of doctrines. They
are in fact the normal manifestations of Power, and differ
not at all in their nature from Henry VIII's confiscation of
the monasteries. The same principle is at work; the hunger
for authority, the thirst for resources; and in all of these
operations the same characteristics are present, including
the rapid elevation of the dividers of the spoils. Whether it
is Socialist or whether it is not, Power must always be at war
with the capitalist authorities and despoil the capitalists of
their accumulated wealth; in doing so it obeys the law of its
nature.[34]

WHAT THE STATE FEARS

What the State fears above all, of course, is any fundamental threat to its own power and its own existence. The
death of a State can come about in two major ways: (a)
through conquest by another State, or (b) through revolutionary overthrow by its own subjects—in short, by war or
revolution. War and revolution, as the two basic threats,
invariably arouse in the State rulers their maximum efforts
and maximum propaganda among the people. As stated
above, any way must always be used to mobilize the people to
come to the State's defense in the belief that they are defending themselves. The fallacy of the idea becomes evident when
conscription is wielded against those who refuse to "defend"
themselves and are, therefore, forced into joining the State's
military band: needless to add, no "defense" is permitted
them against this act of "their own" State.

In war, State power is pushed to its ultimate, and, under
the slogans of "defense" and "emergency," it can impose a
tyranny upon the public such as might be openly resisted in
time of peace. War thus provides many benefits to a State,

---

[34]de Jouvenel, *On Power,* p. 171.

and indeed every modern war has brought to the warring peoples a permanent legacy of increased State burdens upon society. War, moreover, provides to a State tempting opportunities for conquest of land areas over which it may exercise its monopoly of force. Randolph Bourne was certainly correct when he wrote that "war is the health of the State," but to any particular State a war may spell either health or grave injury.[35]

We may test the hypothesis that the State is largely interested in protecting *itself* rather than its subjects by asking: which category of crimes does the State pursue and punish most intensely—those against private citizens or those against *itself?* The gravest crimes in the State's lexicon are almost invariably not invasions of private person or property, but dangers to its *own* contentment, for example, treason, desertion of a soldier to the enemy, failure to register for the draft, subversion and subversive conspiracy, assassination of rulers and such economic crimes against the State as counterfeiting its money or evasion of its income tax. Or compare the degree of zeal devoted to pursuing the man who assaults a policeman, with the attention that the State pays to the assault of an ordinary citizen. Yet, curiously, the State's openly assigned priority to its *own* defense against the public

---

[35]We have seen that essential to the State is support by the intellectuals, and this includes support against their two acute threats. Thus, on the role of American intellectuals in America's entry into World War I, see Randolph Bourne, "The War and the Intellectuals," in *The History of a Literary Radical and Other Papers* (New York: S.A. Russell, 1956), pp. 205–22. As Bourne states, a common device of intellectuals in winning support for State actions is to channel any discussion within the limits of basic State policy and to discourage any fundamental or total critique of this basic framework.

strikes few people as inconsistent with its presumed *raison d'etre.*[36]

HOW STATES RELATE TO ONE ANOTHER

Since the territorial area of the earth is divided among different States, inter-State relations must occupy much of a State's time and energy. The natural tendency of a State is to expand its power, and externally such expansion takes place by conquest of a territorial area. Unless a territory is stateless or uninhabited, any such expansion involves an inherent conflict of interest between one set of State rulers and another. Only one set of rulers can obtain a monopoly of coercion over any given territorial area at any one time: complete power over a territory by State X can only be obtained by the expulsion of State Y. War, while risky, will be an ever-present tendency of States, punctuated by periods of peace and by shifting alliances and coalitions between States.

---

[36]As Mencken puts it in his inimitable fashion:

> This gang ("the exploiters constituting the government") is well nigh immune to punishment. Its worst extortions, even when they are baldly for private profit, carry no certain penalties under our laws. Since the first days of the Republic, less than a few dozen of its members have been impeached, and only a few obscure understrappers have ever been put into prison. The number of men sitting at Atlanta and Leavenworth for revolting against the extortions of the government is always ten times as great as the number of government officials condemned for oppressing the taxpayers to their own gain. (Mencken, *A Mencken Chrestomathy*, pp. 147–48)

For a vivid and entertaining description of the lack of protection for the individual against incursion of his liberty by his "protectors," see H.L. Mencken, "The Nature of Liberty," in *Prejudices: A Selection* (New York: Vintage Books, 1958), pp. 138–43.

We have seen that the "internal" or "domestic" attempt to limit the State, in the seventeenth through nineteenth centuries, reached its most notable form in constitutionalism. Its "external," or "foreign affairs," counterpart was the development of "international law," especially such forms as the "laws of war" and "neutrals' rights."[37] Parts of international law were originally purely private, growing out of the need of merchants and traders everywhere to protect their property and adjudicate disputes. Examples are admiralty law and the law merchant. But even the governmental rules emerged voluntarily and were not imposed by any international super-State. The object of the "laws of war" was to limit inter-State destruction *to the State apparatus itself*, thereby preserving the innocent "civilian" public from the slaughter and devastation of war. The object of the development of neutrals' rights was to preserve private civilian international commerce, even with "enemy" countries, from seizure by one of the warring parties. The overriding aim, then, was to limit the extent of any war, and, particularly to limit its destructive impact on the private citizens of the neutral and even the warring countries.

The jurist F.J.P. Veale charmingly describes such "civilized warfare" as it briefly flourished in fifteenth-century Italy:

> The rich burghers and merchants of medieval Italy were too busy making money and enjoying life to undertake the hardships and dangers of soldiering themselves. So they adopted the practice of hiring mercenaries to do their fighting for them, and, being thrifty, businesslike folk, they dismissed their mercenaries immediately after their services could be dispensed with. Wars were, therefore, fought by

---

[37]This is to be distinguished from modern international law, with its stress on maximizing the extent of war through such concepts as "collective security."

armies hired for each campaign. . . . For the first time, sol-
diering became a reasonable and comparatively harmless
profession. The generals of that period maneuvered against
each other, often with consummate skill, but when one had
won the advantage, his opponent generally either retreated
or surrendered. It was a recognized rule that a town could
only be sacked if it offered resistance: immunity could
always be purchased by paying a ransom. . . . As one natural
consequence, no town ever resisted, it being obvious that a
government too weak to defend its citizens had forfeited their
allegiance. Civilians had little to fear from the dangers of
war which were the concern only of professional soldiers.[38]

The well-nigh absolute separation of the private civilian
from the State's wars in eighteenth-century Europe is highlighted by Nef:

> Even postal communications were not successfully
> restricted for long in wartime. Letters circulated without
> censorship, with a freedom that astonishes the twentieth-
> century mind. . . . The subjects of two warring nations
> talked to each other if they met, and when they could not
> meet, corresponded, not as enemies but as friends. The
> modern notion hardly existed that . . . subjects of any enemy

---

[38]F.J.P. Veale, *Advance to Barbarism* (Appleton, Wis.: C.C. Nelson,
1953), p. 63. Similarly, Professor Nef writes of the War of Don Carlos
waged in Italy between France, Spain, and Sardinia against Austria, in the
eighteenth century:

> at the siege of Milan by the allies and several weeks later at
> Parma . . . the rival armies met in a fierce battle outside the
> town. In neither place were the sympathies of the inhabi-
> tants seriously moved by one side or the other. Their only
> fear was that the troops of either army should get within the
> gates and pillage. The fear proved groundless. At Parma the
> citizens ran to the town walls to watch the battle in the open
> country beyond. (John U. Nef, *War and Human Progress*
> [Cambridge, Mass.: Harvard University Press, 1950], p. 158.
> Also cf. Hoffman Nickerson, *Can We Limit War?* [New
> York: Frederick A. Stoke, 1934])

country are partly accountable for the belligerent acts of their rulers. Nor had the warring rulers any firm disposition to stop communications with subjects of the enemy. The old inquisitorial practices of espionage in connection with religious worship and belief were disappearing, and no comparable inquisition in connection with political or economic communications was even contemplated. Passports were originally created to provide safe conduct in time of war. During most of the eighteenth century it seldom occurred to Europeans to abandon their travels in a foreign country which their own was fighting.[39]

And trade being increasingly recognized as beneficial to both parties; eighteenth-century warfare also counterbalances a considerable amount of "trading with the enemy."[40]

How far States have transcended rules of civilized warfare in this century needs no elaboration here. In the modern era of total war, combined with the technology of total destruction, the very idea of keeping war limited to the State apparati seems even more quaint and obsolete than the original Constitution of the United States.

When States are not at war, agreements are often necessary to keep frictions at a minimum. One doctrine that has gained curiously wide acceptance is the alleged "sanctity of treaties." This concept is treated as the counterpart of the "sanctity of contract." But a treaty and a genuine contract have nothing in common. A contract transfers, in a precise manner, titles to private property. Since a government does not, in any proper sense, "own" its territorial area, any agreements that it concludes do not confer titles to property. If, for

---

[39]Nef, *War and Human Progress*, p. 162.

[40]Ibid., p. 161. On advocacy of trading with the enemy by leaders of the American Revolution, see Joseph Dorfman, *The Economic Mind in American Civilization* (New York: Viking Press, 1946), vol. 1, pp. 210–11.

example, Mr. Jones sells or gives his land to Mr. Smith, Jones's heir cannot legitimately descend upon Smith's heir and claim the land as rightfully his. The property title has already been transferred. Old Jones's contract is automatically binding upon young Jones, because the former had already transferred the property; young Jones, therefore, has no property claim. Young Jones can only claim that which he has inherited from old Jones, and old Jones can only bequeath property which he still owns. But if, at a certain date, the government of, say, Ruritania is coerced or even bribed by the government of Waldavia into giving up some of its territory, it is absurd to claim that the governments or inhabitants of the two countries are forever barred from a claim to reunification of Ruritania on the grounds of the sanctity of a treaty. Neither the people nor the land of northwest Ruritania are owned by either of the two governments. As a corollary, one government can certainly not bind, by the dead hand of the past, a later government through treaty. A revolutionary government which overthrew the king of Ruritania could, similarly, hardly be called to account for the king's actions or debts, for a government is not, as is a child, a true "heir" to its predecessor's property.

HISTORY AS A RACE BETWEEN STATE POWER AND SOCIAL POWER

Just as the two basic and mutually exclusive interrelations between men are peaceful cooperation or coercive exploitation, production or predation, so the history of mankind, particularly its economic history, may be considered as a contest between these two principles. On the one hand, there is creative productivity, peaceful exchange and cooperation; on the other, coercive dictation and predation over those social relations. Albert Jay Nock happily termed these contesting forces: "social power" and "State power."[41] Social power is man's power over nature, his cooperative transformation of nature's resources and insight into nature's laws, for the benefit of all participating individuals. Social power is the *power over nature*, the living standards achieved by men in mutual exchange. State power, as we have seen, is the coercive and parasitic seizure of this production—a draining of the fruits of society for the benefit of nonproductive (actually antiproductive) rulers. While social power is over nature, State power is *power over man*. Through history, man's productive and creative forces have, time and again, carved out new ways of transforming nature for man's benefit. These have been the times when social power has spurted ahead of State power, and when the degree of State encroachment over society has considerably lessened. But always, after a greater or smaller time lag, the State has moved into these new areas, to cripple and confiscate social power once more.[42] If the seventeenth through the nineteenth centuries were, in many countries of the West, times of accelerating social power, and a corollary increase in freedom, peace, and material welfare, the twentieth century has been primarily an age in which

---

[41]On the concepts of State power and social power, see Albert J. Nock, *Our Enemy the State* (Caldwell, Idaho: Caxton Printers, 1946). Also see Nock, *Memoirs of a Superfluous Man* (New York: Harpers, 1943), and Frank Chodorov, *The Rise and Fall of Society* (New York: Devin-Adair, 1959).

[42]Amidst the flux of expansion or contraction, the State always makes sure that it seizes and retains certain crucial "command posts" of the economy and society. Among these command posts are a monopoly of violence, monopoly of the ultimate judicial power, the channels of communication and transportation (post office, roads, rivers, air routes), irrigated water in Oriental despotisms, and education—to mold the opinions of its future citizens. In the modern economy, money is the critical command post.

State power has been catching up—with a consequent reversion to slavery, war, and destruction.[43]

In this century, the human race faces, once again, the virulent reign of the State—of the State now armed with the fruits of man's creative powers, confiscated and perverted to its own aims. The last few centuries were times when men tried to place constitutional and other limits on the State, only to find that such limits, as with all other attempts, have failed. Of all the numerous forms that governments have taken over the centuries, of all the concepts and institutions that have been tried, none has succeeded in keeping the State in check. The problem of the State is evidently as far from solution as ever. Perhaps new paths of inquiry must be explored, if the successful, final solution of the State question is ever to be attained.[44]

---

[43] This parasitic process of "catching up" has been almost openly proclaimed by Karl Marx, who conceded that socialism must be established through seizure of capital *previously accumulated* under capitalism.

[44] Certainly, one indispensable ingredient of such a solution must be the sundering of the alliance of intellectual and State, through the creation of centers of intellectual inquiry and education, which will be independent of State power. Christopher Dawson notes that the great intellectual movements of the Renaissance and the Enlightenment were achieved by working outside of, and sometimes against, the entrenched universities. These academia of the new ideas were established by independent patrons. See Christopher Dawson, *The Crisis of Western Education* (New York: Sheed and Ward, 1961).

4
JUSTICE AND
PROPERTY RIGHTS

THE FAILURE OF UTILITARIANISM

U ntil very recently, free-market economists paid little
attention to the entities actually being exchanged on
the very market they have advocated so strongly.
Wrapped up in the workings and advantages of freedom of
trade, enterprise, investment, and the price system, economists tended to lose sight of the things being exchanged on
that market. Namely, they lost sight of the fact that when
$10,000 is being exchanged for a machine, or $1 for a hula
hoop, what is actually being exchanged is the *title of ownership*
to each of these goods. In short, when I buy a hula hoop for
$1, what I am actually doing is exchanging my title of own-
ership to the dollar in exchange for the ownership title to the
hula hoop; the retailer is doing the exact opposite.[1] But this

---

[1]Economists failed to heed the emphasis on titles of ownership underlying exchange stressed by the social philosopher Spencer Heath. Thus:
"Only those things which are *owned* can be exchanged or used as instru-
ments of service or exchange. This exchange is not transportation; it is
the transfer of ownership or title. This is a social and not a physical
process." Spencer Heath, *Citadel, Market, and Altar* (Baltimore, Md.:
Science of Society Foundation, 1957), p. 48.

means that economists' habitual attempts to be *wertfrei*, or at the least to confine their advocacy to the processes of trade and exchange, cannot be maintained. For if myself and the retailer are indeed to be free to trade the dollar for the hula hoop without coercive interference by third parties, then this can only be done if these economists will proclaim the justice and the propriety of my original ownership of the dollar and the retailer's ownership of the hula hoop.

In short, for an economist to say that X and Y should be free to trade Good A for Good B unmolested by third parties, he must *also* say that X legitimately and properly owns Good A and that Y legitimately owns Good B. But this means that the free-market economist must have some sort of theory of justice in property rights; he can scarcely say that X properly owns Good A without asserting some sort of theory of justice on behalf of such ownership.

Suppose, for example, that as I am about to purchase the hula hoop, the information arrives that the retailer had really stolen the hoop from Z. Surely not even the supposedly *wertfrei* economist can continue to blithely endorse the proposed exchange of ownership titles between myself and the retailer. For now we find that the retailer's, Y's, title of ownership is improper and unjust, and that he must be forced to return the hoop to Z, the original owner. The economist can then only endorse the proposed exchange between myself and Z, rather than Y, for the hula hoop, since he has to acknowledge Z as the proper owner of title to the hoop.

In short, we have two mutually exclusive claimants to the ownership of the hoop. If the economist agrees to endorse only Z's sale of the hoop, then he is implicitly agreeing that Z has the just, and Y the unjust, claim to the hoop. And even if he continues to endorse the sale by Y, then he is implicitly maintaining *another* theory of property titles: namely, that theft is justified. Whichever way he decides, the economist cannot escape a judgment, a theory of justice in the ownership of property. Furthermore, the economist is not really finished when he proclaims the injustice or theft and endorses Z's proper title. For what is the justification for Z's title to the hoop? Is it only because he is a nonthief?

In recent years, free-market economists Ronald Coase and Harold Demsetz have begun to redress the balance and to focus on the importance of a clear and precise demarcation of property rights for the market economy. They have demonstrated the importance of such demarcation in the allocation of resources and in preventing or compensating for unwanted imposition of "external costs" from the actions of individuals. But Coase and Demsetz have failed to develop any theory of justice in these property rights; or, rather, they have advanced two theories: one, that it "doesn't matter" how the property titles are allocated, so long as they are allocated precisely; and, two, that the titles should be allocated to minimize "total social transaction costs," since a minimization of costs is supposed to be a *wertfrei* way of benefitting all of society.

There is no space here for a detailed critique of the Coase–Demsetz criteria. Suffice it to say that in a conflict over property titles between a rancher and a farmer for the same piece of land, even if the allocation of title "doesn't matter" for the allocation of resources (a point which itself could be challenged), it certainly matters from the point of view of the rancher and the farmer. And second, that it is impossible to weigh "total social costs" if we fully realize that all costs are subjective to the individual and, therefore, cannot be compared interpersonally.[2] Here the important point is that

---

[2] For a welcome recent emphasis on the subjectivity of cost, see James M. Buchanan, *Cost and Choice* (Chicago: Markham, 1969).

Coase and Demsetz, along with all other utilitarian free-market economists, implicitly or explicitly leave it to the hands of government to define and allocate the titles to private property.

It is a curious fact that utilitarian economists, generally so skeptical of the virtues of government intervention, are so content to leave the fundamental underpinning of the market process—the definition of property rights and the allocation of property titles—wholly in the hands of government. Presumably they do so because they themselves have no theory of justice in property rights; and, therefore, place the burden of allocating property titles into the hands of government. Thus, if Smith, Jones, and Doe each own property and are about to exchange their titles, utilitarians simply assert that if these titles are *legal* (that is, if the government puts the stamp of approval upon them), then they consider those titles to be justified. It is only if someone violates the government's definition of legality (for example, in the case of Y, the thieving retailer) that utilitarians are willing to agree with the general and the governmental view of the injustice of such action. But this means, of course, that, once again, the utilitarians have failed in their wish to escape having a theory of justice in property. Actually they do have such a theory, and it is the surely simplistic one that *whatever government defines as legal is right*.

As in so many other areas of social philosophy, then, we see that utilitarians, in pursuing their vain goal of being *wertfrei*, of "scientifically" abjuring any theory of justice, actually *have* such a theory: namely, putting their stamp of approval on whatever the process by which the government arrives at its allocation of property titles. Furthermore, we find that, as on many similar occasions, utilitarians in their vain quest for the *wertfrei* really conclude by endorsing as right and just whatever the government happens to decide; that is, by blindly apologizing for the *status quo.*[3]

Let us consider the utilitarian stamp of approval on government allocation of property titles. Can this stamp of approval possibly achieve even the limited utilitarian goal of certain and precise allocation of property titles? Suppose that the government endorses the existing titles to their property held by Smith, Jones, and Doe. Suppose, then, that a faction of government calls for the confiscation of these titles and redistribution of that property to Roe, Brown, and Robinson. The reasons for this program may stem from any number of social theories or even from the brute fact that Roe, Brown, and Robinson have greater political power than the original trio of owners. The reaction to this proposal by free-market economists and other utilitarians is predictable: they will oppose this proposal on the ground that definite and certain property rights, so socially beneficial, are being endangered. But suppose that the government, ignoring the protests of our utilitarians, proceeds anyway and redistributes these titles to property. Roe, Brown, and Robinson are *now* defined by the government as the proper and legal owners, while any claims to that property by the original trio of Smith, Jones, and Doe are considered improper and illegitimate, if not subversive. What now will be the reaction of our utilitarians?

It should be clear that, since the utilitarians only base their theory of justice in property on whatever the government defines as legal, they can have no groundwork whatever for

---

[3]I do not mean to imply here that no social science or economic analysis can be *wertfrei,* only that any attempt whatever to apply the analysis to the political arena, however remote, must involve and imply some sort of ethical position.

any call for restoring the property in question to its original owners. They can only, willy-nilly, and, despite any emotional reluctance on their part, simply endorse the *new* allocation of property titles as defined and endorsed by government. Not only must utilitarians endorse the *status quo* of property titles, but also they must endorse whatever *status quo* exists and however rapidly the government decides to shift and redistribute such titles. Furthermore, considering the historical record, we may indeed say that relying upon government to be the guardian of property rights is like placing the proverbial fox on guard over the chicken coop.

We see, therefore, that the supposed defense of the free market and of property rights by utilitarians and free-market economists is a very weak reed indeed. Lacking a theory of justice that goes beyond the existing *imprimatur* of government, utilitarians can only go along with every change and shift of government allocation after they occur, no matter how arbitrary, rapid, or politically motivated such shifts might be. And, since they provide no firm roadblock to governmental reallocations of property, the utilitarians, in the final analysis, can offer no real defense of property rights themselves. Since governmental redefinitions can and will be rapid and arbitrary, they cannot provide long-run certainty for property rights; and, therefore, they cannot even ensure the very social and economic efficiency which they themselves seek.[4] All this is implied in the pronouncements of utilitarians that any future free society must confine itself to whatever definitions of property titles the government may happen to be endorsing at that moment.

---

[4]On the arbitrariness and uncertainty of all legislative law, see Bruno Leoni, *Freedom and the Law* (Los Angeles: Nash, 1972).

Let us consider a hypothetical example of the failure of the utilitarian defense of private property. Suppose that somehow government becomes persuaded of the necessity to yield to a clamor for a free-market, laissez-faire society. Before dissolving itself, however, it redistributes property titles, granting the ownership of the entire territory of New York to the Rockefeller family, of Massachusetts to the Kennedy family, etc. It then dissolves, ending taxation and all other forms of government intervention in the economy. However, while taxation has been abolished, the Rockefeller, Kennedy, etc., families proceed to dictate to all the residents in what is now "their" territory, exacting what are now called "rents" over all the inhabitants.[5] It seems clear that our utilitarians could have no intellectual armor with which to challenge this new dispensation; indeed, they would have to endorse the Rockefeller, Kennedy, etc., holdings as "private property" equally deserving of support as the ordinary property titles which they had endorsed only a few months previously. All this because the utilitarians have no theory of justice in property beyond endorsement of whatever *status quo* happens to exist.

Consider, furthermore, the grotesque box in which the utilitarian proponent of freedom places himself in relation to the institution of human slavery. Contemplating the institution of slavery, and the "free" market that once existed in buying, selling, and renting slaves, the utilitarian who must rely on the legal definition of property can only endorse slavery on the ground that the slave masters had purchased their slave titles legally and in good faith. Surely, any endorsement of a "free" market in slaves indicates the inadequacy of utilitarian

---

[5]The point here is not, of course, to criticize all rents *per se*, but rather to call into question the legitimacy of property titles (here landed property) derived from the coercive actions of government.

concepts of property and the need for a theory of justice to provide a groundwork for property rights and a critique of existing official titles to property.

TOWARD A THEORY OF JUSTICE IN PROPERTY

Utilitarianism cannot be supported as a groundwork for property rights or, *a fortiori*, for the free-market economy. A theory of justice must be arrived at which goes beyond government allocations of property titles, and which can, therefore, serve as a basis for criticizing such allocations. Obviously, in this space I can only outline what I consider to be the correct theory of justice in property rights. This theory has two fundamental premises: (1) the absolute property right of each individual in his own person, his own body; this may be called the *right of self-ownership*; and (2) the absolute right in material property of the person who first finds an unused material resource and then in some way occupies or transforms that resource by the use of his personal energy. This might be called the *homestead principle*—the case in which someone, in the phrase of John Locke, has "mixed his labour" with an unused resource. Let Locke summarize these principles:

> . . . every man has a *property* in his own *person*. This nobody has any right to but himself. The *labour* of his body and the *work* of his hands, we may say, are properly his. Whatsoever, then, he removes out of the state that nature hath provided and left it in, he hath mixed his labour with it, and joined to it something that is his own, and thereby makes it his property. It being by him removed from the common state nature placed it in, it hath by this labour something annexed to it that excludes the common right of other men.[6]

---

[6]John Locke, "An Essay Concerning the True, Original, Extent and End of Civil Government," in E. Barker, ed., *Social Contract* (New York: Oxford University Press, 1948), pp. 17–18.

Let us consider the first principle: the right to self-ownership. This principle asserts the absolute right of each man, by virtue of his (or her) being a human being, to "own" his own body; that is, to control that body free of coercive interference. Since the nature of man is such that each individual must use his mind to learn about himself and the world, to select values, and to choose ends and means in order to survive and flourish, the right to self-ownership gives each man the right to perform these vital activities without being hampered and restricted by coercive molestation.

Consider, then, the alternatives—the consequences of denying each man the right to own his own person. There are only two alternatives: either (1) a certain class of people, A, have the right to own another class, B; or (2) everyone has the right to own his equal quotal share of everyone else. The first alternative implies that, while class A deserves the rights of being human, class B is in reality subhuman and, therefore, deserves no such rights. But since they are indeed human beings, the first alternative contradicts itself in denying natural human rights to one set of humans. Moreover, allowing class A to own class B means that the former is allowed to exploit and, therefore, to live parasitically at the expense of the latter; but, as economics can tell us, this parasitism itself violates the basic economic requirement for human survival: production and exchange.

The second alternative, which we might call "participatory communalism" or "communism," holds that every man should have the right to own his equal quotal share of everyone else. If there are three billion people in the world, then everyone has the right to own one-three-billionth of every other person. In the first place, this ideal itself rests upon an absurdity—proclaiming that every man is entitled to own a part of everyone else and yet is not entitled to own himself.

Second, we can picture the viability of such a world—a world in which no man is free to take any action whatever without prior approval or indeed command by everyone else in society. It should be clear that in that sort of "communist" world, no one would be able to do anything, and the human race would quickly perish. But if a world of zero self-ownership and one-hundred-percent other-ownership spells death for the human race, then any steps in that direction also contravene the natural law of what is best for man and his life on earth.

Finally, however, the participatory communist world cannot be put into practice. It is physically impossible for everyone to keep continual tabs on everyone else and, thereby, to exercise his equal quotal share of partial ownership over every other man. In practice, then, any attempt to institute universal and equal other-ownership is utopian and impossible, and supervision and, therefore, control and ownership of others would necessarily devolve upon a specialized group of people who would thereby become a "ruling class." Hence, in practice, any attempt at communist society will automatically become class rule, and we would be back at our rejected first alternative.

We conclude, then, with the premise of absolute universal right of self-ownership as our first principle of justice in property. This principle, of course, automatically rejects slavery as totally incompatible with our primary right.[7]

---

[7]Equally to be rejected is a grotesque proposal by Professor Kenneth E. Boulding, which, however, is a typical suggestion of a market-oriented utilitarian economist. This is a scheme for the government to allow only a certain maximum number of baby-permits per mother, but then to allow a "free" market in the purchase and sale of these baby rights. This plan, of course, denies the right of every mother over her own body.

Let us now turn to the more complex case of property in material objects. For even if every man has the right to self-ownership, people are not floating wraiths; they are not self-subsistent entities; they can only survive and flourish by grappling with the earth around them. They must, for example, stand on land areas; they must also, in order to survive, transform the resources given by nature into "consumer goods," into objects more suitable for their use and consumption. Food must be grown and eaten, minerals must be mined and then transformed into capital, and finally into useful consumer goods, etc. Man, in other words, must own not only his own person, but also material objects for his control and use. How, then, should property titles in these objects be allocated?

Let us consider, as our first example, the case of a sculptor fashioning a work of art out of clay and other materials, and let us simply assume for the moment that he owns these materials while waiving the question of the justification for their ownership. Let us examine the question: *who* should own the work of art as it emerges from the sculptor's fashioning? The sculpture is, in fact, the sculptor's "creation," not in the sense that he has created matter *de novo*, but in the sense that he has transformed nature-given matter—the clay—into another form dictated by his own ideas and fashioned by his own hands and energy. Surely, it is a rare person who, with the case put thus, would say that the sculptor does *not* have the property right in his own product. For if every

---

Boulding's plan may be found in Kenneth E. Boulding, *The Meaning of the 20th Century* (New York: Harper and Row, 1964). For a discussion of the plan, see Edwin G. Dolan, *TANSTAAFL: The Economic Strategy for Environmental Crisis* (New York: Holt, Rinehart, and Winston, 1971), p. 64.

man has the right to own his own body, and if he must grapple with the material objects of the world in order to survive, then the sculptor has the right to own the product which he has made, by his energy and effort, a veritable extension of his own personality. He has placed the stamp of his person upon the raw material by "mixing his labour" with the clay.

As in the case of the ownership of people's bodies, we again have three logical alternatives: (1) either the transformer, the "creator," has the property right in his creation; or (2) another man or set of men have the right to appropriate it by force without the sculptor's consent; or (3) the "communal" solution—every individual in the world has an equal, quotal share in the ownership of the sculpture. Again, put baldly, there are very few who would not concede the monstrous injustice of confiscating the sculptor's property, either by one or more others, or by the world as a whole. For by what right do they do so? By what right do they appropriate to themselves the product of the creator's mind and energy? (Again, as in the case of bodies, any confiscation in the supposed name of the world as a whole would, in practice, devolve into an oligarchy of confiscators.)

But the case of the sculptor is not qualitatively different from all cases of "production." The man or men who extracted the clay from the ground and sold it to the sculptor were also "producers"; they, too, mixed their ideas and their energy and their technological know-how with the nature-given material to emerge with a useful product. As producers, the sellers of the clay and of the sculptor's tools also mixed their labor with natural materials to transform them into more useful goods and services. All the producers are, therefore, entitled to the ownership of their product.

The chain of material production logically reduces back, then, from consumer goods and works of art to the first producers who gathered or mined the nature-given soil and resources to use and transform them by means of their personal energy. And use of the soil logically reduces back to the legitimate ownership by first users of previously unowned, unused, virginal, nature-given resources. Let us again quote Locke:

> He that is nourished by the acorns he picked up under an oak, or the apples he gathered from the trees in the wood, has certainly appropriated them to himself. Nobody can deny but the nourishment is his. I ask then, when did they begin to be his? When he digested? or when he ate? or when he boiled? or when he brought them home? or when he picked them up? And 'tis plain, if the first gathering made them not his, nothing else could. That labour put the distinction between them and common. That added something to them more than Nature, the common mother of all, had done, and so they became his private right. And will anyone say he had no right to those acorns or apples he thus appropriated because he had not the consent of all mankind to make them his? Was it a robbery thus to assume to himself what belonged to all in common? If such a consent as that was necessary, man had starved, notwithstanding the plenty God had given him. . . . Thus, the grass my horse has bit, the turfs my servant has cut, and the ore I have digged in my place, where I have a right to them in common with others, become my property without the assignation or consent of any body. The labour that was mine, removing them out of that common state they were in, hath fixed my property in them.[8]

If every man owns his own person and therefore his own labor, and if by extension he owns whatever material property he has "created" or gathered out of the previously unused, unowned "state of nature," then what of the logically final question: who has the right to own or control the earth *itself?* In short, if the gatherer has the right to own the acorns or

---

[8]Locke, *An Essay Concerning the True, Original, Extent, and End of Civil Government*, p. 18.

berries he picks, or the farmer the right to own his crop of wheat or peaches, who has the right to own the land on which these things have grown? It is at this point that Henry George and his followers, who would have gone all the way so far with our analysis, leave the track and deny the individual's right to own the piece of land itself, the ground on which these activities have taken place. The Georgists argue that, while every man should own the goods which he produces or creates, since Nature or God created the land itself, no individual has the right to assume ownership of that land. Yet, again, we are faced with our three logical alternatives: either the land itself belongs to the pioneer, the first user, the man who first brings it into production; or it belongs to a group of others, or it belongs to the world as a whole, with every individual owning an equal quotal part of every acre of land. George's option for the last solution hardly solves his moral problem: for if the land itself should belong to God or Nature, then why is it more moral for every acre in the world to be owned by the world as a whole, than to concede individual ownership? In practice, again, it is obviously impossible for every person in the world to exercise his ownership of his three-billionth portion of every acre of the world's surface; in practice, a small oligarchy would do the controlling and owning, rather than the world as a whole.

But apart from these difficulties in the Georgist position, our proposed justification for the ownership of ground land is the same as the justification for the original ownership of all other property. For as we have indicated, no producer really "creates" matter; he takes nature-given matter and transforms it by his personal energy in accordance with his ideas and his vision. But this is precisely what the pioneer—the "homesteader"—does, when he brings previously unused land into his private ownership. Just as the man who makes steel out of iron ore transforms that ore out of his know-how and with his energy, and just as the man who takes the iron out of the ground does the same, so too, does the homesteader who clears, fences, cultivates or builds upon the land. The homesteader, too, has transformed the character and usefulness of the nature-given soil by his labor and his personality. The homesteader is just as legitimately the owner of the property as the sculptor or the manufacturer; he is just as much a "producer" as the others.

Moreover, if a producer is not entitled to the fruits of his labor, who is? It is difficult to see why a newborn Pakistani baby should have a moral claim to a quotal share of ownership of a piece of Iowa land that someone has just transformed into a wheatfield and vice versa, of course, for an Iowan baby and a Pakistani farm. Land in its original state is unused and unowned. Georgists and other land communalists may claim that the entire world population "really" owns it, but if no one has yet used it, it is in the real sense owned and controlled by no one. The pioneer, the homesteader, the first user and transformer of this land, is the man who first brings this simple valueless thing into production and use. It is difficult to see the justice of depriving him of ownership in favor of people who have never gotten within a thousand miles of the land and who may not even know of the existence of the property over which they are supposed to have a claim. It is even more difficult to see the justice of a group of outside oligarchs owning the property, and at the expense of expropriating the creator or the homesteader who had originally brought the product into existence.

Finally, no one can produce anything without the cooperation of ground land, if only as standing room. No man can produce or create anything by his labor alone; he must have the cooperation of land and other natural raw materials. Man comes into the world with just himself and the world around him—the land and natural resources given him by nature. He takes these resources and transforms them by his labor and mind and energy into goods more useful to man. Therefore, if an individual cannot own original ground land, neither can he in the full sense own any of the fruits of his labor. Now that his labor has been inextricably mixed with the land, he cannot be deprived of one without being deprived of the other.

The moral issue involved here is even clearer if we consider the case of animals. Animals are "economic land," since they are original nature-given resources. Yet, will anyone deny full title to a horse to the man who finds and domesticates it? This is no different from the acorns and berries which are generally conceded to the gatherer. Yet in land, too, the homesteader takes the previously "wild," undomesticated land, and "tames" it by putting it to productive use. Mixing his labor with land sites should give him just as clear a title as in the case of animals.

From our two basic axioms, the right of every man to self-ownership and the right of every man to own previously unused natural resources that he first appropriates or transforms by his labor—the entire system of justification for property rights can be deduced. For if anyone justly owns the land himself and the property which he finds and creates, then he, of course, has the right to exchange that property for the similarly acquired just property of someone else. This establishes the right of free exchange of property, as well as the right to give one's property away to someone who agrees to receive it. Thus, X may own his person and labor and the farm he clears on which he grows wheat; Y owns the fish he catches; Z owns the cabbages he grows and the land under it. But then X has the right to exchange some of his wheat for some of Y's fish (if Y agrees) or Z's cabbages and when X and

Y make a voluntary agreement to exchange wheat for fish, then that fish becomes X's justly acquired property to do with what he wishes, and the wheat becomes Y's just property in precisely the same way. Further, a man may, of course, exchange not only the tangible objects he owns, but also his own labor which, of course, he owns as well. Thus, Z may sell his labor services of teaching farmer X's children in return for some of the farmer's produce.

We have thus established the property-right justification for the free-market process. For the free-market economy, as complex as the system appears to be on the surface, is yet nothing more than a vast network of voluntary and mutually agreed upon two-person or two-party exchanges of property titles such as we have seen occurs between wheat and cabbage farmers, or between the farmer and the teacher. In the developed free-market economy, the farmer exchanges his wheat for money. The wheat is bought by the miller who processes and transforms the wheat into flour. The miller sells the bread to the wholesaler, who in turn sells it to the retailer, who finally sells it to the consumer. In the case of the sculptor, he buys the clay and the tools from the producers who dug the clay out of the ground or those who bought the clay from the original miners, and he bought his tools from the manufacturers who, in turn, purchased the raw material from the miners of iron ore.

How "money" enters the equation is a complex process, but it should be clear here that, conceptually, the use of money is equivalent to any useful commodity that is exchanged for wheat, flour, etc. Instead of money, the commodity exchanged could be cloth, iron, or whatever. At each step of the way, mutually beneficial exchanges of property titles—to goods, services, or money—are agreed upon and transacted.

And what of the capital–labor relationship? Here, too, as in the case of the teacher selling his services to the farmer, the

laborer sells his services to the manufacturer who has purchased the iron ore or to the shipper who has bought logs
from the loggers. The capitalist performs the function of saving money to buy the raw material, and then pays the labor-
ers in advance of sale of the product to the eventual cus-
tomers.

Many people, including such utilitarian free-market advocates as John Stuart Mill, have been willing to concede the
propriety and the justice (if they are not utilitarians) of the
producer owning and earning the fruits of his labor. But they
balk at one point: inheritance. If Roberto Clemente is ten
times as good and "productive" a ball player as Joe Smith,
they are willing to concede the justice of Clemente's earning
ten times the amount; but what, they ask, is the justification
for someone whose only merit is being born a Rockefeller
inheriting far more wealth than someone born a Rothbard?

There are several answers that could be given to this question. For example, the natural fact is that every individual
must, of necessity, be born into a different condition, at a different time or place, and to different parents. Equality of birth
or rearing, therefore, is an impossible chimera. But in the context of our theory of justice in property rights, the answer is to
focus not on the recipient, not on the child Rockefeller or the
child Rothbard, but to concentrate on the giver, the man who
bestows the inheritance. For if Smith and Jones and
Clemente have the right to their labor and their property and
to exchange the titles to this property for the similarly
obtained property of others, then they also have the right to
give their property to whomever they wish. The point is not
the right of "inheritance" but the right of bequest, a right
which derives from the title to property itself. If Roberto
Clemente owns his labor and the money he earns from it,
then he has the right to give that money to the baby
Clemente.

Armed with a theory of justice in property rights, let us now apply it to the often vexed question of how we should regard existing titles to property.

Toward a Critique of Existing Property Titles

Among those who call for the adoption of a free market and a free society, the utilitarians, as might be expected, wish to validate all existing property titles, as so defined by the government. But we have seen the inadequacy of this position, most clearly in the case of slavery, but similarly in the validation that it gives to any acts of governmental confiscation or redistribution, including our hypothetical Kennedy and Rockefeller "private" ownership of the territorial area of a state. But how much of a redistribution from existing titles would be implied by the adoption of our theory of justice in property, or of any attempt to put that theory into practice? Isn't it true, as some people charge, that all existing property titles, or at least all land titles, were the result of government grants and coercive redistribution? Would all property titles, therefore, be confiscated in the name of justice? And who would be granted these titles?

Let us first take the easiest case: where existing property has been stolen, as acknowledged by the government (and, therefore, by utilitarians) as well as by our theory of justice. In short, suppose that Smith has stolen a watch from Jones. In that case, there is no difficulty in calling upon Smith to relinquish the watch and to give it back to the true owner, Jones. But what of more difficult cases—in short, where existing property titles are ratified by State confiscation of a previous victim? This could apply either to money, or especially to land titles, since land is a constant, identifiable, fixed quotal share of the earth's surface.

Suppose, first, for example, that the government has either taken land or money from Jones by coercion (either by taxation or its imposed redefinition of property) and has granted the land to Smith or, alternatively, has ratified Smith's direct act of confiscation. What would our policy of justice say then? We would say, along with the general view of crime, that the aggressor and unjust owner, Smith, must be made to disgorge the property title (either land or money) and give it over to its true owner, Jones. Thus, in the case of an identifiable unjust owner and the identifiable victim or just owner, the case is clear: a restoration to the victim of his rightful property. Smith, of course, must not be compensated for this restitution, since compensation would either be enforced unjustly on the victim himself or on the general body of taxpayers. Indeed, there is a far better case for the additional punishment of Smith, but there is no space here to develop the theory of punishment for crime or aggression.

Suppose, next, a second case, in which Smith has stolen a piece of land from Jones but that Jones has died; he leaves, however, an heir, Jones II. In that case, we proceed as before; there is still the identifiable aggressor, Smith, and the identifiable heir of the victim, Jones II, who now is the inherited just owner of the title. Again, Smith must be made to disgorge the land and turn it over to Jones II.

But suppose a third, more difficult case. Smith is still the thief, but Jones and his entire family and heirs have been wiped out, either by Smith himself or in the natural course of events. Jones is intestate; what then should happen to the property? The first principle is that Smith, being the thief, cannot keep the fruits of his aggression; but, in that case, the property becomes unowned and becomes up for grabs in the same way as any piece of unowned property. The "homestead principle" becomes applicable in the sense that the first user or occupier of the newly-declared unowned property becomes the just and proper owner. The only stipulation is that Smith himself, being the thief, is not eligible for this homesteading.[9]

Suppose now a fourth case, and one generally more relevant to problems of land title in the modern world. Smith is not a thief, nor has he directly received the land by government grant; but his title is derived from his ancestor who did so unjustly appropriate title to the property; the ancestor, Smith I, let us say, stole the property from Jones I, the rightful owner. What should be the disposition of the property now? The answer, in our view, completely depends on whether or not Jones's heirs, the surrogates of the identifiable victims, still exist. Suppose, for example, that Smith VI legally "owns" the land, but that Jones VI is still extant and identifiable. Then we would have to say that, while Smith VI himself is not a thief and not punishable as such, his title to the land, being solely derived from inheritance passed down from Smith I, does not give him true ownership, and that he, too, must disgorge the land—without compensation—and yield it into the hands of Jones VI.

But, it might be protested, what of the improvements that Smiths II–VI may have added to the land? Doesn't Smith VI deserve compensation for these legitimately owned additions to the original land received from Jones I? The answer depends on the movability or separability of these improvements. Suppose, for example, that Smith steals a car from Jones and sells it to Robinson. When the car is apprehended, then Robinson, though he purchased it in good faith from

---

[9]Neither is the government eligible. There is no space here to elaborate my view that government can never be the just owner of property. Suffice it to say here that the government gains its revenue from tax appropriation from production rather than from production itself and, hence, that the concept of just property can never apply to government.

Smith, has no title better than Smith's which was nil and, therefore, he must yield up the car to Jones without compensation. (He has been defrauded by Smith and must try to extract compensation out of Smith, not out of the victim Jones.) But suppose that Robinson, in the meantime, has improved the car? The answer depends on whether these improvements are separable from the car itself. If, for example, Robinson has installed a new radio which did not exist before, then he should certainly have the right to take it out before handing the car back to Jones. Similarly, in the case of land, to the extent that Smith VI has simply improved the land itself and mixed his resources inextricably with it, there is nothing he can do; but if, for example, Smith VI or his ancestors built new buildings upon the land, then he should have the right to demolish or cart away these buildings before handing the land over to Jones VI.

But what if Smith I did indeed steal the land from Jones I, but that all of Jones's descendants or heirs are lost in antiquity and cannot be found? What should be the status of the land then? In that case, since Smith VI is not himself a thief, he becomes the legitimate owner of the land on the basis of our homestead principle. For if the land is "unowned" and up for grabs, then Smith VI himself has been occupying and using it, and, therefore, he becomes the just and rightful owner on the homestead basis. Furthermore, all of his descendants have clear and proper title on the basis of being his heirs.

It is clear, then, that even if we can show that the origin of most existing land titles are in coercion and theft, the existing owners are still just and legitimate owners if (a) they themselves did not engage in aggression, and (b) if no identifiable heirs of the original victims can be found. In most cases of current land title this will probably be the case. *A fortiori,* of course, if we simply don't know whether the original land titles were acquired by coercion, then our homestead principle gives the current property owners the benefit of the doubt and establishes them as just and proper owners as well. Thus, the establishment of our theory of justice in property titles will not usually lead to a wholesale turnover of landed property.

In the United States, we have been fortunate enough to largely escape continuing aggression in land titles. It is true that originally the English Crown gave land titles unjustly to favored persons (for example, the territory roughly of New York State to the ownership of the Duke of York), but fortunately these grantees were interested enough in quick returns to subdivide and sell their lands to the actual settlers. As soon as the settlers purchased their land, their titles were legitimate, and so were the titles of all those who inherited or purchased them. Later on, the United States government unfortunately laid claim to all virgin land as the "public domain," and then unjustly sold the land to speculators who had not earned a homestead title. But eventually these speculators sold the land to the actual settlers, and from then on, the land title was proper and legitimate.[10]

In South America and much of the undeveloped world, however, matters are considerably different. For here, in many areas, an invading State conquered the lands of peasants, and then parcelled out such lands to various warlords as their "private" fiefs, from then on to extract "rent" from the hapless peasantry. The descendants of the conquistadores still presume to own the land tilled by the descendants of the original

---

[10]This legitimacy, of course, does not apply to the vast amount of land in the West still owned by the federal government which it refuses to throw open to homesteading. Our response to this situation must be that the government should throw open all of its public domain to private homesteading without delay.

peasants, people with a clearly just claim to ownership of the land. In this situation justice requires the vacating of the land titles by these "feudal" or "coercive" landholders (who are in a position equivalent to our hypothetical Rockefellers and Kennedys) and the turning over of the property titles, without compensation, to the individual peasants who are the "true" owners of their land.

Much of the drive for "land reform" by the peasantry of the undeveloped world is precisely motivated by an instinctive application of our theory of justice: by the apprehension of the peasants that the land they have tilled for generations is "their" land and that the landlord's claim is coercive and unjust. It is ironic that, in these numerous cases, the only response of utilitarian free-market advocates is to defend existing land titles, regardless of their injustice, and to tell the peasants to keep quiet and "respect private property." Since the peasants are convinced that the property is their private title, it is no wonder that they fail to be impressed; but since they find the supposed champions of property rights and free-market capitalism to be their staunch enemies, they generally are forced to turn to the only organized groups that, at least rhetorically, champion their claims and are willing to carry out the required rectification of property titles—the socialists and communists. In short, from simply a utilitarian consideration of consequences, the utilitarian free-marketeers have done very badly in the undeveloped world, the result of their ignoring the fact that others than themselves, however inconveniently, do have a passion for justice. Of course, after socialists or communists take power, they do their best to collectivize peasant land, and one of the prime struggles of Socialist society is that of the State versus the peasantry. But even those peasants who are aware of socialist duplicity on the land question may still feel that with the socialists and communists they at least have a fighting chance. And sometimes, of course, the peasants have been able to win and to force communist regimes to keep hands off their newly gained private property: notably in the case of Poland and Yugoslavia.

The utilitarian defense of the *status quo* will then be least viable—and, therefore, the least utilitarian—in those situations where the *status quo* is the most glaringly unjust. As often happens, far more than utilitarians will admit, justice and genuine utility are here linked together.

To sum up, all existing property titles may be considered just under the homestead principle, *provided*: (a) that there may never be any property in people; (b) that the existing property owner did not himself steal the property; and particularly (c) that any identifiable just owner (the original victim of theft or his heir) must be accorded his property.

5
WAR, PEACE,
AND THE STATE

The libertarian movement has been chided by William F. Buckley, Jr., for failing to use its "strategic intelligence" in facing the major problems of our time. We have, indeed, been too often prone to "pursue our busy little seminars on whether or not to demunicipalize the garbage collectors" (as Buckley has contemptuously written), while ignoring and failing to apply libertarian theory to the most vital problem of our time: war and peace. There *is* a sense in which Libertarians have been utopian rather than strategic in their thinking, with a tendency to divorce the ideal system which we envisage from the realities of the world in which we live. In short, too many of us have divorced theory from practice, and have then been content to hold the pure libertarian society as an abstract ideal for some remotely future time, while in the concrete world of today we follow unthinkingly the orthodox "conservative" line. To live liberty, to begin the hard but essential strategic struggle of changing the unsatisfactory world of today in the direction of our ideals, we must realize and demonstrate to the world that libertarian theory can be brought sharply to bear upon all of the world's crucial problems. By coming to grips with these problems, we can demonstrate that libertarianism is not just a beautiful ideal somewhere on Cloud Nine, but a tough-minded body of truths that enables us to take our stand and to cope with the whole host of issues of our day.

Let us then, by all means, use our strategic intelligence. Although, when he sees the result, Mr. Buckley might well wish that we had stayed in the realm of garbage collection. Let us construct a libertarian theory of war and peace.

The fundamental axiom of libertarian theory is that no one may threaten or commit violence ("aggress") against another man's person or property. Violence may be employed only against the man who commits such violence; that is, only defensively against the aggressive violence of another.[1] In short, no violence may be employed against a nonaggressor. Here is the fundamental rule from which can be deduced the entire *corpus* of libertarian theory. [2]

Let us set aside the more complex problem of the State for awhile and consider simply relations between "private" individuals. Jones finds that he or his property is being invaded, aggressed against, by Smith. It is legitimate for Jones, as we have seen, to repel this invasion by defensive violence of his own. But now we come to a more knotty question: is it within

---

[1]There are some libertarians who would go even further and say that no one should employ violence even in defending himself against violence. However, even such Tolstoyans, or "absolute pacifists," would concede the defender's right to employ defensive violence and would merely urge him not to exercise that right. They, therefore, do not disagree with our proposition. In the same way, a Libertarian temperance advocate would not challenge a man's right to drink liquor, only his wisdom in exercising that right.

[2]We shall not attempt to justify this axiom here. Most Libertarians and even Conservatives are familiar with the rule and even defend it; the problem is not so much in arriving at the rule as in fearlessly and consistently pursuing its numerous and often astounding implications.

the right of Jones to commit violence against innocent third parties as a corollary to his legitimate defense against Smith? To the Libertarian, the answer must be clearly, no. Remember that the rule prohibiting violence against the persons or property of innocent men is absolute: it holds regardless of the subjective *motives* for the aggression. It is wrong and criminal to violate the property or person of another, even if one is a Robin Hood, or starving, or is doing it to save one's relatives, *or* is defending oneself against a third man's attack. We may understand and sympathize with the motives in many of these cases and extreme situations. We may later mitigate the guilt if the criminal comes to trial for punishment, but we cannot evade the judgment that this aggression is still a criminal act, and one which the victim has every right to repel, by violence if necessary. In short, A aggresses against B because C is threatening, or aggressing against, A. We may understand C's "higher" culpability in this whole procedure; but we must still label this aggression as a criminal act which B has the right to repel by violence.

To be more concrete, if Jones finds that his property is being stolen by Smith, he has the right to repel him and try to catch him; but he has *no* right to repel him by bombing a building and murdering innocent people or to catch him by spraying machine gun fire into an innocent crowd. If he does this, he is as much (or more of) a criminal aggressor as Smith is.

The application to problems of war and peace is already becoming evident. For while war in the narrower sense is a conflict between States, in the broader sense we may define it as the outbreak of open violence between people or groups of people. If Smith and a group of his henchmen aggress against Jones and Jones and his bodyguards pursue the Smith gang to their lair, we may cheer Jones on in his endeavor; and we, and others in society interested in repelling aggression, may contribute financially or personally to Jones's cause. But Jones has *no* right, any more than does Smith, to aggress against anyone else in the course of his "just war": to steal others' property in order to finance his pursuit, to conscript others into his posse by use of violence or to kill others in the course of his struggle to capture the Smith forces. If Jones should do any of these things, he becomes a criminal as *fully* as Smith, and he too becomes subject to whatever sanctions are meted out against criminality. In fact, if Smith's crime was theft, and Jones should use conscription to catch him, or should kill others in the pursuit, Jones becomes more of a criminal than Smith, for such crimes against another person as enslavement and murder are surely far worse than theft. (For while theft injures the extension of another's personality, enslavement injures, and murder obliterates, that personality itself.)

Suppose that Jones, in the course of his "just war" against the ravages of Smith, should kill a few innocent people, and suppose that he should declaim, in defense of this murder, that he was simply acting on the slogan, "Give me liberty or give me death." The absurdity of this "defense" should be evident at once, for the issue is not whether Jones was willing to risk death personally in his defensive struggle against Smith; the issue is whether he was willing to kill other people in pursuit of his legitimate end. For Jones was in truth acting on the completely indefensible slogan: "Give me liberty or give *them* death" surely a far less noble battle cry.[3]

---

[3]Or, to bring up another famous antipacifist slogan, the question is not whether "we would be willing to use force to prevent the rape of our sister," but whether, to prevent that rape, we are willing to kill innocent people and perhaps even the sister herself.

The Libertarian's basic attitude toward war must then be: it is legitimate to use violence against criminals in defense of one's rights of person and property; it is completely impermissible to violate the rights of *other* innocent people. War, then, is only proper when the exercise of violence is rigorously limited to the individual criminals. We may judge for ourselves how many wars or conflicts in history have met this criterion.

It has often been maintained, and especially by Conservatives, that the development of the horrendous modern weapons of mass murder (nuclear weapons, rockets, germ warfare, etc.) is only a difference of *degree* rather than *kind* from the simpler weapons of an earlier era. Of course, one answer to this is that when the degree is the number of human lives, the difference is a very big one.[4] But another answer that the Libertarian is particularly equipped to give is that while the bow and arrow and even the rifle can be pinpointed, if the will be there, against actual criminals, modern nuclear weapons cannot. Here is a crucial difference in kind. Of course, the bow and arrow could be used for aggressive purposes, but it could also be pinpointed to use only against aggressors. Nuclear weapons, even "conventional" aerial bombs, cannot be. These weapons are *ipso facto* engines of indiscriminate mass destruction. (The only exception would be the extremely rare case where a mass of people who were all criminals inhabited a vast geographical area.) We must,

---

[4]William Buckley and other Conservatives have propounded the curious moral doctrine that it is no worse to kill millions than it is to kill one man. The man who does either is, to be sure, a murderer; but surely it makes a huge difference how many people he kills. We may see this by phrasing the problem thus: after a man has already killed one person, does it *make any difference* whether he stops killing now or goes on a further rampage and kills many dozen more people? Obviously, it does.

therefore, conclude that the use of nuclear or similar weapons, or the threat thereof, is a sin and a crime against humanity for which there can be no justification.

This is why the old cliché no longer holds that it is not the arms but the will to use them that is significant in judging matters of war and peace. For it is precisely the characteristic of modern weapons that they cannot be used selectively, cannot be used in a libertarian manner. Therefore, their very existence must be condemned, and nuclear disarmament becomes a good to be pursued for its own sake. And if we will indeed use our strategic intelligence, we will see that such disarmament is not only a good, but the highest political good that we can pursue in the modern world. For just as murder is a more heinous crime against another man than larceny, so mass murder—indeed murder so widespread as to threaten human civilization and human survival itself—is the worst crime that any man could possibly commit. And that crime is now imminent. And the forestalling of massive annihilation is far more important, in truth, than the demunicipalization of garbage disposal, as worthwhile as that may be. Or are Libertarians going to wax properly indignant about price control or the income tax, and yet shrug their shoulders at or even positively advocate the ultimate crime of mass murder?

If nuclear warfare is totally illegitimate even for individuals defending themselves against criminal assault, how much more so is nuclear or even "conventional" warfare between States!

It is time now to bring the State into our discussion. The State is a group of people who have managed to acquire a virtual monopoly of the use of violence throughout a given territorial area. In particular, it has acquired a monopoly of aggressive violence, for States generally recognize the right of individuals to use violence (though not against States, of course) in self-defense.[5] The State then uses this monopoly to wield power over the inhabitants of the area and to enjoy the material fruits of that power. The State, then, is the only organization in society that regularly and openly obtains its monetary revenues by the use of *aggressive* violence; all other individuals and organizations (except if delegated that right by the State) can obtain wealth only by peaceful production and by voluntary exchange of their respective products. This use of violence to obtain its revenue (called "taxation") is the keystone of State power. Upon this base the State erects a further structure of power over the individuals in its territory, regulating them, penalizing critics, subsidizing favorites, etc. The State also takes care to arrogate to itself the compulsory monopoly of various critical services needed by society, thus keeping the people in dependence upon the State for key services, keeping control of the vital command posts in society and also fostering among the public the myth that *only* the State can supply these goods and services. Thus the State is careful to monopolize police and judicial service, the ownership of roads and streets, the supply of money, and the postal service, and effectively to monopolize or control education, public utilities, transportation, and radio and television.

Now, since the State arrogates to itself the monopoly of violence over a territorial area, so long as its depredations and extortions go unresisted, there is said to be "peace" in the

---

[5]Professor Robert L. Cunningham has defined the State as the institution with "a monopoly on initiating open physical coercion." Or, as Albert Jay Nock put it similarly if more caustically, "The State claims and exercises the monopoly of crime. . . . It forbids private murder, but itself organizes murder on a colossal scale. It punishes private theft, but itself lays unscrupulous hands on anything it wants."

area, since the only violence is one-way, directed by the State downward against the people. Open conflict within the area only breaks out in the case of "revolutions" in which people resist the use of State power against them. Both the quiet case of the State unresisted and the case of open revolution may be termed "vertical violence": violence of the State against its public or vice versa.

In the modern world, each land area is ruled over by a State organization, but there are a number of States scattered over the earth, each with a monopoly of violence over its own territory. No super-State exists with a monopoly of violence over the entire world; and so a state of "anarchy" exists between the several States. (It has always been a source of wonder, incidentally, to this writer how the same Conservatives who denounce as lunatic any proposal for eliminating a monopoly of violence over a given territory and thus leaving private individuals without an overlord, should be equally insistent upon leaving *States* without an overlord to settle disputes between them. The former is always denounced as "crackpot anarchism"; the latter is hailed as preserving independence and "national sovereignty" from "world government.") And so, except for revolutions, which occur only sporadically, the open violence and two-sided conflict in the world takes place *between* two or more States, that is, in what is called "international war" (or "horizontal violence").

Now there are crucial and vital differences between inter-State warfare on the one hand and revolutions against the State or conflicts between private individuals on the other. One vital difference is the shift in geography. In a revolution, the conflict takes place *within* the same geographical area: both the minions of the State and the revolutionaries inhabit the same territory. Inter-State warfare, on the other hand, takes place between two groups, each having a monopoly over its own geographical area; that is, it takes place between inhabitants of different territories. From this difference flow several important consequences: (1) in inter-State war the scope for the use of modern weapons of destruction is far greater. For if the "escalation" of weaponry in an intra-territorial conflict becomes too great, each side will blow itself up with the weapons directed against the other. Neither a revolutionary group nor a State combatting revolution, for example, can use nuclear weapons against the other. But, on the other hand, when the warring parties inhabit different territorial areas, the scope for modern weaponry becomes enormous, and the entire arsenal of mass devastation can come into play. A second consequence (2) is that while it is *possible* for revolutionaries to pinpoint their targets and confine them to their State enemies, and thus avoid aggressing against innocent people, pinpointing is far less possible in an inter-State war.[6] This is true even with older weapons; and, of course, with modern weapons there can be no pinpointing whatever. Furthermore, (3) since each State can mobilize all the people and resources in its territory, the other State comes to regard all the citizens of the opposing country as at least temporarily its enemies and to treat them accordingly by extending the war to them. Thus, all of the consequences of inter-territorial war make it almost inevitable that inter-State war will involve aggression by each side against the innocent civilians—the private individuals—of the other. This inevitability becomes absolute with modern weapons of mass destruction.

---

[6]An outstanding example of pinpointing by revolutionaries was the invariable practice of the Irish Republican Army, in its later years, of making sure that only British troops and British government property were attacked and that no innocent Irish civilians were injured. A guerrilla revolution not supported by the bulk of the people, of course, is far more likely to aggress against civilians.

If one distinct attribute of inter-State war is inter-territoriality, another unique attribute stems from the fact that each State lives by taxation over its subjects. Any war against another State, therefore, involves the increase and extension of taxation–aggression over its own people.[7] Conflicts between private individuals can be, and usually are, voluntarily waged and financed by the parties concerned. Revolutions can be, and often are, financed and fought by voluntary contributions of the public. But State wars can only be waged through aggression against the taxpayer.

All State wars, therefore, involve increased aggression against the State's own taxpayers, and almost all State wars (*all*, in modern warfare) involve the maximum aggression (murder) against the innocent civilians ruled by the enemy State. On the other hand, revolutions are generally financed voluntarily and may pinpoint their violence to the State rulers, and private conflicts may confine their violence to the actual criminals. The Libertarian must, therefore, conclude that, while some revolutions and some private conflicts *may* be legitimate, State wars are *always* to be condemned.

Many Libertarians object as follows: "While we too deplore the use of taxation for warfare, and the State's monopoly of defense service, we have to recognize that these conditions exist, and while they do, we must support the State in just wars of defense." The reply to this would go as follows: "Yes, as you say, unfortunately States exist, each having a monopoly of violence over its territorial area." What

---

[7] If it be objected that a war *could* theoretically be financed solely by a State's lowering of nonwar expenditures, then the reply still holds that taxation remains greater than it *could* be without the war effect. Moreover, the purport of this article is that Libertarians should be opposed to government expenditures *whatever* the field, war or nonwar.

then should be the attitude of the Libertarian toward conflicts between these States? The Libertarian should say, in
effect, to the State: "All right, you exist, but as long as you
exist at least confine your activities to the area which you
monopolize." In short, the Libertarian is interested in reducing as much as possible the area of State aggression against
all private individuals. The only way to do this, in international affairs, is for the people of each country to pressure
their own State to confine its activities to the area which it
monopolizes and not to aggress against other State-monopo-
lists. In short, the objective of the Libertarian is to confine any
existing State to as small a degree of invasion of person and
property as possible. And this means the total avoidance of
war. The people under each State should pressure "their"
respective States not to attack one another, and, if a conflict
should break out, to negotiate a peace or declare a cease-fire
as quickly as physically possible.

Suppose further that we have that rarity—an unusually
clear-cut case in which the State is actually trying to defend the
property of one of its citizens. A citizen of country A travels or
invests in country B, and then State B aggresses against his
person or confiscates his property. Surely, our libertarian
critic would argue, here is a clear-cut case where State A
should threaten or commit war against State B in order to
defend the property of "its" citizen. Since, the argument
runs, the State has taken upon itself the monopoly of defense
of its citizens, it then has the obligation to go to war on
behalf of any citizen, and libertarians have an obligation to
support this war as a just one.

But the point again is that each State has a monopoly of violence and, therefore, of defense only over its territorial area. It
has no such monopoly; in fact, it has no power at all, over any
other geographical area. Therefore, if an inhabitant of country

A should move to or invest in country B, the libertarian must argue that he thereby takes his chances with the State-monopolist of country B, and it would be immoral and criminal for State A to tax people in country A *and* kill numerous innocents in country B in order to defend the property of the traveler or investor.[8]

It should also be pointed out that there is no defense against nuclear weapons (the only current "defense" is the threat of mutual annihilation) and, therefore, that the State *cannot* fulfill any sort of defense function so long as these weapons exist.

The libertarian objective, then, should be, regardless of the specific causes of any conflict, to pressure States not to launch wars against other States and, should a war break out, to pressure them to sue for peace and negotiate a cease-fire and peace treaty as quickly as physically possible. This objective, incidentally, is enshrined in the international law of the eighteenth and nineteenth centuries, that is, the ideal that no State could aggress against the territory of another—in short, the "peaceful coexistence" of States.[9]

---

[8]There is another consideration which applies rather to "domestic" defense within a State's territory: the less the State can successfully defend the inhabitants of its area against attack by criminals, the *more* these inhabitants may come to learn the inefficiency of state operations, and the more they will turn to non-State methods of defense. Failure by the State to defend, therefore, has educative value for the public.

[9]The international law mentioned in this paper is the old-fashioned libertarian law as had voluntarily emerged in previous centuries and has nothing to do with the modern statist accretion of "collective security." Collective security forces a maximum escalation of every local war into a worldwide war—the precise reversal of the libertarian objective of *reducing* the scope of any war as much as possible.

Suppose, however, that despite libertarian opposition, war has begun and the warring States are not negotiating a peace. What, then, should be the libertarian position? Clearly, to reduce the scope of assault of innocent civilians as much as possible. Old-fashioned international law had two excellent devices for this: the "laws of war," and the "laws of neutrality" or "neutrals' rights." The laws of neutrality are designed to keep any war that breaks out confined to the warring States themselves, without aggression against the States or particularly the peoples of the other nations. Hence the importance of such ancient and now forgotten American principles as "freedom of the seas" or severe limitations upon the rights of warring States to blockade neutral trade with the enemy country. In short, the libertarian tries to induce neutral States to *remain* neutral in any inter-State conflict and to induce the warring States to observe fully the rights of neutral citizens. The "laws of war" were designed to limit as much as possible the invasion by warring States of the rights of the civilians of the respective warring countries. As the British jurist F.J.P. Veale put it:

> The fundamental principle of this code was that hostilities between civilized peoples must be limited to the armed forces actually engaged. . . . It drew a distinction between combatants and noncombatants by laying down that the sole business of the combatants is to fight each other and, consequently, that noncombatants must be excluded from the scope of military operations.[10]

In the modified form of prohibiting the bombardment of all cities not in the front line, this rule held in Western European wars in recent centuries until Britain launched the

---

[10]F.J.P. Veale, *Advance to Barbarism* (Appleton, Wis.: C.C. Nelson, 1953), p. 58.

strategic bombing of civilians in World War II. Now, of course, the entire concept is scarcely remembered, the very nature of nuclear war resting on the annihilation of civilians.

In condemning all wars, regardless of motive, the Libertarian knows that there may well be varying degrees of guilt among States for any specific war. But the overriding consideration for the Libertarian is the condemnation of any State participation in war. Hence his policy is that of exerting pressure on all States not to start a war, to stop one that has begun and to reduce the scope of any persisting war in injuring civilians of either side or no side.

A neglected corollary to the libertarian policy of peaceful coexistence of States is the rigorous abstention from any foreign aid; that is, a policy of nonintervention between States (= "isolationism" = "neutralism"). For any aid given by State A to State B (1) increases tax aggression against the people of country A and (2) aggravates the suppression by State B of its own people. If there are any revolutionary groups in country B, then foreign aid intensifies this suppression all the more. Even foreign aid to a revolutionary group in B—more defensible because directed to a voluntary group opposing a State rather than a State oppressing the people—must be condemned as (at the very least) aggravating tax aggression at home.

Let us see how libertarian theory applies to the problem of *imperialism*, which may be defined as the aggression by State A over the people of country B, and the subsequent maintenance of this foreign rule. Revolution by the B people against the imperial rule of A is certainly legitimate, provided again that revolutionary fire be directed only against the rulers. It has often been maintained—even by Libertarians—that Western imperialism over undeveloped countries should be supported as more watchful of property rights than any successor native government would be. The first reply is that judging what might follow the *status quo* is purely speculative, whereas existing imperialist rule is all too real and culpable. Moreover, the libertarian here begins his focus at the wrong end—at the alleged benefit of imperialism to the native. He should, on the contrary, concentrate first on the Western taxpayer, who is mulcted and burdened to pay for the wars of conquest, and then for the maintenance of the imperial bureaucracy. On this ground alone, the libertarian must condemn imperialism.[11]

Does opposition to all war mean that the libertarian can never countenance change—that he is consigning the world to a permanent freezing of unjust regimes? Certainly not. Suppose, for example, that the hypothetical state of "Waldavia" has attacked "Ruritania" and annexed the western part of the country. The Western Ruritanians now long to be reunited with their Ruritanian brethren. How is this to be achieved? There is, of course, the route of peaceful negotiation

---

[11]Two other points about Western imperialism: first, its rule is not nearly so liberal or benevolent as many libertarians like to believe. The only property rights respected are those of the Europeans; the *natives* find their best lands stolen from them by the imperialists and their labor coerced by violence into working the vast landed estates acquired by this theft.

Second, another myth holds that the "gunboat diplomacy" of the turn of the century was a heroic libertarian action in defense of the property rights of Western investors in backward countries. Aside from our above strictures against going beyond any State's monopolized land area, it is overlooked that the bulk of gunboat moves were in defense, *not* of private investments, but of Western holders of government bonds. The Western powers coerced the smaller governments into increasing tax aggression on their own people, in order to pay off foreign bondholders. By no stretch of the imagination was this an action on behalf of private property—quite the contrary.

between the two powers, but suppose that the Waldavian imperialists prove adamant. Or, libertarian Waldavians can put pressure on their government to abandon its conquest in the name of justice. But suppose that this, too, does not work. What then? We must still maintain the illegitimacy of Ruritania's mounting a war against Waldavia. The legitimate routes are (1) revolutionary uprisings by the oppressed Western Ruritanian people, and (2) aid by private Ruritanian groups (or, for that matter, by friends of the Ruritanian cause in other countries) to the Western rebels—either in the form of equipment or of volunteer personnel.[12]

We have seen throughout our discussion the crucial importance, in any present-day libertarian peace program, of the elimination of modern methods of mass annihilation. These weapons, against which there can be no defense, assure maximum aggression against civilians in any conflict with the clear prospect of the destruction of civilization and even of the human race itself. Highest priority on any libertarian agenda, therefore, must be pressure on all States to agree to general and complete disarmament down to police levels, with particular stress on nuclear disarmament. In short, if we are to use our strategic intelligence, we must conclude that the dismantling of the greatest menace that has ever confronted the life and liberty of the human race is indeed far more important than demunicipalizing the garbage service.

---

[12]The Tolstoyan wing of the libertarian movement could urge the Western Ruritanians to engage in *nonviolent* revolution, for example, tax strikes, boycotts, mass refusal to obey government orders or a general strike—especially in arms factories. Cf. the work of the revolutionary Tolstoyan, Bartelemy De Ligt, *The Conquest of Violence: An Essay On War and Revolution* (New York: Dutton, 1938).

We cannot leave our topic without saying at least a word about the domestic tyranny that is the inevitable accompaniment of war. The great Randolph Bourne realized that "war is the health of the State."[13] It is in war that the State really comes into its own: swelling in power, in number, in pride, in absolute dominion over the economy and the society. Society becomes a herd, seeking to kill its alleged enemies, rooting out and suppressing all dissent from the official war effort, happily betraying truth for the supposed public interest. Society becomes an armed camp, with the values and the morale— as Albert Jay Nock once phrased it—of an "army on the march."

The root myth that enables the State to wax fat off war is the canard that war is a defense *by* the State *of* its subjects. The facts, of course, are precisely the reverse. For if war is the health of the State, it is also its greatest danger. A State can only "die" by defeat in war or by revolution. In war, therefore, the State frantically mobilizes the people to fight for *it* against another State, under the pretext that *it* is fighting for them. But all this should occasion no surprise; we see it in other walks of life. For which categories of crime does the State pursue and punish most intensely—those against private citizens or those against *itself*? The gravest crimes in the State's lexicon are almost invariably not invasions of person and property, but dangers to its *own* contentment: for example, treason, desertion of a soldier to the enemy, failure to register for the draft, conspiracy to overthrow the government. Murder is pursued haphazardly unless the victim be a *policeman*, or *Gott zoll hüten*, an assassinated Chief of State;

---

[13]See Randolph Bourne, "Unfinished Fragment on the State," in *Untimely Papers* (New York: B.W. Huebsch, 1919).

failure to pay a private debt is, if anything, almost encouraged, but income tax evasion is punished with utmost severity; counterfeiting the State's money is pursued far more relentlessly than forging private checks, etc. All this evidence demonstrates that the State is far more interested in preserving its own power than in defending the rights of private citizens.

A final word about conscription: of all the ways in which war aggrandizes the State, this is perhaps the most flagrant and most despotic. But the most striking fact about conscription is the absurdity of the arguments put forward on its behalf. A man must be conscripted to defend his (or someone else's?) liberty against an evil State beyond the borders. Defend his liberty? How? By being coerced into an army whose very *raison d'etre* is the expunging of liberty, the trampling on all the liberties of the person, the calculated and brutal dehumanization of the soldier and his transformation into an efficient engine of murder at the whim of his "commanding officer"?[14] Can any conceivable foreign State do anything worse to him than what "his" army is now doing for his alleged benefit? Who is there, O Lord, to defend him against his "defenders"?

---

[14]To the old militarist taunt hurled against the pacifist: "Would you use force to prevent the rape of your sister?" the proper retort is: "Would you rape your sister if ordered to do so by your commanding officer?"

6
THE FALLACY OF
THE PUBLIC SECTOR

We have heard a great deal in recent years of the "public sector," and solemn discussions abound through the land on whether or not the public sector should be increased *vis-à-vis* the "private sector." The very terminology is redolent of pure science, and, indeed, it emerges from the supposedly scientific, if rather grubby, world of "national income statistics." But the concept is hardly *Wertfrei*, in fact, it is fraught with grave, and questionable, implications.

In the first place, we may ask: "public sector" of *what*? Of something called the "national product." But note the hidden assumptions: that the national product is something like a pie, consisting of several "sectors," and that these sectors, public and private alike, are added to make the product of the economy as a whole. In this way, the assumption is smuggled into the analysis that the public and private sectors are equally productive, equally important, and on an equal footing altogether, and that "our" deciding on the proportions of public to private sector is about as innocuous as any individual's decision on whether to eat cake or ice cream. The State is considered to be an amiable service agency, somewhat akin to the corner grocer, or rather to the neighborhood lodge, in which "we" get together to decide how much "our government" should do for (or to) us. Even those neoclassical economists who tend to favor the free market and free society often regard the State as a generally inefficient, but still amiable, organ of social service, mechanically registering "our" values and decisions.

One would not think it difficult for scholars and laymen alike to grasp the fact that government is not like the Rotarians or the Elks; that it differs profoundly from all other organs and institutions in society; namely, that it lives and acquires its revenues by coercion and not by voluntary payment. The late Joseph Schumpeter was never more astute than when he wrote:

> The theory which construes taxes on the analogy of club dues or of the purchase of the services of, say, a doctor only proves how far removed this part of the social sciences is from scientific habits of mind.[1]

Apart from the public sector, what constitutes the productivity of the "private sector" of the economy? The productivity of the private sector does not stem from the fact that people are rushing around doing something, anything, with their resources; it consists in the fact that they are using these resources to satisfy the needs and desires of the consumers.

---

[1]In the preceding sentence, Schumpeter wrote:

> The friction or antagonism between the private and the public sphere was intensified from the first by the fact that . . . the state has been living on a revenue which was being produced in the private sphere for private purposes and had to be deflected from these purposes by political force.

Precisely. Joseph A. Schumpeter, *Capitalism, Socialism, and Democracy* (New York: Harper and Bros., 1942), p. 198.

Businessmen and other producers direct their energies, on the free market, to producing those products which will be most rewarded by the consumers; and the sale of these products may, therefore, roughly "measure" the importance which the consumers place upon them. If millions of people bend their energies to producing horses-and-buggies, they will, in this day and age, not be able to sell them, and hence the productivity of their output will be virtually zero. On the other hand, if a few million dollars are spent in a given year on product X, then statisticians may well judge that these millions constitute the productive output of the X part of the "private sector" of the economy.

One of the most important features of our economic resources is their scarcity; land, labor, and capital good factors are all scarce, and may all be put to varied possible uses. The free market uses them "productively" because the producers are guided, on the market, to produce what the consumers most need, automobiles, for example, rather than buggies. Therefore, while the statistics of the total output of the private sector seem to be a mere adding of numbers, or counting units of output, the measures of output actually involve the important qualitative decision of considering as "product" what the consumers are willing to buy. A million automobiles, sold on the market, are productive because the consumers so considered them; a million buggies, remaining unsold, would not have been "product" because the consumers would have passed them by.

Suppose, now, that into this idyll of free exchange enters the long arm of government. The government, for some reasons of its own, decides to ban automobiles altogether (perhaps because the many tailfins offend the aesthetic sensibilities of the rulers) and to compel the auto companies to produce the equivalent in buggies instead. Under such a strict regimen, the consumers would be, in a sense, compelled to purchase buggies because no cars would be permitted. However, in this case, the statistician would surely be purblind if he blithely and simply recorded the buggies as being just as "productive" as the previous automobiles. To call them equally productive would be a mockery; in fact, given plausible conditions, the "national product" totals might not even show a statistical decline when they had actually fallen drastically.

And yet the highly-touted "public sector" is in even worse straits than the buggies of our hypothetical example. For most of the resources consumed by the maw of government have not even been seen, much less used, by the consumers who were at least allowed to ride in their buggies. In the private sector a firm's productivity is gauged by how much the consumers voluntarily spend on its product. But in the public sector, the government's "productivity" is measured— *mirabile dictu*—by how much it spends! Early in their construction of national product statistics, the statisticians were confronted with the fact that the government, unique among individuals and firms, could not have its activities gauged by the voluntary payments of the public—because there were little or none of such payments. Assuming, without any proof, that government must be as productive as anything else, they then settled upon its expenditures as a gauge of its productivity. In this way, not only are government expenditures just as useful as private, but all the government need do in order to increase its "productivity" is to add a large chunk to its bureaucracy. Hire more bureaucrats and see the productivity of the public sector rise! Here, indeed, is an easy and happy form of social magic for our bemused citizens.

The truth is exactly the reverse of the common assumptions. Far from adding cozily to the private sector, the public sector can only feed off the private sector; it necessarily lives parasitically upon the private economy. But this means that the productive resources of society—far from satisfying the wants of consumers—are now directed, by compulsion, away from these wants and needs. The consumers are deliberately thwarted, and the resources of the economy diverted from them to those activities desired by the parasitic bureaucracy and politicians. In many cases, the private consumers obtain nothing at all, except perhaps propaganda beamed to them at their own expense. In other cases, the consumers receive something far down on their list of priorities like the buggies of our example. In either case, it becomes evident that the "public sector" is actually antiproductive; that is, subtracts from rather than adds to the private sector of the economy. For the public sector lives by continuous attack on the very criterion that is used to gauge productivity: the voluntary purchases of consumers.

We may gauge the fiscal impact of government on the private sector by subtracting government expenditures from the national product. For government payments to its own bureaucracy are hardly additions to production; and government absorption of economic resources takes them out of the productive sphere. This gauge, of course, is only fiscal; it does not begin to measure the antiproductive impact of various government regulations, which cripple production and exchange in other ways than absorbing resources. It also does not dispose of numerous other fallacies of the national product statistics. But, at least, it removes such common myths as the idea that the productive output of the American economy increased during World War II. Subtract the government deficit instead of adding it, and we see that the real productivity of the economy declined, as we would rationally expect during a war.

In another of his astute comments, Joseph Schumpeter wrote, concerning anticapitalist intellectuals:

> . . . capitalism stands its trial before judges who have the
> sentence of death in their pockets. They are going to pass

> it, whatever the defense they may hear; the only success vic-
> torious defense can possibly produce is a change in the
> indictment.[2]

The indictment has certainly been changing. In the 1930s,
we heard that government must expand because capitalism
had brought about mass poverty. Now, under the aegis of
John Kenneth Galbraith, we hear that capitalism has sinned
because the masses are too affluent. Where once poverty was
suffered by "one-third of a nation," we must now bewail the
"starvation" of the public sector.

By what standards does Dr. Galbraith conclude that the
private sector is too bloated and the public sector too anemic,
and, therefore, that government must exercise further coercion to rectify its own malnutrition? Certainly, his standard is
not historical. In 1902, for example, net national product of
the United States was $22.1 billion; government expenditure
(Federal, state, and local) totaled $1.66 billion or 7.1 percent
of the total product. In 1957, on the other hand, net national
product was $402.6 billion, and government expenditures
totaled $125.5 billion, or 31.2 percent of the total product.
Government's fiscal depredation on the private product has,
therefore, multiplied from four- to five-fold over the present
century. This is hardly "starvation" of the public sector. And
yet, Galbraith contends that the public sector is being
increasingly starved, relative to its status in the nonaffluent
nineteenth century!

What standards, then, does Galbraith offer us to discover
when the public sector will finally be at its optimum? The
answer is nothing but personal whim:

> There will be question as to what is the test of balance—at
> what point may we conclude that balance has been achieved

---

[2]Schumpeter, *Capitalism, Socialism, and Democracy*, p. 144.

> in the satisfaction of private and public needs. The answer
> is that no test can be applied, for none exists. . . . The pres-
> ent imbalance is clear. . . . This being so, the direction in
> which we move to correct matters is utterly plain.[3]

To Galbraith, the imbalance of today is "clear." Clear, why? Because he looks around him and sees deplorable conditions wherever government operates. Schools are overcrowded, urban traffic is congested, the streets littered and rivers are polluted; he might have added that crime is increasingly rampant and the courts of justice clogged. All of these are areas of government operation and ownership. The one supposed solution for these glaring defects is to siphon more money into the government till.

But how is it that only government agencies clamor for more money and denounce the citizens for reluctance to supply more? Why do we never have the private enterprise equivalents of traffic jams (which occur on government streets), mismanaged schools, water shortages, etc.? The reason is that private firms acquire the money that they deserve from two sources: voluntary payment for the services by consumers and voluntary investment by investors in expectation of consumer demand. If there is an increased demand for a privately-owned good, consumers pay more for the product, and investors invest more in its supply, thus "clearing the market" to everyone's satisfaction. If there is an increased demand for a publicly-owned good (water, streets, subway, etc.), all we hear is annoyance at the consumer for wasting precious resources, coupled with annoyance at the taxpayer for balking at a higher tax load. Private enterprise makes it its business to court the consumer and to satisfy his most urgent

---

[3]John Kenneth Galbraith, *The Affluent Society* (Boston: Houghton Mifflin, 1958), pp. 320–21.

demands; government agencies denounce the consumer as a troublesome user of their resources. Only a government, for example, would look fondly upon the prohibition of private cars as a "solution" for the problem of congested streets. Government's numerous "free" services, moreover, create permanent excess demand over supply and, therefore, permanent "shortages" of the product. Government, in short, acquiring its revenue by coerced confiscation rather than by voluntary investment and consumption, is not and cannot be run like a business. Its inherent gross inefficiencies, the impossibility for it to clear the market, will insure its being a mare's nest of trouble on the economic scene.[4]

In former times, the inherent mismanagement of government was generally considered a good argument for keeping as many things as possible out of government hands. After all, when one has invested in a losing proposition, one tries to refrain from pouring good money after bad. And yet, Dr. Galbraith would have us redouble our determination to pour the taxpayer's hard-earned money down the rathole of the "public sector," and uses the very defects of government operation as his major argument!

Dr. Galbraith has two supporting arrows in his bow. First, he states that, as people's living standards rise, the added goods are not worth as much to them as the earlier ones. This is standard knowledge; but Galbraith somehow deduces from this decline that people's private wants are now worth nothing to them. But, if that is the case, then why should *government* "services," which have expanded at a much faster

---

[4]For more on the inherent problems of government operations, see Murray N. Rothbard, "Government in Business," in *Essays on Liberty* (Irvington-on-Hudson, N.Y.: Foundation for Economic Education, 1958), vol. 4, pp. 183–87.

rate, still be worth so much as to require a further shift of resources to the public sector? His final argument is that private wants are all artificially induced by business advertising which automatically "creates" the wants that it supposedly serves. In short, people, according to Galbraith, would, if let alone, be content with nonaffluent, presumably subsistence-level living; *advertising* is the villain that spoils this primitive idyll.

Aside from the philosophical problem of how A can "create" B's wants and desires without B's having to place his own stamp of approval upon them, we are faced here with a curious view of the economy. Is everything above subsistence "artificial"? By what standard? Moreover, why in the world should a business go through the extra bother and expense of inducing a change in consumer wants, when it can profit by serving the consumer's existing, "uncreated" wants? The very "marketing revolution" that business is now undergoing, its increased and almost frantic concentration on "market research," demonstrates the reverse of Galbraith's view. For if by advertising, business production automatically creates its own consumer demand, there would be no need whatever for market research—and no worry about bankruptcy either. In fact, far from the consumer in an affluent society being more of a "slave" to the business firm, the truth is precisely the opposite: for as living standards rise above subsistence, the consumer gets more particular and choosey about what he buys. The businessman must pay even greater court to the consumer than he did before; hence the furious attempts of market research to find out what the consumers want to buy.

There is an area of our society, however, where Galbraith's strictures on advertising may almost be said to apply—but it is in an area that he curiously never mentions. This is the enormous amount of advertising and propaganda *by government*.

This is advertising that beams to the citizen the virtues of a product which, unlike business advertising, he never has a chance to test. If cereal company X prints a picture of a pretty girl declaiming that "Cereal X is yummy," the consumer, even if doltish enough to take this seriously, has a chance to test that proposition personally. Soon his own taste determines whether he will buy or not. But, if a government agency advertises its own virtues over the mass media, the citizen has no direct test to permit him to accept or reject the claims. If any wants are artificial, they are those generated by government propaganda. Furthermore, business advertising is, at least, paid for by investors, and its success depends on the voluntary acceptance of the product by the consumers. Government advertising is paid for by means of taxes extracted from the citizens, and hence can go on, year after year, without check. The hapless citizen is cajoled into applauding the merits of the very people who, by coercion, are forcing him to pay for the propaganda. This is truly adding insult to injury. If Dr. Galbraith and his followers are poor guides for dealing with the public sector, what standard does our analysis offer instead? The answer is the old Jeffersonian one: "that government is best which governs least." Any reduction of the public sector, any shift of activities from the public to the private sphere, is a net moral and economic gain.

Most economists have two basic arguments on behalf of the public sector which we may only consider very briefly here. One is the problem of "external benefits." A and B often benefit, it is held, if they can force C into doing something. Much can be said in criticism of this doctrine; but suffice it to say here that any argument proclaiming the right and goodness of, say, three neighbors, who yearn to form a string quartet, forcing a fourth neighbor at bayonet point to learn and play the viola, is hardly deserving of sober comment. The second argument is more substantial; stripped of technical jargon, it states that some essential services simply cannot be supplied by the private sphere and that, therefore, government supply of these services is necessary. And yet, every single one of the services supplied by government has been, in the past, successfully furnished by private enterprise. The bland assertion that private citizens *cannot* possibly supply these goods is never bolstered, in the works of these economists, by any proof whatever. How is it, for example, that economists, so often given to pragmatic or utilitarian solutions, do not call for social "experiments" in this direction? Why must political experiments always be in the direction of more government? Why not give the free market a county, or even a state or two, and see what it can accomplish?

7
KID LIB

Among the many highly touted "liberations" of recent years, sometimes genuine and more often spurious, "kid lib" seems to be waiting in the wings. In fact, one libertarian publication claims that "kid lib" is the next wave of the future. What "kid lib" is supposed to be is now unclear; and I suspect it may amount to little more than the supposed "right" to kick every adult in the shins and to enjoy a guaranteed annual income to be provided by long-suffering parents and the longer-suffering taxpayer. But, nevertheless, kid lib highlights the difficult and vexing problem of children's rights; what, indeed, are the rights of children and of parents?

There has been very little thinking among libertarians about the children question. The reason is clear, for libertarians are well trained to handle the problems of adults; each adult is clearly possessed with the right of self-ownership. So far so good. But what of the newborn babe? It is evident that the baby has no *de facto* power of self-ownership; and since adult rights in natural law derive from adult powers and faculties, who does own the baby? And if the baby must in some sense be "owned" by one or more adults, if he must be directed and controlled, who draws the line and where? At what point or in what zone does the child acquire his full rights, his rights of self-ownership? Suddenly? Gradually? At age 21, or what? Libertarian answers have ranged from the progressives, who wish to give children the right to run roughshod over everyone in the name of "freedom," to some anarchists who concluded that children were to be the absolute property of their creators, their parents, who therefore had the right to kill their children if they so desired.

As in so many other fuzzy areas of demarcation of rights, as for example in the problem of "free speech" and the shouting of "Fire!" in a crowded theater, the answer to perplexing questions of rights is invariably to be found in focusing on the rights of property. Where do the property rights lie? In the first place, the overriding fact of parent–child relations is that the child lives on the property of his parents. The child lives either in a house owned by his parents or in an apartment rented by them. Therefore, as in the case of any other "guest" living on someone else's property, he must obey the rules set down by the property owners for remaining on that property. In short, the parents have the perfect legal and moral right to lay down rules for their children, just as they would have the right to lay down rules for the behavior of their longstanding house guest, Uncle Ezra. Furthermore, there is nothing morally wrong with laying down such rules. On the contrary, any property owner is bound to lay down rules for the use of his property.

We have already said enough to demolish the progressive's cry for absolute "freedom" for children: that children should be allowed to run wild in the house, to make noise, kick adults in the shins, and generally behave in an obnoxious manner. No well-regulated piece of property, including a household, can be run intelligently in such a manner. And so it is perfectly proper, legally and morally, for the parents to prohibit noise, offensive behavior, etc., as part of the rules for persons living on their property. When the child becomes older, it is equally legitimate for the parents to insist on curfews, to prohibit noise, wild parties, sexual hijinks, etc., on the property as well. In moral and legal theory, there is no freedom except freedom for the property owner; and hence, such rules for the use of property are not infringements on the rights of the child.

Ludwig von Mises settled an analogous case when he demolished the "traffic-laws" argument for government, the common argument being that you have to have traffic laws, and, therefore, why not other government interventions in the economy? Mises replied that every owner of a piece of property will and must lay down rules for its use; and so, if the government owns the roads, it will lay down rules for traffic. But if private parties owned the streets and roads, *they* would lay down such rules, and hence there is no case here for government intervention in private affairs. In the same way, the owner of the house or apartment will lay down the rules for its use.

The focus on property rights also provides us with the solution to the thorny problem of when the child can own and regulate himself. The answer is: when he leaves his parents' household. When he gets out of his parents' property, he then removes himself from his parents' property jurisdiction. But this means that the child must always have, regardless of age, the absolute freedom to run away, to get out from under. It is grotesque to think that the parents can actually own the child's body as well as physical property; it is advocating slavery and denying the fundamental right of self-ownership to permit such ownership of others, regardless of age. Therefore, the child must always be free to run away; he then becomes a self-owner whenever he chooses to exercise his right to run-away freedom.

This means that the fundamental tyranny of the parent over the child is not imposing curfews or getting him to eat spinach or preventing cohabitation in the back room; the fundamental tyranny is the current legal power of the parent to seize a child who has run away and drag him back home by force. The parent should, of course, have the right to try to persuade or cajole the kid to return, but he should never have the right to force him to do so, for that is kidnapping and a high crime that violates every person's absolute right to his body.

Asserting every child's right to run-away freedom does not imply, of course, that the libertarian advocates running away; that is purely a question of the individual situation of the parent and child. But we must recognize that inherent in even the best of parent–child relations is an essential "class struggle," a struggle rooted in the necessary existential fact that the kid is born into an environment created not by himself but by his parents. And even in the best of circumstances, tastes, values, interests, attitudes will differ from every individual to another, and therefore from every parent to every child. In the natural course of events, then, most children will, upon growing up, seek to create their own environment by leaving the parental nest. That is the way of nature, from the animal kingdom to man.

The absolute right to run away, then; but this means, of course, that the child cannot continue to exert a legal or moral claim upon the parents' continued economic support. In fact, it is rather absurd for the parent to continue supporting the child under those circumstances; independence replacing dependence is a worthy and noble goal, but it must necessarily include being economically independent as well. The child, indeed, has the right either to support himself or to find other adults who will support him voluntarily. In short, he has the right, once out from under the parental roof, to find foster parents who will care for him voluntarily and under whose jurisdiction he voluntarily places himself until he wishes to strike out on his own.

The right to run away clears up most parent–child problems for the libertarian, but two questions remain: (1) what is the moral role of the parent–property-owner so long as the child remains in the parental home; and (2) as a subquestion, what is the moral and the legal role of the parent during those very early years when the child cannot physically leave the parental property? In short, given the parent's legal right to regulate the kid at home, what is his moral duty as parent, and how extensive is his legal right to regulation?

During the early years of babyhood, when the child is helpless and has few if any powers of self-ownership, he indeed becomes a kind of property of his creators, his parents. Some adult must be in charge of each baby, and there are only two alternatives: his parent–creators or outside adults seizing the kid from his parents by force. Surely, the latter is totally illegitimate, whether done by the State or by other parties. We may say that the act of creation gives the parent, and not outside adults, jurisdiction over the baby. And yet, this ownership cannot be absolute, cannot involve the right of the parent to mutilate, maim, or murder the child, for this would be criminal aggression against the body of the child, who, being an independent human entity, cannot come under the absolute jurisdiction of anyone. The role of the parent, then, is to be, not an absolute owner, but a trustee-owner or guardian, with the right to regulate the child but not to aggress against his person (as by forcibly preventing him from running away).

If, then, outside adults find that parents are mutilating or assaulting their children, they do have the right to step in and stop this aggression, as any outside parties do when they see aggression taking place. They have the right, too, to rescue the kid from this aggression and remove it from its subjection to parent–criminals.

The moral duty or responsibility of the parents to their children stems also from their act of voluntary creation, from their responsibility for bringing helpless babies into the world. Their moral responsibility is to raise these children, to bring them from their natural state of infant dependency to the status of rational, self-owning, independent adults. Their moral responsibility is to rear the children to the status of independence. What, then, does this imply? It implies caring, provision of food, shelter, education, etc., to the best of the parents' love and ability. And it implies something else: it implies the moral duty as well as the right of the parents to train the children in the values, self-discipline, and techniques which are needed to become a fully mature adult.

We see here the fundamental flaw in the progressive notion that parents should allow their young children unlimited freedom to do as they wish and not to "impose" training, values, or education on them. For the young child, still not in possession of knowledge, values, self-discipline, or much rationality, is hardly in a position to be able to decide what he should be doing or wishing. Failure to function as rational "authorities" or failure to provide that training and those values to the best of their ability, is a tragic abdication of the basic parental responsibility—which is not simply to provide food and shelter but also mental and moral training. This moral abdication accounts for the tragedies of our current "child-centered" culture, in which the parents make themselves the literal slaves of the untutored and inchoate whims of the child; while the child, yearning for direction and guidance by his parents, only finds these parents dancing in attendance upon his every blind caprice. Later on, the abdication of parental authority subjects the child to the blind tyranny of his own, equally ill-formed, peer group. The individual then becomes often permanently subjected to the tyranny of his "crowd" or "gang," and later to the rest of society.

One of the wisest and most brilliant critiques of progressive education was written by the great libertarian–theorist Isabel Paterson. Paterson quotes the writer Lafcadio Hearn on the contrast between old-fashioned Western education, which first trained the child by parental authority until the child was fit for independence, after which he became a self-starting, self-owning individual; and the Japanese (read progressive) system, which gives children unlimited freedom, only to subject these undisciplined children to greater and greater control as they become adults. Mrs. Paterson quotes Hearn that, in the West, education began in early childhood:

> with the repressive part of moral training. . . . It is important to inculcate the duties of behavior, the "must" and "must not" of individual obligation as soon as possible. Later on, more liberty is allowed. The well-grown boy is made to understand that his future will depend upon his personal effort and capacity; and he is therefore left, in great measure, to take care of himself, being occasionally admonished and warned, as seems needful. . . . Throughout the whole course of mental and moral training, competition is not only expected but required. . . . The aim is the cultivation of individual ability and personal character the creation of an independent and forceful being.

In contrast:

> Japanese education has always been conducted on the reverse plan. Its object has never been to train the individual for independent action, but to train him for cooperative action. . . . Constraint among us begins with childhood, and gradually relaxes; constraint in Far Eastern training begins later, and thereafter gradually tightens . . . by the common opinion of his class; and a skillful teacher is able to direct that opinion. . . . The ruling power is always class sentiment. . . . It is always the rule of the many over the one; and the power is formidable.

The result in Japan is that "the individual was completely sacrificed to the community." Mrs. Paterson then points out that progressive education is an application of this Japanese system.

> Class activities, group interests, social influences have become predominant. And the prevailing philosophy with which pupils are indoctrinated is that of "instrumentalism," which denies that there can be any universal or permanent moral values or standards.

Mrs. Paterson adds that the most striking result of all this is what Hearn found in Japan: a "sinister absence of moral freedom"—the absence of the right to act according to one's own convictions of justice. "When called upon to think," the children cannot, "because they have been trained to accept the class, the group or the 'social trend,' as the sole authority."[1]

Parents, then, have not only the moral right but the moral obligation and responsibility to raise their young children in preparation for adulthood, to care for, shelter, educate, and train their persons and their character. But suppose some parents do not perform such moral obligations? Can we say that the law—that outside enforcement agencies—have the right to step in and force the parents to raise their children properly? The answer must be no. For the libertarian, the law can only be negative, can only prohibit aggressive and

---

[1]Isabel Paterson, "Our Japanized Educational System," in *The God of the Machine* (New York: G.P. Putman's Sons, 1943), pp. 251–54. Those libertarians who may feel that it is a contradiction for a libertarian to call for parental authority are suffering from the grave modern confusion between authority and coercion, or power. Thus, libertarians accept the authority of sound values, civilization, and especially reason; it is those who refuse to accept such authority who turn instead to outside coercion and violence. On the confusion between authority and power, see the brilliant article by Robert A. Nisbet, "The Nemesis of Authority," *The Intercollegiate Review* (Winter–Spring, 1972): 3–13.

criminal acts by one person upon another. It cannot compel *positive* acts, regardless of how praiseworthy or even necessary such actions may be. And so a parent may be a moral monster for not caring for his child properly, but the law cannot compel him to do otherwise. It cannot be emphasized too strongly that there is a host of moral rights and duties which are properly beyond the province of the law.

In a purely libertarian society, the young child is not as bereft as might at first appear. For in such a society, every parent would have the right to sell their guardianship rights to others. In short, there would be a free market in babies and other children. What? A free market in babies? Isn't this equivalent to slavery, to the treating of babies as mere objects? No, what it would mean is that parents who now neglect or dislike their children would be able to sell their offspring to those parents who would desire and care for them properly. Every party involved would gain by the actions of such a market: the child would be shifted from cruel or neglectful parents to those who would desire and care for it; the neglecting parent would acquire the preferred amount of money instead of the unwanted child; and the new foster parents would at last be able to adopt a child. William Rickenbacker, in his column in *National Review*, has, in fact, recently advocated such a free-baby market.

In actual fact, of course, we have a baby market now, except that it is regulated by government—which imposes a maximum baby price of zero. A parent is not allowed to sell his kid; he can only give it away for nothing. As with all maximum price controls, fixing the price at zero means a great shortage of valuable babies on the baby market; as a result, government-licensed adoption agencies are granted the monopoly privilege of acquiring and rationing out those babies to the foster parents clamoring at their doors. Often,

would-be foster parents must grovel before the social workers at the adoption agency, prove they are "fit parents," pay a
fee to the agency, etc. The result is that unwanted babies
remain with bad parents, and good foster parents are
deprived of the right to care for and bring up offspring. In
the free-baby market, of course, there would be no title to
absolute ownership of the baby; only guardianship rights
would be traded.

Typical of State repression of the baby market and its consequences was an incident some years ago in New York City.
The New York press heralded the fact that an evil, enslaving
"baby ring" had been broken up by the vigilant government
authorities. Babies were being smuggled in from Greece by
diligent entrepreneurs, and sold (horrors!) to relatively affluent foster parents in New York City. The busting of this baby
ring, I suppose, gave the snoops and enforcers a sense of high
accomplishment. But what exactly did they accomplish? They
busted up a situation where babies were being sold by their
impoverished parents in Greece, there to leave a life of starvation, for a life of comfort, love and care in New York; both
sets of parents, as well as the babies themselves, benefitted
from the transaction; yet busybody Big Brother had to step in
and outlaw voluntary arrangements for mutual benefit.

Parents, then, have the legal right and the moral obligation to nurture their children as guardians, as trustee-"owners"; no law or enforcing agency has the right to seize these
children from their creators or regulate them except as they
are being aggressed against by their parents. Above all, every
child must always have the right to run away to freedom, to
get out from under parental property—otherwise enslavement is indeed involved.

In the present society, of course, the State imposes many
aggressions against parents and children alike. Through

compulsory attendance laws, the state governments force
children either into public schools or into those private
schools certified as legitimate and proper by the state authorities. The whipsawing of the kid is reinforced by child labor
laws, which prevent the child from entering the labor force
even if he and his parents wish to do so. By coercively keeping kids out of the labor force, the State cuts the unemployment rate (by the way that rate is defined), and keeps out
competition that might lower restrictive union wage rates.
All this, of course, is supposedly done for the child's "benefit," even though the kid in question may be suited neither in
ability nor in interest for continued schooling. This idea that
every child must have a higher schooling is strictly a modern
concept; in all past ages it was taken for granted that the child
not suited for schooling was far better off being allowed to
enter the labor force. In recent years, this supposedly "reactionary" view has been brought back to prominence by such
"New Left" educational theorists as Paul Goodman and Ivan
Filich. The abolition of compulsory attendance laws would
free children and parents alike, and the abolition of the public school system would remove an enormous weight of taxes
off parents (and nonparents!) and allow them to purchase
that amount of schooling and in those forms which they particularly desire. What is needed, above all, is the liberation of
both child and parent from the domination of the State apparatus.

8
THE GREAT WOMEN'S LIBERATION ISSUE: SETTING IT STRAIGHT

I t is high time, and past due, that someone blew the whistle on "Women's Liberation." Like the environment, women's lib is suddenly and raucously everywhere. It has become impossible to avoid being assaulted, day in and day out, by the noisy blather of the women's movement. Special issues of magazines, TV news programs, and newspapers have been devoted to this new-found "Problem"; and nearly two dozen books on women's lib are being scheduled for publication this year by major publishers. In all this welter of verbiage, not one article, not one book, not one program has dared to present the opposition case. The injustice of this one-sided tidal wave should be evident. Not only is it evident, but the lack of published opposition negates one of the major charges of the women's lib forces: that the society and economy are groaning under a monolithic male "sexist" tyranny. If the men are running the show, how is it that they do not even presume to print or present anyone from the other side? Yet the "oppressors" remain strangely silent, which leads one to suspect, as we will develop further below, that perhaps the "oppression" is on the other side.

In the meanwhile, the male "oppressors" are acting, in the manner of liberals everywhere, like scared, or guilt-ridden, rabbits. When the one hundred viragoes of women's lib bullied their way into the head offices of the *Ladies' Home Journal*, did the harried editor-in-chief, John Mack Carter, throw these aggressors out on their collective ear, as he should have done? Did he, at the very least, abandon his office for the day and go home? No, instead he sat patiently for eleven hours while these harridans heaped abuse upon him and his magazine and his gender, and then meekly agreed to donate to them a special section of the *Journal*, along with $10,000 ransom. In this way, spineless male liberalism meekly feeds the appetite of the aggressors and paves the way for the next set of outrageous "demands." *Rat* magazine, an underground tabloid, caved in even more spectacularly and simply allowed itself to be taken over permanently by a "women's liberation collective."

Why, in fact, this sudden upsurge of women's lib? Even the most fanatic virago of the women's movement concedes that this new movement has not emerged in response to any sudden clamping down of the male boot upon the collective sensibilities of the American female. Instead, the new uprising is part of the current degeneracy of the New Left, which, as its one-time partly libertarian politics, ideology, and organization have collapsed, has been splintering into absurd and febrile forms, from Maoism to Weathermanship to mad bombings to women's lib. The heady wine of "liberation" for every crackpot group has been in the air for some time, sometimes deserved but more often absurd, and now the New Left women have gotten into the act. We need not go quite so far as the recent comment of Professor Edward A. Shils, eminent sociologist at the University of Chicago, that he now expects a "dog liberation front," but it is hard to fault the annoyance behind his remark. Throughout the whole gamut of "liberation," the major target has been the harmless, hardworking, adult WASP American male, William Graham Sumner's *Forgotten Man*; and now this hapless Dagwood Bumstead figure is being battered yet once more. How long will it be before the put-upon, long-suffering average American at last loses his patience and rises up in his wrath to do some effective noise-making on his own behalf?

The current women's movement is divisible into two parts. The older slightly less irrational wing began in 1963 with the publication of Betty Friedan's *The Feminine Mystique* and her organization of NOW (the National Organization for Women). NOW concentrates on alleged economic discrimination against women. For example: the point that while the median annual wage for all jobs in 1968 was almost $7,700 for men, it only totaled $4,500 for women, 58 percent of the male figure. The other major point is the quota argument: that if one casts one's eye about various professions, top management positions, etc., the quota of women is far lower than their supposedly deserved 51 percent share of the total population. The quota argument may be disposed of rapidly; for it is a two-edged sword. If the low percentage of women in surgery, law, management, etc., is proof that the men should posthaste be replaced by females, then what are we to do with the Jews, for example, who shine far above their assigned quota in the professions, in medicine, in academia, etc.? Are they to be purged?

The lower average income for women can be explained on several grounds, none of which involve irrational "sexist" discrimination. One is the fact that the overwhelming majority of women work a few years and then take a large chunk of their productive years, to raise children, after which they may or may not decide to return to the labor force. As a result, they tend to enter, or to find, jobs largely in those industries and in that type of work that does not require a long-term commitment to a career. Furthermore, they tend to find jobs in those occupations where the cost of training new people, or of losing old ones, is relatively low. These tend to be lower-paying occupations than those that require a long-term commitment or where costs of training or turnover are high. This general tendency to take out years for child raising also accounts for a good deal of the failure to promote women to higher-ranking and, therefore, higher-paying jobs and hence for the low female "quotas" in these areas. It is easy to hire secretaries who do not intend to make the job their continuing life work; it is not so easy to promote people up the academic or the corporate ladder who do not do so. How does a dropout for motherhood get to *be* a corporate president or a full professor?

While these considerations account for a good chunk of lower pay and lower ranked jobs for women, they do not fully explain the problem. In the capitalist market economy, women have full freedom of opportunity; irrational discrimination in employment tends to be minimal in the free market, for the simple reason that the employer also suffers from such discriminatory practice. In the free market, every worker tends to earn the value of his product, his "marginal productivity." Similarly, everyone tends to fill the job he can best accomplish, to work at his most productive efforts. Employers who persist in paying below a person's marginal product will hurt themselves by losing their best workers and hence losing profits for themselves. If women have persistently lower pay and poorer jobs, even after correcting for the motherhood-dropout, then the simple reason must be that their marginal productivity tends to be lower than men's.

It should be emphasized that, in contrast to the women's lib forces who tend to blame capitalism as well as male tyrants for centuries-old discrimination, it was precisely capitalism and the "capitalist revolution" of the eighteenth and nineteenth centuries that freed women from male oppression and set each woman free to find her best level. It was the feudal and precapitalist, pre-market society that was marked by male oppression; it was that society where women were chattels of their fathers and husbands, where they could own no property of their own, etc.[1] Capitalism set women free to find their own level, and the result is what we have today. The women's libs retort that women possess the full potential of equality of output and productivity with men, but that they have been browbeaten during centuries of male oppression. But the conspicuous lack of rising to the highest posts under capitalism still remains. There are few women doctors, for example. Yet medical schools nowadays not only don't discriminate against women, they bend over backwards to accept them (that is, they discriminate in their favor); yet the proportion of women doctors is still not noticeably high.

---

[1]Ludwig von Mises has written, in *Socialism: An Economic and Sociological Analysis* (New Haven, Conn.: Yale University Press, 1951), pp. 95–96:

> As the idea of contract enters the Law of Marriage, it breaks the rule of the male, and makes the wife a partner with equal rights. From a one-sided relationship resting on force, marriage thus becomes a mutual agreement. . . . Nowadays the position of the woman differs from the position of the man only in so far as their peculiar ways of earning a living differ. . . . Woman's position in marriage was improved as the principle of violence was thrust back, and as the idea of contract advanced in other fields of the Law of Property it necessarily transformed the property relations between the married couple. The wife was freed from the power of her husband for the first time when she gained legal rights ever the wealth which she brought into marriage and which she acquired during marriage. . . . That marriage unites one man and one woman, that it can be entered into only with the free will of both parties . . . that the rights of husband and wife are essentially the same— these principles develop from the contractual attitude to the problem of married life.

Here the female militants fall back on another argument: that centuries of being "brainwashed" by a male-dominated culture have made most women passive, accepting their allegedly inferior role, and even liking and enjoying their major role as homemakers and child raisers. And the real problem for the raucous females, of course, is that the overwhelming majority of women do embrace the "feminine mystique," do feel that their sole careers are those of housewife and mother. Simply to write off these evident and strong desires by most women as "brainwashing" proves far too much; for we can always dismiss any person's values, no matter how deeply held, as the result of "brainwashing." The "brainwashing" contention becomes what the philosophers call "operationally meaningless," for it means that the female militants refuse to accept any evidence, logical or empirical, of whatever kind, that might prove their contentions to be wrong. Show them a woman who loves domesticity, and they dismiss this as "brainwashing"; show them a militant, and they claim that this proves that women are yearning for "liberation." In short, these militants regard their flimsy contentions as unworthy of any sort of proof, but this is the groundless method of mystics rather than an argument reflecting scientific truth.

And so the high rate of conversion claimed by women's liberationists proves nothing either; may not this be the result of "brainwashing" by the female militants? After all, if you are a redhead, and a Redheaded Liberation League suddenly emerges and shouts at you that you are eternally oppressed by vile nonredheads, some of you might well join in the fray—which proves nothing at all about whether or not redheads are *objectively* oppressed.

I do not go so far as the extreme male "sexists" who contend that women *should* confine themselves to home and children and that any search for alternative careers is unnatural.

On the other hand, I do not see much more support for the opposite contention that domestic-type women are violating *their* natures. There is in this, as in all matters, a division of labor; and in a free-market society, every individual will enter those fields and areas of work which he or she finds most attractive. The proportion of working women is far higher than even twenty years ago, and that is fine; but it is still a minority of females, and that's fine too. Who are you or I to tell anyone, male or female, what occupation he or she should enter?

Furthermore, the women's libs have fallen into a logical trap in their charge of centuries of male brainwashing. For if this charge be true, then *why have* men been running the culture over eons of time? Surely, this cannot be an accident. Isn't this evidence of male superiority?

The Friedanites, who call stridently for equality of income and position, have, however, been outpaced in recent months by the more militant women's liberationists, or "new feminists," women who work with the older movement but consider them conservative "Aunt Toms." These new militants, who have been getting most of the publicity, persistently liken their alleged oppression to that of blacks and, like the black movement, reject equality and integration for a radical change in society. They call for the revolutionary abolition of alleged male rule and its supposed corollary, the family. Displaying a deepseated and scarcely concealed hatred of men *per se*, these females call for all-women communes, State-run children, test-tube babies, or just simply the "cutting up of men," as the real founder of militant women's lib, Valerie Solanis, put it in her SCUM (Society for Cutting Up Men) Manifesto. Solanis became the culture-heroine of the New Feminism in 1968 when she shot and almost killed the painter and filmmaker, Andy Warhol. Instead of being dismissed (as she would be by any rational person) as a lone nut, the liberated females wrote articles praising Solanis as the "sweet assassin" who tried to dispose of the "plastic male" Warhol. We should have known at that point of the travails that lay in store.

I believe that modern American marriages are, by and large, conducted on a basis of equality, but I also believe that the opposite contention is far closer to the truth than that of the New Feminists: namely, that it is *men*, not women, who are more likely to be the oppressed class, or gender, in our society, and that it is far more the men who are the "blacks," the slaves, and women their masters. In the first place, the female militants claim that marriage is a diabolical institution by which husbands enslave their wives and force them to rear children and do housework. But let us consider: in the great majority of the cases, *who* is it that insists on marriage, the man or the woman? Everyone knows the answer. And if this great desire for marriage is the result of male brainwashing, as the women's libs contend, then how is it that so many men resist marriage, resist this prospect of their lifelong seat upon the throne of domestic "tyranny"?

Indeed, as capitalism has immensely lightened the burden of housework through improved technology, many wives have increasingly constituted a kept leisure class. In the middle-class neighborhood in which I live, I see them, these "oppressed" and hard-faced viragoes, strutting down the street in their mink stoles to the next bridge or mah-jongg game, while their husbands are working themselves into an early coronary down in the garment district to support their helpmeets.

In these cases, then, who are the "niggers": the wives or the husbands? The women's libs claim that men are the masters because they are doing most of the world's work. But, if we look back at the society of the slave South, who indeed did the work? It is always the slaves who do the work, while the masters live in relative idleness off the fruits of their labor. To the extent that husbands work and support the family, while wives enjoy a kept status, who then are the masters?

There is nothing new in this argument, but it is a point that has been forgotten amidst the current furor. It has been noted for years—and especially by Europeans and Asians—that too many American men live in a matriarchy, dominated first by Momism, then by female teachers, and then by their wives. Blondie and Dagwood have long symbolized for sociologists an all-too prevalent American matriarchy, a matriarchy contrasted with the European scene where the women, though more idle than in the United States, do not run the home. The henpecked American male has long been the butt of perceptive humor. And, finally, when the male dies, as he usually does, earlier than his spouse, she inherits the entire family assets, with the result that far more than 50 percent of the *wealth* of America is owned by women. *Income*—the index of hard and productive work—is less significant here than ownership of ultimate wealth. Here is another inconvenient fact which the female militants brusquely dismiss as of no consequence. And, finally, if the husband should seek a divorce, he is socked with the laws of alimony, which he is forced to pay and pay to support a female whom he no longer sees, and, if he fails to pay, faces the barbaric penalty of imprisonment— the only instance remaining in our legal structure of imprisonment for nonpayment of "debt." Except, of course, that this is a "debt" which the man had never voluntarily incurred. Who, then, are the slaves?

And as for men forcing women to bear and rear children, *who*, again, in the vast majority of cases, is the party in the marriage most eager to have children? Again, everyone knows the answer.

When, as they do at times, the female militants acknowledge matriarchal dominance by the American female, their defense, as usual, is to fall back on the operationally meaningless: that the *seeming* dominance of the wife is only the reflection of her quintessential passivity and subordination, so that women have to seek various roads to bitchiness and manipulation as their route to . . . power. Beneath their seeming power, then, these wives are psychologically unhappy. Perhaps, but I suppose that one could argue that the slavemaster in the Old South was also psychologically uneasy because of his unnaturally dominant role. But the politico-economic fact of his dominance remained, and this is the major point.

The ultimate test of whether women are enslaved or not in the modern marriage is the one of "natural law": to consider what would happen if indeed the women's libs had their way and there were no marriage. In that situation, and in a consequently promiscuous world, what would happen to the children? The answer is that the only visible and demonstrable parent would be the mother. Only the mother would have the child, and therefore *only the mother* would be stuck with the child. In short, the women militants who complain that they are stuck with the task of raising the children should heed the fact that, in a world without marriage, they would *also* be stuck with the task of earning all of the income for their children's support. I suggest that they contemplate this prospect long and hard before they continue to clamor for the abolition of marriage and the family.

The more thoughtful of the female militants have recognized that their critical problem is finding a solution for the raising of children. Who is going to do it? The moderates answer: governmental provision of day-care centers, so that women can be freed to enter the labor force. But the problem here, aside from the general problem of socialism or statism, is this: why hasn't the free market provided day-care centers fairly inexpensively, as it does for any product or service in mass demand? No one has to clamor for government provision of motels, for example. There are plenty of them. The economist is compelled to answer: either that the demand for mothers to go to work is not nearly as great as the New Feminists would have us believe, or some controls by government—perhaps requirements for registered nurses or licensing laws—are artificially restricting the supply. Whichever reason, then, *more* goverment is clearly not the answer.

The more radical feminists are not content with such a piddling solution as day-care centers (besides who but *women*, other women this time, would be staffing these centers?). What they want, as Susan Brownmiller indicates in her *New York Sunday Times Magazine* article (March 15, 1970), is total husband–wife equality in all things, which means equally shared careers, equally shared housework, and equally shared child rearing. Brownmiller recognizes that this would have to mean *either* that the husband works for six months and the wife for the next six months, with each alternating six months of child rearing, or that each work half of every day and so alternate the child rearing each halfday. Whichever path is chosen, it is all too clear that this total equality could only be pursued if both parties are willing to live permanently on a hippie, subsistence, part-time-job level. For what career of any importance or quality can be pursued in such a fleeting and haphazard manner? Above the hippie level, then, this alleged "solution" is simply absurd.

If our analysis is correct and we are already living in a matriarchy, then the true significance of the new feminism is *not*, as they would so stridently have it, the "liberation" of women from their oppression. May we not say that, not content with kept idleness and subtle domination, these women are reaching eagerly for total power? Not content with being supported and secure, they are now attempting to force their passive and long-suffering husbands to do most of the house-work and child-rearing as well. I know personally several couples where the wife is a militant liberationist and the husband has been brainwashed by his spouse to be an Uncle Tom and a traitor to his gender. In all these cases, after a long hard day at the office or at teaching to support the family, the husband sits at home teaching the kids while the wife is out at women's lib meetings, there to plot their accession to total power and to denounce their husbands as sexist oppressors. Not content with the traditional mah-jongg set, the New Woman is reaching for the final castrating blow—to be accepted, I suppose, with meek gratitude by their male-liberal spouses.

There is still the extremist women's lib solution: to abandon sex, or rather heterosexuality, altogether. There is no question but that this at least would solve the child-rearing problem. The charge of lesbianism used to be considered a venomous male-chauvinist smear against the liberated woman. But in the burgeoning writings of the New Feminists there has run an open and increasing call for female homosexuality. Note, for example, Rita Mae Brown, writing in the first "liberated" issue of *Rat* (February 6, 1970):

> For a woman to vocally assert her heterosexuality is to emphasize her "goodness" by her sexual activity with men. That old sexist brainwashing runs deep even into the consciousness of the most ardent feminist who will quickly tell you she loves sleeping with men. In fact, the worst thing you can call a woman in our society is a lesbian. Women are so male identified that they quake at the mention of this three-syllable word. The lesbian is, of course, the woman who has no need of men. When you think about it, what is so terrible about two women loving each other? To the insecure male, this is the supreme offense, the most outrageous blasphemy committed against the sacred scrotum.
>
> After all, just what would happen if we all wound up loving each other. Good things for us but it would mean each

man would lose his personal "nigger" . . . a real and great loss if you are a man. . . .

> To love another woman is an acceptance of sex which is a severe violation of the male culture (sex as exploitation) and, therefore, carries severe penalties. . . . Women have been taught to abdicate the power of our bodies, both physically in athletics and self-defense, and sexually. To sleep with another woman is to confront the beauty and power of your own body as well as hers. You confront the experience of your sexual self-knowledge. You also confront another human being without the protective device of role. This may be too painful for most women as many have been so brutalized by heterosexual role play that they cannot begin to comprehend this real power. It is an overwhelming experience. I vulgarize it when I call it a freedom high. No wonder there is such resistance to lesbianism.

Or this, in the same issue, by "A Weatherwoman":

> Sex becomes entirely different without jealousy. Women who never saw themselves making it with women begin digging each other sexually. . . . What weatherman is doing is creating new standards for men and women to relate to. We are trying to make sex nonexploitative. . . . We are making something new, with the common denominator being the revolution.

Or, finally, still in the same issue, by Robin Morgan:

> Let it all hang out. Let it seem bitchy, catty, dykey, frustrated, crazy, Solanisesque, nutty, frigid, ridiculous, bitter, embarrassing, man-hating, libelous. . . . Sexism is not the fault of women—kill your fathers, not your mothers.

And so, at the hard inner core of the Women's Liberation Movement lies a bitter, extremely neurotic if not psychotic, man-hating lesbianism. The quintessence of the New Feminism is revealed.

Is this spirit confined to a few extremists? Is it unfair to tar the whole movement with the brush of the Lesbian Rampant? I'm afraid not. For example, one motif now permeating the entire movement is a strident opposition to men treating women as "sex objects." This supposedly demeaning, debasing, and exploitative treatment extends from pornography to beauty contests, to advertisements of pretty models using a product, all the way to wolf whistles and admiring glances at girls in miniskirts. But surely the attack on women as "sex objects" is simply an attack on sex, period, or rather, on hetero-sex. These new monsters of the female gender are out to destroy the lovely and age-old custom—delighted in by normal women the world over—of women dressing to attract men and succeeding at this pleasant task. What a dull and dreary world these termagants would impose upon us! A world where all girls look like unkempt wrestlers, where beauty and attractiveness have been replaced by ugliness and "unisex," where delightful femininity has been abolished on behalf of raucous, aggressive, and masculine feminism.

Jealousy of pretty and attractive girls does, in fact, lie close to the heart of this ugly movement. One point that should be noted, for example, in the alleged economic discrimination against women: the fantastic upward mobility, as well as high incomes, available to the strikingly pretty girl. The Women's Libs may claim that models are exploited, but if we consider the enormous pay that the models enjoy—as well as their access to the glamorous life—and compare it with their opportunity cost foregone in other occupations such as waitress or typist—the charge of exploitation is laughable indeed. Male models, whose income and opportunities are far lower than those of females, might well envy the privileged female position! Furthermore, the potential for upward mobility for pretty, lower-class girls is enormous, infinitely more so than for lower-class men: we might cite Bobo Rockefeller and Gregg Sherwood Dodge (a former pin-up model who married the multimillionaire scion of the Dodge family) as merely conspicuous examples. But these cases, far from counting as an argument against them, arouse the female liberationists to still greater fury, since one of their real complaints is against those more attractive girls who by virtue of their attractiveness have been more successful in the inevitable competition for men—a competition that must exist whatever the form of government or society (provided, of course, that it remains heterosexual).

Woman as "sex objects"? Of course they are sex objects and, praise the Lord, they always will be. (Just as men, of course, are sex objects to women.) As for the wolf whistles, it is impossible for any meaningful relationship to be established on the street or by looking at ads, and so in these roles women properly remain solely as sex objects. When deeper relationships are established between men and women, they each become *more* than sex objects to each other; they each hopefully become love objects as well. It would seem banal even to bother mentioning this, but in today's increasingly degenerate intellectual climate no simple truths can any longer be taken for granted.

Contrast to the strident women's liberationists the charming letter in the *New York Sunday Times* (March 29, 1970) by Susan L. Peck, commenting on the Brownmiller article. After asserting that she, for one, welcomes male admiration, Mrs. Peck states that "To some this might sound square, but I do not harbor a mad, vindictive desire to see my already hardworking, responsible husband doing the household ironing." After decrying the female maladjustment exhibited in the "liberation movement," Mrs. Peck concludes: "I, for one, adore men and I'd rather see than be one!" Hooray, and hopefully Mrs. Peck speaks for the silent majority of American womanhood.

As for the women's liberationists, perhaps we might begin to take their constantly repeated analogies with the black movement more seriously. The blacks have, indeed, moved from integration to black power, but the logic of black power is starkly and simply: black nationalism—an independent black nation. If our New Feminists wish to abandon male–female "integrationism" for liberation, then this logically implies Female Power, in short, Female Nationalism. Shall we then turn over some virgin land, maybe the Black Hills, maybe Arizona, to these termagants? Yes, let them set up their karate-chopping Amazonian Women's Democratic People's Republic and bad cess to them. The infection of their sick attitudes and ideology would then be isolated and removed from the greater social body, and the rest of us, dedicated to good old-fashioned heterosexuality, could then go about our business undisturbed. It is high time that we heed the ringing injunction of William Butler Yeats:

> Down the fanatic, down the clown;
> Down, down, hammer them down,

and that we echo the joyous cry of the elderly Frenchman in the famous joke.

As a female militant in France addressed a gathering on women's liberation, asserting, "There is only a very small difference between men and women," the elderly Frenchman leaped to his feet, shouting, *"Vive la petite difference!"*[2]

---

[2] Professor Leonard P. Liggio has brought to my attention two vitally important points in explaining why the women's lib agitation has emerged at this time from within the New Left. The first is that the New Left women were wont to sleep promiscuously with the males in the movement and found to their shock and dismay that they were not being treated as more than mere "sex objects." In short, after lacking the self-respect to treat themselves as more than sex objects, these New Left women found to their dismay that the men were treating them precisely as they regarded themselves! Instead of realizing that their own promiscuous behavior was at the root of the problem, these women bitterly blamed the men, and Women's Liberation was born.

The second point is that almost all the agitation comes not from working class, but rather from middle-class wives, who find themselves

———————————

tied to the home and kept from satisfying outside jobs by the demands of children and housework. He notes that this condition could be readily cured by abolishing restrictions on immigration, so that cheap and high-quality maids and governesses would once more be available at rates that middle-class wives could afford. And this, of course, would be a libertarian solution as well.

9
CONSERVATION IN
THE FREE MARKET

It should be no news by this time that intellectuals are fully as subject to the vagaries of fashion as are the hemlines of women's skirts. Apparently, intellectuals tend to be victims of a herd mentality. Thus, when John Kenneth Galbraith published his best-selling *The Affluent Society* in 1958, every intellectual and his brother was denouncing America as suffering from undue and excessive affluence; yet, only two or three years later, the fashion suddenly changed, and the very *same* intellectuals were complaining that America was rife with poverty. In all too many of these ideological sprees, capitalism is blamed for whatever illness is being focused on at the moment; the same capitalism supposedly responsible for making us all surfeited with material goods in 1958 was to be equally guilty for rendering the nation poverty-stricken in 1961.

Another leading example was the "stagnation thesis," propounded by many economists in the late thirties and early forties. The stagnation thesis held that capitalism had come to the end of its rope, since there was no room for any further technological inventions and, therefore, for capital investment. Capitalism was therefore doomed to perpetual and growing mass unemployment. After this notion had faded away, the early and mid-sixties produced precisely the opposite damning indictment of the capitalist system. Numerous intellectuals, including the self-same proclaimers of the stagnation thesis, now asserted that imminent automation and cybernation were going to lead quickly to permanent and growing mass unemployment for practically everyone because there would be no work for any mere men to do. Happily, the automation hysteria has faded away in the intellectual fashions of recent years. But we can see that in many of these cases, through the rampant contradictions, there runs one crucial thread: whatever the problem, the market economy is held to be the culprit.[1]

The latest intellectual craze, which has taken on the proportions of a deluge in a very short time, is The Environment, otherwise known as Ecology or the Quality of Life. In the last two months, it has been impossible to pick up a newspaper or magazine without being bombarded by the Ravaged Environment Problem. Whatever the dimensions of that problem, it is hard to believe that it has escalated from negligible to endemic proportions within one or two months' time. And, yet, there it is.

---

[1]The great economist Joseph Schumpeter put the case brilliantly in discussing modern intellectuals: "Capitalism stands its trial before judges who have the sentence of death in their pockets. They are going to pass it, whatever the defense they may hear; the only success victorious defense can possibly produce is a change in the indictment." Joseph A. Schumpeter, *Capitalism, Socialism, and Democracy* (New York: Harper and Bros., 1942), p. 144.

One amusing note is that the same man, George Terborgh, economist for the Machinery and Allied Products Institute, produced the leading refutations of both of these fallacies, writing *The Bogey of Economic Maturity* in 1945, followed by *The Automation Hysteria* twenty years later.

On the Left, acutely pressing questions which have been properly agitating them for several years, such as Vietnam and the draft, have suddenly and magically disappeared, as leftists and student protesters now picket and demonstrate on behalf of the environment and clean air. Conservatives have happily seized on the issue in order to draw the teeth of dissent; after all, who in the world—left, right, or center—is going to come out squarely in favor of ugliness, garbage or air pollution? Establishment organs happily proclaim that The Environment will be *the* political "issue" of the 1970s. President Nixon eagerly scrambled to make the "quality of life" the major theme of his State of the Union Address. Thus:

> The great question of the seventies is: Shall we surrender to our surroundings or shall we make our peace with nature and begin to make reparations for the damage we have done to our air, to our land, and to our water? Restoring nature to its natural state is a cause beyond . . . factions. It has become a common cause of all the people of this country. . . . The program I shall propose to Congress will be the most comprehensive and costly program in this field in America's history. . . . Each of us must resolve that each day he will leave his home, his property, the public places of the city or town a little cleaner, a little better. . . . I propose that before these problems become insoluble the nation develop a national growth policy. . . . We will carry our concern with the quality of life in America to the farm as well as the suburb, to the village as well as the city.

What are we, then, to make of this Environment Question? The first thing we must do is to isolate and distinguish the different problems raised; we must, above all, resist the exhortations of the environment hysterics to throw a whole slew of totally different problems into one overall grab bag. We must, in short, do the opposite of what *Fortune* magazine tells us to do in its special issue on the environment (February, 1970):

> Looked at one by one, many of our present depredations seem relatively easy to correct. But when we put the horrors

in a row—the drab and clumsy cities, the billboards, the scum-choked lakes, the noise, the poisoned air and water, the clogged highways, the mountainous and reeking dumps—their cumulative effect drives us toward the conclusion that some single deep-seated flaw. . . .

The Left, of course, has found—surprise—its single deep-seated flaw: capitalism, in this case "capitalist greed," which has ravaged and destroyed our resources, etc. That capitalism is not the problem should be evident from the fact that the Soviet Union has created a far more "ravaged" environment, certainly in proportion to its industrial activity, than the United States. The famous poisoning of the Soviet's Lake Baikal is a sharp case in point.

Let us then distinguish the very different problems involved. There is, first, the esthetic question. Countless "environmentalists" have been complaining bitterly about the "ugliness" of life in the United States, about the "ugly" cities, "hideous" buildings, etc. In the first place, esthetics brings us adrift without a rudder on a sea of diverse individual values and tastes. One man's "ugliness" is another's "beauty," and vice versa. My own observation is that most of the bellyachers about the ugliness of our cities and singers of paeans to the unspoiled wilderness, stubbornly remain ensconced in these very cities. Why don't they leave? There are, even today, plenty of rural and even wilderness areas for them to live in and enjoy. Why don't they go there and leave those of us who like and enjoy the cities in peace? Furthermore, if they got out, it would help relieve the urban "overcrowding" which they also complain about. Second, much of the ugliness of the buildings and the landscape, by most esthetic definitions, has been created by such governmental programs as urban renewal, with its wanton destruction of urban homes, stores, and community neighborhoods, to be replaced by barracks-like developments built through subsidies and the confiscatory power of eminent domain. Furthermore, what buildings in this country are typically more ugly than those housing the organs of government, from the Pentagon to your local post office?[2] Or what of such government programs as the proliferating highways and expressways, which gut the landscape and tear down neighborhoods along the way?

Another charge against the cities is that they are terribly "overcrowded." Here again, we have an unsupported value judgment by the critics. How much crowding is "overcrowding"? As Jane Jacobs points out, high concentration of dwelling units per acre and high land coverage are essential to the diversity, growth, and vitality of the best and most generally liked areas of the big cities. She notes that it is in the lower-density suburban areas where stores and businesses must cater only to majority economic demand and which lead to a flat sameness of life and neighborhood; it is the high-density areas that make profitable a large spectrum of stores and services catering to a wide range of minority tastes. And, once more, there is nothing to prevent the critics of crowds from hightailing it to the wilderness.

The environmental critics are also sadly deficient in historical knowledge. They fail to realize that the cities of a century and several centuries ago were far more crowded and unpleasant than they are today by anyone's esthetic standards. In those olden days, streets were far narrower, cobblestone

---

[2]On the destruction of the neighborhoods, see Jane Jacobs, *The Death and Life of Great American Cities* (New York: Vintage Books, 1963). Also see her recent scintillating discussion of the primary importance of free-market cities, *The Economy of Cities* (New York: Random House, 1969), and the appreciative review by Richard Sennett, "The Anarchism of Jane Jacobs," *New York Review of Books* (January 1, 1970).

pavements were far noisier, modern sewage was nonexistent so that rank odors and epidemics were rampant, dogs and sometimes livestock roamed the streets, heat was overpowering with no refuge in air conditioning, etc. Our environmentalists place their greatest blame on modern technology, and yet it is precisely modern technology that has permitted the growth of the far more populous cities of today with far greater health, ease, and comfort for each inhabitant.

The critics seem also to be reaching for compulsory birth control as their means of checking population growth. And yet far too much has been made of the population question. South America and Africa are, by any criteria of density, highly underpopulated, and yet they are largely poverty-stricken and living on a bare subsistence level. By the same mechanical criteria, Japan, like India, would be highly "over-populated," and yet Japan, unlike India, with great ingenuity and enterprise has the highest industrial growth rate in the world today.

One of the most disquieting features of the environmentalist movement is its evident abhorrence of modern technology and its Romanticist back-to-nature philosophy. Technology and civilization are responsible, they say, for crowding, pollution, despoliation of resources, so let us therefore return to unspoiled nature, to Walden Pond, to contemplation in a far-off glade. None of these critics of modern culture and civilization seem to realize that the back-to-nature path would not only mean shuffling off the benefits of civilization, but would also mean starvation and death for the vast bulk of mankind, who are dependent on the capital and the division of labor of the modern industrial market economy. Or are our modern Romantics operating on a death, as opposed to a life, premise? It very much looks that way.

Take, for example, the standard conservationist complaints about the "destruction" of natural resources by the modern economy. It is true that if the American continent had never been populated and settled, many millions of square miles of forest would have remained intact. But so what? Which are more important, people or trees? For if a flourishing conservationist lobby in 1600 had insisted that the existing wilderness remain intact, the American continent would not have had room for more than a handful of fur trappers. If man had not been allowed to use these forests, then these resources would have been *truly wasted*, because they could not be used. What good are resources if man is barred from using them to achieve his ends?[3]

Furthermore, it is little realized that growing technology not only uses up, but also *adds* to, usable natural resources. Before the development of the automobile and of modern machinery, the vast pools of petroleum under the earth were totally valueless to man; they were useless, black liquid. With the development of modern technology and industry, they suddenly became useful resources.

Then there is the common argument that any time a natural resource is used, any time a tree is chopped down, we are depriving future generations of its use. And yet this argument proves far too much. For if we are to be prohibited from felling a tree because some future generation is deprived of doing so, then this future generation, when it becomes "present," also cannot use the tree for fear of its future generations, and so on to prove that the resource can never be used

---

[3]On the widely accepted conservationist myth that deforestation has led to greater floods, see Gordon B. Dodds, "The Stream-Flow Controversy: A Conservation Turning Point," *Journal of American History* (June, 1969): 59–69.

by man at all—surely a profoundly "antihuman" thesis, since man in general is kept in subservience to a resource which he can never use. Furthermore, even if the future is allowed to use the resources, if we consider that living standards usually rise from one generation to the next, this means that we must hobble ourselves for the sake of a future which will be richer than we are. But surely the idea that the relatively poorer must sacrifice themselves for the benefit of the richer is a peculiar kind of ethic by anyone's ethical standard.

If, then, every present generation may properly use resources, we reduce the whole conservation question to a far more sober and less hysterical dimension. How much, then, of any resource should be used in any given generation and how much conserved for posterity? The environmentalists and conservationists totally fail to realize that the free-market economy contains within itself an automatic principle for deciding the proper degree of conservation.

Let us consider, for example, a typical copper mine. We do not find copper miners, once they have found and opened a vein of ore, rushing to mine all the copper immediately; instead, the copper mine is conserved and used gradually, from year to year. Why is that? Because the mine owners realize that if they, for example, triple this year's production of copper, they will indeed triple this year's revenue, *but* they will also deplete the mine and therefore lower the monetary value of the mine as a whole. The monetary value of the mine is based on the expected future income to be earned from the production of copper, and if the mine is unduly depleted, the value of the mine, and therefore the selling price of the shares of stock in the mine, will fall. Every mine owner, then, has to weigh the advantages of immediate income from copper production against the loss of capital value of the mine as a whole. Their decision is determined by their expectation of future yields and demands for their product, the prevailing and expected rates of interest, etc. If, for example, copper is expected to be rendered obsolete in a few years by a new synthetic metal, they will rush to produce more copper now when it is more highly valued and save far less for the future when it will have little value—thus benefitting the consumers and the economy as a whole. If, on the other hand, various veins of copper are expected to run out soon in the world as a whole, and copper is, therefore, expected to have a higher value in the future, less will be produced now and more withheld for future mining—again benefitting the consumers and the overall economy. Thus, we see that the market economy contains a marvelous built-in mechanism whereby the resource owners' decision on present as against future production will benefit not only their own income and wealth, but also that of the mass of consumers and of the national and world economy.

We find, in fact, no one complaining about capitalism's "ravaging" of copper or iron resources. What, then, is the problem in such cases as forests? Why are the forests or the fisheries "ravaged" but not minerals? The problem is that the areas where overproduction *does* exist are precisely those where the built-in market mechanism has been *prevented* from operating by the force of government. Specifically, these are the areas where private property has not been allowed in the *resource itself*, but only in their daily or annual use.

Suppose, for example, that the government had decreed, from the beginning of iron or copper mining, that private property cannot exist in the mines themselves but that instead the government or the "public" retained ownership of the mines and that private business could only lease them and use them from month to month. Clearly, this would mean that private business, not being able to own the capital value of the mines themselves, would try to use up these mines as rapidly as possible, since they would earn only present but not future income. Private mine owners would try to use up the mines quickly, for if they did not, other miners would gain the benefit of future copper ore. As private copper miners rushed to produce as much copper as possible immediately, leftists would begin to point to "greedy" capitalism's unconscionable ravaging of our precious copper supply. But the fault would lie, not in the market economy, but precisely in the fact that the government had prevented the market, and private property rights, from functioning in the copper resources as a whole.

This is precisely what has happened in those areas: forests, fisheries, petroleum, where overproduction and wastage of resources have actually occurred.[4] The bulk of the forests in the United States has been reserved to the ownership of the federal government; private firms can only lease the forests for current use. This means, of course, that business firms have every incentive to use the forests as rapidly as possible and to conserve nothing for future use. Furthermore, if forests as a whole were owned by private firms, these firms would have every economic incentive—none of which now exists—to develop techniques for *increasing* the resource and for enhancing its long-run productivity, so that current annual production *and* the resource as a whole could both increase at the same time. As things now stand, there is no such incentive to develop resource-enhancing and sustaining technology.

---

[4]On all this, see Anthony Scott, *Natural Resources: The Economics of Conservation* (Toronto: University of Toronto Press, 1955).

The same situation, in even more aggravated form, exists in the case of ocean fisheries. Governments have never allowed private property rights in parts of the ocean; they have only allowed private persons and firms to *use* the fish resource by catching and capturing the fish, but never to own the fish resource—the waters themselves. Is it any wonder that there is grave danger of depletion of the fisheries?

Let us consider the analogy of property and use in the land. In primitive times, man did not transform the land itself; in the primitive hunting and gathering economy, he only used the fruits of the natural soil or land: hunting wild animals, picking wild fruits or seeds for food. In this hunting and gathering stage, and with the population low in relation to the resources, the land itself was not scarce and so the concept of private property in the land did not arise. Only after man began to transform the land (agriculture) did the concept and the institution of private property in the land arise. But now man's use of fish has begun to make this resource scarce, and it will continue to be more and more scarce so long as private property is not allowed to exist in the parts of the ocean itself. For since no one can own any part of the ocean, no one will have the incentive to conserve it; furthermore, there is now no economic incentive to develop the great untapped resource of *aquaculture*. If private property rights existed in the ocean, there would be a fantastic flowering of aquaculture, a flowering which would not only use the enormous untapped resources of the ocean, but also would enormously increase the resources through such techniques as fertilizing, "fencing" off parts of the ocean, etc. Thus, the supply of fish could be increased enormously by simple fertilizing techniques (just as fertilizers led to an incredible increase in the supply of agricultural food). But no one person or firm is going to fertilize a part of the ocean when the fruits of this investment can be captured by some competing

fisherman who does not have to respect the first man's property rights. Even now, in our present primitive stage of aquaculture technique, electronic fencing of parts of the ocean
which segregated fish by size could greatly increase the supply of fish simply by preventing big fish from eating little
ones. And if private property in the ocean were permitted, an
advanced technology of aquaculture would soon develop
which could increase the long-range as well as immediate
productivity of the sea in numerous ways which we cannot
now even foresee.

Thus, the problem of resources in fish and the sea is not
to put further shackles on the profit motive, the technology,
and the economic growth; rather, the proper path is the
reverse: to free man's energies to use, multiply, and develop
the vast untapped resources of the ocean through an extension of private property rights from land to the sea.[5]

This brings us to the area where the environmentalists
indeed have their strongest case, but a case which they do not
really understand, the whole field of *pollution*: of air, water,
food (pesticides), and noise. Of course, there is a grave problem of the befouling of our air and water resources. But the
root of the problem does not lie in capitalist greed, modern
technology, or in private property and the free market; on the
contrary, it lies, once again, in the fact that government has
failed to apply or protect the rights of private property.
Rivers are, in essence, owned by no one; and so, of course,
industry, farmers, and government alike have poured poisons
into those rivers. Clean water and clean air have become
scarce resources, and yet, as in the case of fisheries, they still

---

[5]See the imaginative pamphlet by Gordon Tullock, "The Fisheries—
Some Radical Proposals" (Columbia: University of South Carolina
Bureau of Business and Economic Research, 1962).

may not be owned by private persons. If there were full private property rights on the rivers, for example, the owners
would not permit their pollution.[6] As to the seemingly insol-
uble question of the air, it needs to be recognized that factories, automobiles and incinerators that pour poisons into the
air are damaging the private property of each one of us: not
only the orchards of the farmers and the buildings of real
estate owners, but the lungs and bodies of everyone. Surely
every man's private property in his own body is his most precious resource; and the fact that air pollutants injure that private property should be enough for us to obtain court injunctions preventing that pollution from taking place.

The question to ask, then, is why haven't the courts
applied the common-law defense of property rights to an air
pollution that injures material property and the persons of
every one of us. The reason is that, from the beginnings of
modern air pollution, the courts made a conscious decision
not to protect, for example, the orchards of farmers from the
smoke of nearby factories or locomotives. They said, in
effect, to the farmers: yes, your private property is being
invaded by this smoke, but we hold that "public policy" is
more important than private property, and public policy
holds factories and locomotives to be good things. These
goods were allowed to override the defense of property rights
resulting in pollution disaster. The remedy is both "radical"
and crystal clear, and it has nothing to do with multibillion-
dollar palliative programs at the expense of the taxpayers
which do not even meet the real issue. The remedy is simply
to enjoin anyone from injecting pollutants into the air, and

---

[6]On possible private property rights in the rivers, see, among other
works, Jack Hirshleifer, James C. DeNaven, and Jerome W. Milliman,
Water Supply: Economics, Technology, and Policy (Chicago: University of
Chicago Press, 1960), chap. 9.

thereby invading the rights of persons and property. Period. The argument that such an injunction prohibition would add to the cost of industrial production is as reprehensible as the pre-Civil War argument that the abolition of slavery would add to the costs of growing cotton, and therefore, should not take place. For this means that the polluters are able to impose the high costs of pollution upon those whose property rights they are allowed to invade with impunity.

Furthermore, the cost argument overlooks the crucial fact that if air pollution is allowed to proceed with impunity, there again is no economic incentive to develop a technology which would either prevent or cure air pollution. If, however, industry and government were prohibited from pollution invasion, they would soon develop techniques whereby production could proceed without polluting the air. Even now, at our necessarily primitive stage in antipollution technology, techniques exist for the recycling of wastes which would preclude pollution of the air. Thus, sulfur dioxide, one of the major pollutants, could even now be captured and recycled to produce the economically valuable sulfuric acid.[7] The highly pollutant spark ignition automobile engine could well be replaced by a diesel, gas turbine or steam engine, or by an electric car, especially when the economic incentive would exist to develop their technologies to replace the existing engine.

Noise, too, is an invasion of private property; for noise is the creation of sound waves which invade and bombard the property and persons of others. Here, too injunctions to prohibit excessive noise would spur the development and installation of

---

[7]See Jacobs, *The Economy of Cities*, pp. 109ff.; and Jerome Tuccille, "This Desecrated Earth: A Libertarian Analysis of the Air Pollution Problem" (unpublished manuscript).

antinoise devices, such as mufflers, acoustical materials, and even equipment which would create opposing and, therefore, canceling waves of sound to the noise-polluting machinery.

Thus, when we peel away the hysteria, the confusions, and the unsound philosophy of the environmentalists, we find an important bedrock case against the existing system; but the case turns out to be not against capitalism, private property, or modern technology. It is a case against the failure of government to allow and defend the rights of private property against invasion. Pollution and overuse of resources stem directly from the failure of government to defend private property. If property rights were to be defended adequately, we would find that here, as in other areas of our economy and society, private enterprise and modern technology would come not as a curse to mankind but as its salvation.

10
THE MEANING
OF REVOLUTION

I n his vitally important article on this issue,[1] Karl Hess
properly refers to the genuine libertarian movement as a
"revolutionary" movement. This raises the point that very
few Americans understand the true meaning of the word
"revolution."

Most people, when they hear the world "revolution,"
think immediately and only of direct acts of physical con-
frontation with the State: raising barricades in the streets,
battling a cop, storming the Bastille or other government
buildings. But this is only one small part of revolution. Revolution is a mighty, complex, long-run process, a complicated
movement with many vital parts and functions. It is the pam-
phleteer writing in his study, it is the journalist, the political
club, the agitator, the organizer, the campus activist, the theoretician, the philanthropist. It is all this and much more.
Each person and group has its part to play in this great complex movement.

---

[1] See Karl Hess, "What the Movement Needs," *The Libertarian Forum*
(July 1, 1969).

Let us take, for example, the major model for Libertarians in our time: the great classical-liberal, or better, "classical radical," revolutionary movement of the seventeenth, eighteenth, and nineteenth centuries. These our ancestors created a vast, sprawling, and brilliant revolutionary movement not only in the United States but also throughout the Western world that lasted for several centuries. This was the movement largely responsible for radically changing history, for almost destroying history as it was previously known to man. For before these centuries, the history of man, with one or two luminous exceptions, was a dark and gory record of tyranny and despotism; a record of various absolute States and monarchs crushing and exploiting their underlying populations, largely peasants, who lived a brief and brutish life at bare subsistence, devoid of hope or promise. It was classical liberalism and radicalism that brought to the mass of people that hope and promise, and which launched the great process of fulfillment. All that man has achieved today, in progress, in hope, in living standards, we can attribute to that revolutionary movement, to that "revolution." This great revolution was our fathers'; it is now our task to complete its unfinished promise.

This classical revolutionary movement was made up of many parts. It was the libertarian theorists and ideologists, the men who created and wove the strands of libertarian theory and principle: the La Boeties, the Levellers in seventeenth-century England, the eighteenth-century radicals, the philosophes, the physiocrats, the English radicals, the Patrick Henrys, and Tom Paines of the American Revolution; the James Mills and Cobdens of nineteenth-century England, the Jacksonians and abolitionists and Thoreaus in America, the Bastiats and Molinaris in France. The vital scholarly work of Caroline Robbins and Bernard Bailyn, for example, has demonstrated the continuity of libertarian classical-radical ideas and movements, from the seventeenth-century English revolutionaries down through the American Revolution a century and a half later.

Theories blended into activist movements, rising movements calling for individual liberty, a free-market economy, the overthrow of feudalism and mercantilist statism, an end to theocracy and war and their replacement by freedom and international peace. Once in a while, these movements erupted into violent "revolutions" that brought giant steps in the direction of liberty: the English Civil War, the American Revolution, the French Revolution.[2] The result was enormous strides for freedom and the prosperity unleashed by the consequent Industrial Revolution. The barricades, while important, were just one small part of this great process.

Socialism is neither genuinely radical nor truly revolutionary. Socialism is a reactionary reversion, a self-contradictory attempt to achieve classical radical ends: liberty, progress, the withering away or abolition of the State, by using old-fashioned statist and Tory means: collectivism and State control. Socialism is a New Toryism doomed to rapid failure whenever it is tried, a failure demonstrated by the collapse of central planning in the Communist countries of Eastern Europe. Only libertarianism is truly radical. Only we can complete the unfinished revolution of our great forebears, the bringing of the world from the realm of despotism into the realm of freedom. Only we can replace the governance of men by the administration of things.

---

[2]Barrington Moore, Jr., has shown the intimate connection between these violent revolutions and the freedoms that the Western world has been able to take from the State.

11
NATIONAL LIBERATION

T he recent rioting and virtual civil war in Northern Ireland
points out, both for libertarians and for the world at
large, the vital importance of pushing for and attaining
the goal of national liberation for all oppressed people. Aside
from being a necessary condition to the achievement of justice, national liberation is the only solution to the great world
problems of territorial disputes and oppressive national rule.
Yet, all too many anarchists and libertarians mistakenly scorn
the idea of national liberation and independence as simply
setting up more nation–states; they tragically do not realize
that, taking this stand, they become in the concrete, objective
supporters of the bloated, imperialistic nation–states of
today.

Sometimes this mistake has had tragic consequences.
Thus, it is clear from Paul Avrich's fascinating and definitive
book[1] that the anarchists in Russia had at least a fighting
chance to take control of the October Revolution rather than
the Bolsheviks, but that they lost out for two major reasons:
(1) their sectarian view that any kind of definite organization
of their own movement violated anarchist principles; and (2)

---

[1] Paul Avrich, *The Russian Anarchists* (Princeton, N.J.: Princeton University Press, 1967).

their opposition to the national independence movements for the Ukraine and White Russia on the ground that this would simply be setting up other states. In this way, they became the objective defenders of Great Russian imperialism, and this led them to the disastrous course of opposing Lenin's statesmanlike "appeasement peace" of Brest-Litovsk in 1918, where Lenin, for the sake of ending the war with Germany, surrendered Ukrainian and White Russian territory from the Greater Russian imperium. Disastrously, both for their own principles and for their standing in the eyes of the war-weary Russian people, the Russian anarchists called for continuing the war against "German imperialism," thereby somehow identifying with anarchy, the centuries-old land grabs of Russian imperialism.

Let us first examine the whole question of national liberation from the point of view of libertarian principle. Suppose that there are two hypothetical countries, "Ruritania" and "Walldavia." Ruritania invades Walldavia and seizes the northern part of the country. This situation continues over decades or even centuries. But the underlying condition remains: the Ruritanian State has invaded and continues to occupy and exploit, very often trying to eradicate the language and culture of the North Walldavian subject people. There now arises, both in northern and southern Walldavia, a "North Walldavian Liberation Movement." Where should we stand on the matter?

It seems clear to me that Libertarians are bound to give this liberation movement their ardent support. For their object, while it might not be to achieve an ultimate stateless society, is to liberate the oppressed North Walldavians from their Ruritanian State rulers. The fact that we may not agree with the Walldavian rebels on all philosophical or political points is irrelevant. The whole point of their existence—to free the Northern Walldavians from their imperial oppressors—deserves our wholehearted support.

Thus is solved the dilemma of how Libertarians and anarchists should react toward the whole phenomenon of "nationalism." Nationalism is not a unitary, monolithic phenomenon. If it is aggressive, we should oppose it; if liberatory, we should favor it. Thus, in the Ruritanian–Walldavian case, those Ruritanians who defend the aggression or occupation on the grounds of "Greater Ruritania" or "Ruritanian national honor" or whatever, are being aggressive nationalists or "imperialists." Those of either country who favor North Walldavian liberation from the imperial Ruritanian yoke are being liberators and, therefore, deserve our support.

One of the great swindles behind the idea of "collective security against aggression," as spread by the "internationalist" interventionists of the 1920s and ever since, is that this requires us to regard as sacred all of the national boundaries which have been often imposed by aggression in the first place. Such a concept requires us to put our stamp of approval upon the countries and territories created by previous imperial aggression.

Let us now apply our analysis to the problem of Northern Ireland. The Northern Irish rulers, the Protestants, insist on their present borders and institutions; the Southern Irish, or Catholics, demand a unitary state in Ireland. Of the two, the Southern Irish have the better case, for all of the Protestants were "planted" centuries ago into Ireland by English imperialism, at the expense of murdering the Catholic Irish and robbing their lands. But unless documentation exists to enable restoration of the land and property to the heirs of the victims—and it is highly dubious that such exists—the proper libertarian solution has been advanced by neither side and, as far as we can tell, by no one in the public press.

For the present partition line does *not*, as most people believe, divide the Catholic South from the Protestant North. The partition, as imposed by Britain after World War I and accepted by the craven Irish rebel leadership, arbitrarily handed a great deal of Catholic territory to the North. Specifically, over half of the territory of Northern Ireland has a majority of Catholics and should revert immediately to the South: this includes Western Derry (including Derry City), all of Tyrone and Fermanagh, southern Armagh and southern Down. Essentially, this would leave as Northern Ireland only the city of Belfast and the rural areas directly to the north.

While this solution would leave the Catholics of Belfast oppressed by outrageous Protestant discrimination and exploitation, at least the problem of the substantial Catholic minority in Northern Ireland—the *majority* in the areas enumerated above—would be solved, and the whole question of Northern Ireland would be reduced to tolerable dimensions. In this way, the libertarian solution—of applying national self-determination and removing imperial oppression— would at the same time bring about justice and solve the immediate utilitarian question.

12
ANARCHO-COMMUNISM

N ow that the New Left has abandoned its earlier loose, flexible, nonideological stance, two ideologies have been adopted as guiding theoretical positions by New Leftists—Marxism–Stalinism and anarcho-communism. Marxism–Stalinism has unfortunately conquered SDS, but anarcho-communism has attracted many leftists who are looking for a way out of the bureaucratic and statist tyranny that has marked the Stalinist road. Also, many libertarians, who are looking for forms of action and for allies in such actions, have become attracted by an anarchist creed which seemingly exalts the voluntary way and calls for the abolition of the coercive State. It is fatal, however, to abandon and lose sight of one's own principles in the quest for allies in specific tactical actions. Anarcho-communism, both in its original Bakunin–Kropotkin form and in its current irrationalist and "post-scarcity" variety, is poles apart from genuine libertarian principle.

If there is one thing, for example, that anarcho-communism hates and reviles *more* than the State, it is the right of private property. As a matter of fact, the major reason that Anarcho-Communists oppose the State is because they wrongly believe that it is the creator and protector of private property, and, therefore, that the only route toward abolition of property is by destruction of the State apparatus. They totally fail to realize that the State has always been the great enemy and invader of the rights of private property. Furthermore, scorning and detesting the free market, the profit-and-loss economy, private property, and material affluence—all of which are corollaries of each other—Anarcho-Communists wrongly identify anarchism with communal living, with tribal sharing, and with other aspects of our emerging drug-rock "youth culture."

The only good thing that one might say about anarcho-communism is that, in contrast to Stalinism, its form of communism would, supposedly, be voluntary. Presumably, no one would be forced to join the communes, and those who would continue to live individually and to engage in market activities would remain unmolested. Or would they? Anarcho-Communists have always been extremely vague and cloudy about the lineaments of their proposed anarchist society of the future. Many of them have been propounding the profoundly antilibertarian doctrine that the anarcho-communist revolution will have to confiscate and abolish all private property, so as to wean everyone from their psychological attachment to the property they own. Furthermore, it is hard to forget the fact that when the Spanish Anarchists (anarcho-communists of the Bakunin–Kropotkin type) took over large sections of Spain during the Civil War of the 1930s, they confiscated and destroyed all the money in their areas and promptly decreed the death penalty for the use of money. None of this can give one confidence in the good, voluntarist intentions of anarcho-communism.

On all other grounds, anarcho-communism ranges from mischievous to absurd. Philosophically, this creed is an all-out assault on individuality and on reason. The individual's desire for private property, drive to better himself, to specialize, to accumulate profits and income are reviled by all branches of communism. Instead, everyone is supposed to live in communes, sharing all his meager possessions with his fellows and each being careful not to advance beyond his communal brothers. At the root of all forms of communism, compulsory or voluntary, lies a profound hatred of individual excellence, a denial of the natural or intellectual superiority of some men over others, and a desire to tear down every individual to the level of a communal ant-heap. In the name of a phony "humanism," an irrational and profoundly antihuman egalitarianism is to rob every individual of his specific and precious humanity.

Furthermore, anarcho-communism scorns reason, and its corollaries: long-range purpose, forethought, hard work, and individual achievement; instead, it exalts irrational feelings, whim, and caprice—all this in the name of "freedom." The "freedom" of the Anarcho-Communist has nothing to do with the genuine libertarian absence of interpersonal invasion or molestation; it is, instead, a "freedom" that means enslavement to unreason, to unexamined whim, and to childish caprice. Socially and philosophically, anarcho-communism is a misfortune.

Economically, anarcho-communism is an absurdity. The Anarcho-Communist seeks to abolish money, prices and employment, and proposes to conduct a modern economy purely by the automatic registry of "needs" in some central data bank. No one who has the slightest understanding of economics can trifle with this theory for a single second. Fifty years ago, Ludwig von Mises exposed the total inability of a planned, moneyless economy to operate above the most primitive level. He showed that money-prices are indispensable for the rational allocation of all of our scarce resources—labor, land, and capital goods—to the fields and the areas where they are most desired by the consumers and where they could operate with greatest efficiency. The Socialists conceded the correctness of Mises's challenge and set about—in vain—to find a way to have a rational, market-price system within the context of a socialist planned economy.

The Russians, after trying an approach to the communist, moneyless economy in their "War Communism" shortly after the Bolshevik Revolution, reacted in horror as they saw the Russian economy heading toward disaster. Even Stalin never tried to revive it; and since World War II, the East European countries have seen a total abandonment of this communist ideal and a rapid movement toward free markets, a free-price system, profit-and-loss tests, and a promotion of consumer affluence. It is no accident that it was precisely the *economists* in the communist countries who led the rush away from communism, socialism, and central planning and toward free markets. It is no crime to be ignorant of economics, which is, after all, a specialized discipline and one that most people consider to be a "dismal science." But it *is* totally irresponsible to have a loud and vociferous opinion on economic subjects while remaining in this state of ignorance. Yet, this sort of aggressive ignorance is inherent in the creed of anarcho-communism.

The same comment can be made on the widespread belief, held by many New Leftists and by all Anarcho-Communists, that there is no longer a need to worry about economics or production because we are supposedly living in a "post-scarcity" world, where such problems do not arise. But while our condition of scarcity is clearly superior to that of the caveman, we are still living in a world of pervasive economic scarcity. How will we know when the world has achieved "post-scarcity"? Simply, we will know when all the goods and services that we may want have become so superabundant that their prices have fallen to zero, in short, when we can acquire all goods and services as in a Garden of Eden—without effort, without work, without using any scarce resources.

The antirational spirit of anarcho-communism was expressed by Norman O. Brown, one of the gurus of the new "counter-culture":

> The great economist Ludwig von Mises tried to refute socialism by demonstrating that, in abolishing exchange, socialism made economic calculation, and hence economic rationality, impossible. . . . But if Mises is right, then what he discovered is not a refutation but a psychoanalytical justification of socialism. . . . It is one of the sad ironies of contemporary intellectual life that the reply of socialist economists to Mises's arguments was to attempt to show that socialism was not incompatible with "rational economic calculation"— that is to say, that it could retain the inhuman principle of economizing.[1]

The fact that the abandonment of rationality and economics in behalf of "freedom" and whim will lead to the scrapping of modern production and civilization and return us to barbarism does not faze our Anarcho-Communists and other exponents of the new "counter-culture." But what they do not seem to realize is that the result of this return to primitivism would be starvation and death for nearly all of mankind and a grinding subsistence for the ones remaining. If they have their way, they will find that it is difficult indeed to be jolly and "unrepressed" while starving to death.

All this brings us back to the wisdom of the great Spanish philosopher Ortega y Gasset:

---

[1]Norman O. Brown, *Life Against Death* (New York: Random House, 1959), pp. 238–39.

[i]n the disturbances caused by scarcity of food, the mob goes in search of bread, and the means it employs is generally to wreck the bakeries. They may serve as a symbol of the attitude adopted, on a greater and more complicated scale, by the masses of today towards the civilization by which they are supported. . . . Civilization is not "just here," it is not self-supporting. It is artificial. . . . If you want to make use of the advantages of civilization, but are not prepared to concern yourself with the upholding of civilization—you are done. In a trice you find yourself left without civilization. Just a slip, and when you look everything has vanished into air. The primitive forest appears in its native state, just as if curtains covering pure Nature had been drawn back. The jungle is always primitive and vice versa, everything primitive is mere jungle.[2]

---

[2]José Ortega y Gasset, *The Revolt of the Masses* (New York: W.W. Norton, 1932), p. 97.

13
THE SPOONER–TUCKER DOCTRINE: AN ECONOMIST'S VIEW

First, I must begin by affirming my conviction that Lysander Spooner and Benjamin R. Tucker were unsurpassed as political philosophers and that nothing is more needed today than a revival and development of the largely forgotten legacy that they left to political philosophy. By the mid-nineteenth century, the libertarian individualist doctrine had reached the point where its most advanced thinkers in their varying ways (Thoreau, Hodgskin, the early Fichte, the early Spencer) had begun to realize that the State was incompatible with liberty or morality. But they went only so far as to assert the right of the lone individual to opt out of the State's network of power and tax-plunder. In this uncompleted form, their doctrines were not really a threat to the State-apparatus, for few individuals will contemplate opting out of the vast benefits of social living in order to get out from under the State.

It was left to Spooner and Tucker to adumbrate the way in which all individuals could abandon the State and cooperate to their own vast mutual benefit in a society of free and voluntary exchanges and interrelations. By doing this, Spooner and Tucker advanced libertarian individualism from a protest against existing evils to pointing the way to an ideal society toward which we can move; and what is more, they correctly located that ideal in the free market which already partially existed and was providing vast economic and social benefits. Thus, Spooner, Tucker, and their movement not only furnished a goal toward which to move, but they also greatly surpassed previous "utopians" in locating that goal in already-existing institutions rather than in a coercive or impossible vision of a transformed mankind. Their achievement was truly remarkable, and we have not yet risen to the level of their insights.

I cannot conclude a tribute to Spooner and Tucker's political philosophy without quoting a particularly magnificent passage from Spooner's *No Treason No. VI*, which meant a great deal to my own ideological development:

> [i]t is true that the theory of our Constitution is, that all taxes are paid voluntarily; that our government is a mutual insurance company, voluntarily entered into by the people with each other. . . .
>
> But this theory of our government is wholly different from the practical fact. The fact is that the government, like a highwayman, says to a man: "Your money or your life." And many, if not most, taxes are paid under the compulsion of that threat.
>
> The government does not, indeed, waylay a man in a lonely place, spring upon him from the roadside, and, holding a pistol to his head, proceed to rifle his pockets. But the robbery is nonetheless a robbery on that account; and it is far more dastardly and shameful.
>
> The highwayman takes solely upon himself the responsibility, danger, and crime of his own act. He does not pretend that he has any rightful claim to your money, or that he intends to use it for your own benefit. He does not pretend to be anything but a robber. He has not acquired impudence enough to profess to be merely a "protector," and that he takes men's money against their will, merely to enable him to "protect" those infatuated travellers, who feel

perfectly able to protect themselves, or do not appreciate his peculiar system of protection. He is too sensible a man to make such professions as these. Furthermore, having taken your money, he leaves you, as you wish him to do. He does not persist in following you on the road, against your will, assuming to be your rightful "sovereign"; on account of the "protection" he affords you. He does not keep "protecting" you, by commanding you to bow down and serve him; by requiring you to do this, and forbidding you to do that; by robbing you of more money as often as he finds it for his interest or pleasure to do so; and by branding you as a rebel, a traitor, and an enemy to your country, and shooting you down without mercy, if you dispute his authority, or resist his demands. He is too much of a gentleman to be guilty of such impostures, and insults, and villainies as these. In short, he does not, in addition to robbing you attempt to make you either his dupe or his slave.

The proceedings of those robbers and murderers, who call themselves "the government," are directly the opposite of those of the single highwayman.[1]

Who, after reading that superb passage, can ever be a dupe of the State again?

I am, therefore, strongly tempted to call myself an "individualist anarchist," except for the fact that Spooner and Tucker have in a sense preempted that name for their doctrine and that from that doctrine I have certain differences. Politically, these differences are minor, and therefore the system that I advocate is very close to theirs; but economically, the differences are substantial, and this means that my view of the consequences of putting our more or less common system into practice is very far from theirs.

Politically, my differences with Spooner–Tucker individualist anarchism are two-fold. In the first place, there is the role of law and the jury system in the individualist–anarchist

---

[1] Lysander Spooner, *No Treason: The Constitution of No Authority*, No. *VI* (Boston, 1870), pp. 12–13.

society. Spooner–Tucker believed in allowing each individual free-market court and more specifically, each free-market jury, totally free rein over judicial decisions. There would be no rational or objective body of law which the juries would in any sense—even morally—be bound to consult, nor even any judicial precedents, since each jury would have the power to decide both the facts and the law of every case strictly *ad hoc*. With no guides or standards to follow, even juries with the best of will could not be expected to arrive at just or even libertarian decisions.

In my view, law is a valuable good that is no more necessarily produced by the State than is postal or defense service; the State can be separated from lawmaking just as it can be separated from the religious or the economic spheres of life. Specifically, it would not be a very difficult task for Libertarian lawyers and jurists to arrive at a rational and objective code of libertarian legal principles and procedures based on the axiom of defense of person and property, and consequently of no coercion to be used against anyone who is not a proven and convicted invader of such person and property. This code would then be followed and applied to specific cases by privately-competitive and free-market courts and judges, all of whom would be pledged to abide by the code, and who would be employed on the market proportionately as the quality of their service satisfies the consumers of their product. In the present society, juries have the inestimable virtue of being repositories of defense of the private citizen against the State; they are indispensable nuclei of people outside the State-apparatus who can be used for protection of the harried defendant in the State's courts. But in the libertarian society, that special virtue would be gone.[2]

---

[2]Professor Bruno Leoni of the University of Pavia, though far from an anarchist, has recently written a stimulating defense of the superiority

On the problem of justice, however, a reconciliation is possible: Tucker, after all, does say at one point that, "Anarchism does mean exactly the observance and enforcement of the natural law of liberty," and that is precisely what I am calling for.[3]

My second political difference with Spooner–Tucker is on the land question, specifically on the question of property rights in land title. Here, however, I believe that the Tucker position is superior to that of current laissez-faire economists who either take no position on land or else blithely assume that all land titles must be protected simply because some government has declared them "private property"; and superior to the Henry Georgists, who recognize the existence of a land problem but who deny the justice of any private property in ground land. The thesis of the individualist anarchists, developed by Joshua K. Ingalls, was that private ownership of land should be recognized only in those who themselves are using the specific areas of land. Such a theory of property would automatically abolish all rent payments for land, since only the direct user of a piece of land would be recognized as its owner.

While I strongly disagree with this doctrine, it does supply a useful corrective to those libertarians and laissez-faire economists who refuse to consider the problem of land monopoly in the State's arbitrary granting of land titles to its favorites, and therefore who fail completely to tackle what is

---

of the making of law by privately-competitive judges to the arbitrary and changing decrees of a state legislature. He, too, however, fails to recognize the necessity for a rational and libertarian code to provide the standard. See Bruno Leoni, *Freedom and the Law* (Princeton, N.J.: D. Van Nostrand, 1961) and Murray N. Rothbard, "On Freedom and the Law," *New Individualist Review* (Winter, 1962): 37–40.

[3] Benjamin R. Tucker, *Instead of a Book* (New York, 1893), p. 37.

probably the number one problem in the undeveloped countries today. It is not enough to call simply for defense of the "rights of private property"; there must be an adequate theory of justice in property rights, else any property that some State once decreed to be "private" must now be defended by Libertarians, no matter how unjust the procedure or how mischievous its consequences.

In my view, the proper theory of justice in landed property can be found in John Locke: that it first become private property by the use criterion. This rules out State sales of unused and unowned "public domain" to land speculators in advance of use, as conveying any valid title whatever. This much of the way I proceed with Ingalls and the anarchists. But once use and settlement convey proper title, it seems to me a complete violation of the Spooner–Tucker "law of equal liberty" to prevent that legitimate owner from selling his land to someone else.

In short, once a piece of land passes justly into Mr. A's ownership, he cannot be said to truly own that land unless he can convey or sell the title to Mr. B; and to prevent Mr. B from exercising his title simply because he doesn't choose to use it himself but rather rents it out voluntarily to Mr. C, is an invasion of B's freedom of contract and of his right to his justly-acquired private property. In contrast, I can see no rational grounds whatever for the principle that no man can ever get off or rent out his justly acquired property. Tucker's usually spirited and intelligent defense of the free market and of private property is here sadly lacking. Furthermore, such hobbling of land sites or of optimum use of land ownership and cultivation and such arbitrary misallocation of land injures all of society.

But my main quarrel with the Spooner–Tucker doctrine is not political but economic, not the form of our ideal system but the consequences that would follow after such a system is adopted. To that extent, the quarrel is not moral or ethical but scientific. I am the first one to concede that most economists vaingloriously think of their science as proving an open sesame to ethical and political decisions; but where economic matters are under discussion, it is our responsibility to take the findings of economic science into account.

Actually, in contrast to collectivist anarchists and to many other types of radicals, Spooner and Tucker tried to use economics rather than scorn it as excessively rational. Some of their fallacies (for example, the "law of cost," the labor theory of value) were embedded in much of classical economics; and it was their adoption of the labor theory of value that convinced them that rent, interest, and profit were payments exploitatively extracted from the worker. In contrast to the Marxists, however, Spooner and Tucker, understanding many of the virtues of the free market, did not wish to abolish that noble institution; instead, they believed that full freedom would lead, by the workings of economic law, to the peaceful disappearance of these three categories of income. The mechanism for this peaceful abolition Spooner and Tucker found— and here they unfortunately ignored the teachings of classical economics and substituted instead their own fallacies—in the sphere of money.

The two basic interrelated fallacies of Spoonerite theory (and the theory of all schools of writers who have unkindly been labelled by economists as "money-cranks") are a failure to understand the nature of money and the nature of interest.[4] Money-crankism assumes (1) that more and ever more

---

[4]For the sake of simplicity, we will here continue the practice of the classical economists of lumping "interest" and "profits" together. Actually, the rate of profit on the market tends, in the long-run, to equal the rate of interest. Short-run profit (and losses) would continue to exist on

money is needed on the market; (2) that the lower the interest rate the better; and (3) that the interest rate is determined by the quantity of money, the former being inversely proportional to the latter. Given this set of totally fallacious assumptions, the prescription follows: keep increasing the quantity of money and lowering the rate of interest (or profits).

At this point, money-crankism separates into two schools: what we might call the "orthodox," who call on the State to print enough paper money to do the job (for example, Ezra Pound, the Social Credit Movement); and the anarchist or Mutualist, who wants private persons or banks to do the work (for example, Proudhon, Spooner, Greene, Meulen). Actually, within these narrow limits, the statists are far better economists than the anarchists; for while the State can wreak havoc by inflating enormously and by temporarily lowering the rate of interest, the anarchist society would, contrary to anarchist notions, lead to much "harder" money than we have now.

In the first fallacy, it must be concluded that money-cranks are simply pushing to its logical conclusion a fallacy adopted widely by preclassical and by current Keynesian writers. The crucial point is that an increase in the supply of money does not confer any benefit whatever on society. On the contrary, it is a means of exploitation of the bulk of society by the State, State-manipulated banks and their favorites. The reason is that, in contrast to potatoes or steel, an increase of which means that more goods can be consumed and more people benefitted, money does its full social work regardless of its quantity on the market. More money will only dilute

---

the market even if Spooner had his way and the rate of interest (and of long-run profit) fell to zero. The true nature of the distinction between interest and profit was not discovered until the work of Frank H. Knight, *Risk, Uncertainty, and Profit* (Boston, Mass.: Houghton Mifflin, 1921).

the purchasing power, the value in exchange, of each dollar; less money will add to the value of each dollar.

David Hume, one of the greatest economists of all time, went to the heart of this question by asking what would happen if everybody magically woke up one morning with the quantity of money in his possession doubled, tripled, or whatever. It should be clear that everyone's subjective feeling of affluence would fade quickly as the new dollars bid up the prices of goods and services, until these prices have doubled or tripled, and society would be no better off than before. The same would be true if everyone's monetary assets were suddenly halved. Or we can postulate a sudden change of name from "cent" to "dollar," with all denominations increasing proportionately. Would everyone really be one hundred times better off? No; indeed the popularity of inflation through the centuries stems from the very fact that everyone is not getting his money supply doubled or quadrupled all at once. It stems from the fact that inflation of the money supply takes place a step at a time and that the first beneficiaries, the people who get the new money first, gain at the expense of the people unfortunate enough to come last in line.

There was a brilliant *New Yorker* cartoon some years ago that cut to the heart of both the whole inflationist process and the sophisticated rationalizations for plunder and exploitation that have been used to justify it: a group of counterfeiters are happily contemplating their handiwork, and one says: "Retail spending in the neighborhood is about to get a needed shot in the arm." Yes, the people who first receive new injections of money (whether the counterfeiting be legal or illegal) do benefit first (that is, the counterfeiters and those whom they spend the money on, or, as banks, lend the money to), but they do so at the expense of those who receive the money last and who find the prices of things they have to buy shooting up before the new injection filters down to them. There is a "multiplier" effect of injecting new money, but it is an effect that exploits some people for the benefit of others, and being exploitation, it is also a drag and a burden upon genuine production on the free market.

As for the rate of interest, it is not simply the price of money, and it is, therefore, not inversely proportional to its quantity. In the David Hume situation, for example, a four-fold rise in the quantity of money will lead to a fourfold rise in various prices, assets, etc., but there is no reason for this increase to affect the rate of interest. If $1,000 once brought $50 interest per year, $4,000 will now bring $200; the amount of interest will rise fourfold, like everything else, but there is no reason for the rate to change. Lysander Spooner believed that if the supply of money were raised sufficiently (as it supposedly would on the purely free market), the rate of interest would fall to zero; actually, there is no reason for it to change at all.

In the process of inflation, as carried out in the real world, generally the new money first enters the loan market; while that occurs, the rate of interest on the loan market falls; but this fall is strictly temporary, and the market soon restores the rate to its proper level. Indeed, in the later stages of inflation, the rate of interest rises sharply. This process of inflationary distortion of the rate of interest followed by free-market restoration is, in fact, the true meaning of the familiar "business cycle" that has plagued capitalism since the rise of bank credit inflation.[5]

------

[5]The Great Depression of 1929 has been universally blamed on free-market capitalism. For an explanation of this depression based on the above theory of bank credit inflation, see Murray N. Rothbard, *America's Great Depression* (Auburn, Ala.: Mises Institute, 2000).

As for the rate of interest, it is not a function of the quantity of money. It is a function of "time preference," of the rate at which people prefer satisfactions in the present to the same satisfactions in the future. In short, anybody would rather have $100 now than $100 ten years from now (setting aside possible changes in the value of money in the interim or the risk of not getting the money later), because he is better off if he can spend, or simply hold, the money right away.

It should be clear that this phenomenon of time preference is deeply rooted in human nature and the nature of man; it is not in the least a monetary phenomenon but would be just as true in a world of barter. And on the free market, interest is not just a phenomenon of lending, but (in the shape of "long-run" profit) would be fully as true of a world in which everyone invested his own money and nobody loaned or borrowed. In short, capitalists would pay out $100 this year to workers and landowners and then sell the product and reap, say, $110 next year, not because of exploitation, but because all parties prefer any given amount of money this year to next year. Hence, capitalists, to pay out wages and rents in advance and then wait for sale, will do so only if compensated by an "interest" (profit) return; while, for the same reason, workers and landowners are willing to accept this 10 percent discount of their product in order to take their money now and not have to wait for sales to the consumer.

It should be remembered by radicals that, if they wanted to, all workers could refuse to work for wages and instead form their own producers' cooperatives and wait for years for their pay until the products are sold to the consumers; the fact that they do not do so, shows the enormous advantage of the capital investment, wage-paying system as a means of allowing workers to earn money far in advance of the sale of their products. Far from being exploitation of the workers, capital investment and the interest-profit system is an enormous boon to them and to all of society.

The rate of interest or profit on the free market, then, is a reflection of people's time preferences, which in turn determine the degree to which people voluntarily allocate their assets between savings and consumption. A lower rate of interest on the free market is a good sign because it reflects a lower rate of time preference, and hence increased savings and capital invest- ment. But any attempt to force a lower interest rate than that reflecting such voluntary savings causes incalculable damage and leads to depressions in the business cycle. Trying to lower the interest rate and expecting good results is very much like trying to raise the heat in a room by forcing up the thermometer.

Finally, it is important to show the true economic conse- quences of the Spooner–Tucker system put into practice. Without the State to create the conditions and coercions for continued inflation, attempts at inflation and credit expan- sion could not succeed on the free market. Suppose, for example, that I decided to print paper tickets called "two Rothbards," "ten Rothbards," etc., and then tried to use these tickets as money. In the libertarian society I would have the perfect right and freedom to do so. But the question is: who would take the tickets as "money"? Money depends on gen- eral acceptance, and general acceptance of a medium of exchange can begin only with commodities, such as gold and silver. The "dollar," "franc," and other monetary units began not as names in themselves, but as the names of certain units of weight of gold or silver on the free market.

And this is precisely what would happen if the free market were given its head. Gold and silver would be generally used as money, and the various flighty attempts at creating new monetary units out of thin air would . . . vanish into thin air. Any banks which fraudulently printed paper tickets called "dollars," thus implying that these were equivalent to, and therefore backed by, gold and silver, might continue in business a bit longer. But even they, without the State and its legal tender laws and central banks and "deposit insurance" to prop them up, would either disappear through "bank runs" or be confined to very narrow limits. For if a bank issued new paper tickets and loaned them to its clients, as soon as the clients tried to buy goods and services from nonclients of that bank, they would be undone, for the nonclients would no more accept Bank A's notes or deposits as money than anyone would accept my "ten Rothbards."[6]

Thus, a system of free banking, such as envisioned by Spooner and Tucker, far from leading to an indefinite increase of the supply of money and a disappearance of interest, would lead to a far "harder" and more restricted money supply. And to the extent that there would be no government-manipulated credit expansion, there would be a higher rate of interest. The nineteenth-century French economist, Henri Cemuschi, once expressed this very well:

> I believe that what is called freedom of banking would result in a total suppression of banknotes (and also of bank deposits) in France. I want to give everybody the right to issue banknotes so that nobody should take any banknotes any longer.[7]

It seems to be a highly unfortunate trait of libertarian and quasi-libertarian groups to spend the bulk of their time and

---

[6]For a fuller description of the principles of money and banking on the free market and under government intervention, see Murray N. Rothbard, *What Has Government Done to Our Money?* (Auburn, Ala.: Mises Institute, 1990).

[7]Henri Cernuschi, *Conte Le Billet de Banque* (Paris, 1866), p. 55. Quoted in Ludwig von Mises, *Human Action* (Auburn, Ala.: Mises Institute, 1998), p. 443.

energy emphasizing their most fallacious or unlibertarian points. Thus, many Georgists would be fine Libertarians if they would only abandon Georgists' views on land, but, of course, the land question is by far their greatest point of concentration. Similarly, it has been particularly distressing to me as an ardent admirer of Spooner and Tucker to find that their followers have emphasized and concentrated on their totally fallacious monetary views almost to the exclusion of all else and even bring them forth as a panacea for all economic and social ills.

There is, in the body of thought known as "Austrian economics," a scientific explanation of the workings of the free market (and of the consequences of government intervention in that market) which individualist anarchists could easily incorporate into their political and social *Weltanschauung*. But to do this, they must throw out the worthless excess baggage of money-crankism and reconsider the nature and justification of the economic categories of interest, rent and profit.

At least twice in the heyday of anarchism in the United States, individualist anarchists were exposed to critiques of their economic fallacies; but, unfortunately, the lesson, despite the weakness of Tucker's replies, did not take. In the August 1877 issue of Tucker's *Radical Review*, Spooner had written of "The Law of Prices: A Demonstration of the Necessity for an Indefinite Increase of Money." In the November 1877 issue, the economist, Edward Stanwood, wrote an excellent critique, "Mr. Spooner's Island Community." Also, in Tucker's *Instead of a Book*, there are a series of interchanges in which J. Greevz Fisher, the English follower of the quasi-anarchist Auberon Herbert, criticized Tucker's monetary doctrines from the point of view of sound economics.

14
LUDWIG VON MISES AND THE PARADIGM FOR OUR AGE

U nquestionably the most significant and challenging development in the historiography of science in the last decade is the theory of Thomas S. Kuhn. Without defending Kuhn's questionable subjectivist and relativistic philosophy, his contribution is a brilliant *sociological* insight into the ways in which scientific theories change and develop.[1] Essentially, Kuhn's theory is a critical challenge to what might be called the "Whig theory of the history of science." This "Whig" theory, which until Kuhn was the unchallenged orthodoxy in the field, sees the progress of science as a gradual, continuous ever-upward process; year by year, decade by decade, century by century, the body of scientific knowledge gradually grows and accretes through the process of framing hypotheses, testing them empirically, and discarding the invalid and keeping the valid theories. Every

---

[1]Philosophically, Kuhn tends to deny the existence of objective truth and therefore denies the possibility of genuine scientific progress. Thomas S. Kuhn, *The Structure of Scientific Revolution* (2nd ed., Chicago: University of Chicago Press, 1970).

age stands on the shoulders of and sees further and more clearly than every preceding age. In the Whig approach, furthermore, there is no *substantive* knowledge to be gained from reading, say, nineteenth-century physicists or seventeenth-century astronomers; we may be interested in reading Priestley or Newton or Maxwell to see how creative minds work or solve problems, or for insight into the history of the period; but we can never read them to learn something about science which we didn't know already. After all, their contributions are, almost by definition, incorporated into the latest textbooks or treatises in their disciplines.

Many of us, in our daily experience, know enough to be unhappy with this idealized version of the development of science. Without endorsing the validity of Immanuel Velikovsky's theory, for example, we have seen Velikovsky brusquely and angrily dismissed by the scientific community without waiting for the patient testing of the open-minded scientist that we have been led to believe is the essence of scientific inquiry.[2] And we have seen Rachel Carson's critique of pesticides generally scorned by scientists only to be adopted a decade later.

But it took Professor Kuhn to provide a comprehensive model of the adoption and maintenance of scientific belief. Basically, he states that scientists, in any given area, come to adopt a fundamental vision or matrix of an explanatory theory, a vision that Kuhn calls a "paradigm." And whatever the paradigm, whether it be the atomic theory or the phlogiston theory, once adopted the paradigm governs all the scientists

---

[2]On the sociology of the reception of Velikovsky in the scientific community, see Alfred de Grazia, "The Scientific Reception Systems," in A. de Grazia, ed., *The Velikovsky Affair* (New Hyde Park, N.Y.: University Books, 1966), pp. 171–231.

in the field *without* being any longer checked or questioned—as the Whig model would have it. The fundamental paradigm, once established, is no longer tested or questioned, and all further research soon becomes minor applications of the paradigm, minor clearing up of loopholes or anomalies that still remain in the basic vision. For years, decades or longer, scientific research becomes narrow, specialized, always within the basic paradigmatic framework.

But then, gradually, more and more anomalies pile up; puzzles can no longer be solved by the paradigm. But the scientists do not give up the paradigm; quite the contrary, increasingly desperate attempts are made to modify the particulars of the basic theory so as to fit the unpleasant facts and to preserve the framework provided by the paradigm. Only when anomalies pile up to such an extent that the paradigm itself is brought into question, do we have a "crisis situation" in science. And even here, the paradigm is never simply discarded until it can be replaced by a new, competing paradigm which appears to close the loopholes and liquidate the anomalies. When this occurs, there arrives a "scientific revolution," a chaotic period during which one paradigm is replaced by another, and which never occurs smoothly and gradually as the Whig theory only being adopted by the younger and more flexible scientists. Thus, of the co-discoverers of oxygen in the late eighteenth century, Priestley and Lavoisier, Joseph Priestley never, until the day he died, conceded that he had in fact discovered oxygen; to the end he insisted that what he had discovered was merely "dephlogisticated air," thus remaining within the framework of the phlogiston theory.[3]

---

[3]Kuhn, *The Structure of Scientific Revolution*, pp. 53–56.

And so, armed with Kuhn's own paradigm of the history of scientific theories, which is now in the process of replacing the Whig framework, we see a very different picture of the process of science. Instead of a slow and gradual upward march into the light, testing and revising at each step of the way, we see a series of "revolutionary" leaps, as paradigms displace each other only after much time, travail, and resistance. Furthermore, without adopting Kuhn's own philosophical relativism, it becomes clear that, since intellectual vested interests play a more dominant role than continual open-minded testing, it may well happen that a successor paradigm is *less* correct than a predecessor. And if that is true, then we must always be open to the possibility that, indeed, we often know *less* about a given science now than we did decades or even centuries ago. Because paradigms become discarded and are never looked at again, the world may have *forgotten* scientific truth that was once known, as well as added to its stock of knowledge. Reading older scientists now opens up the distinct possibility that we may learn something that we haven't known—or have collectively forgotten—about the discipline. Professor de Grazia states that "much more is discovered and forgotten than is known," and much that has been forgotten may be more correct than theories that are now accepted as true.[4]

If the Kuhn thesis is correct about the physical sciences, where we can obtain empirical and laboratory tests of hypotheses fairly easily, how much more must it be true in philosophy and the social sciences, where no such laboratory tests are possible! For in the disciplines relating to human action, there are no clear and evident laboratory tests available; the truths must be arrived at by the processes of introspection,

---

[4]de Grazia, *The Velikovsky Affair*, p. 197.

"common sense" knowledge and deductive reasoning and such processes, while arriving at solid truths, are not as starkly or compellingly evident as in the physical sciences. Hence, it is all the more easy for philosophers or social scientists to fall into tragically wrong and fallacious paradigms, and thus to lead themselves down the garden path for decades, and even centuries. For once the sciences of human action adopt their fundamental paradigms, it becomes much easier than in the physical sciences to ignore the existence of anomalies, and, therefore, easier to retain erroneous doctrines for a very long time. There is a further well-known difficulty in philosophy and the social sciences which makes systematic error still more likely: the infusion of emotions, value judgments, and political ideologies into the scientific process. The angry treatment accorded to Jensen, Shockley, and the theorists of inequalities of racial intelligence by their fellow scientists, for example, is a case in point. For underlying the bulk of the *scientific* reception of Jensen and Shockley is that even if their theories are true, they should not say so, at least for a century, because of the unfortunate *political* consequences that may be involved. While this sort of stultifying of the quest for scientific truth has happened at times in the physical sciences, it is fortunately far less prevalent there; and whatever the intellectual vested interests at stake, there was at least no ideological and political buttressing for the phlogiston theory or the valence theory in chemistry.

Until recent decades, philosophers and social scientists harbored a healthy recognition of vast differences between their disciplines and the natural sciences; in particular, the classics of philosophy, political theory, and economics were read *not* just for antiquarian interest but for the truths that might lie there. The student of philosophy read Aristotle, Aquinas, or Kant not as an antiquarian game but to learn about the answers to philosophical questions. The student of political theory read Aristotle and Machiavelli in the same light. It was not assumed that, as in the physical sciences, all the contributions of past thinkers have been successfully incorporated into the latest edition of the currently popular textbook; and it was, therefore, not assumed that it was far more important to read the latest journal article in the field than to read the classical philosophers.

In recent decades, however, the disciplines of human action—philosophy and the social sciences—have been frantically attempting to ape the methodology of the physical sciences. There have been many grave flaws in this approach which have increasingly divorced the social sciences from reality: the vain substitute of statistics for laboratory experimentation, the adoption of the positivistic hypothesis-testing model, the unfortunate conquest of all of the disciplines—even history to some extent—by mathematics, are cases in point. But here the important point is that in the aping of the physical sciences, the social disciplines have become narrow specialties; as in the physical sciences, no one reads the classics in the field or indeed is familiar with the history of the discipline further back than this year's journal articles. No one writes systematic treatises anymore; systematic presentations are left for jejune textbooks, while the "real" scholars in the field spend their energy on technical minutiae for the professional journals.

We have seen that even the physical sciences have their problems from uncritical perpetuation of fundamental assumptions and paradigms; but in the social sciences and philosophy this aping of the methods of physical science has been disastrous. For while the social sciences were slow to change their fundamental assumptions in the past, they were eventually *able* to do so by pure reasoning and criticism of the basic paradigm. It took, for example, a long time for "marginal utility" economics to replace classical economics in the late nineteenth century, but it was finally done through such fundamental reasoning and questioning. But no systematic treatise—with one exception to be discussed below—has been written in economics, not a single one, since World War I. And if there are to be no systematic treatises, there can be no questioning of the fundamental assumptions; deprived of the laboratory testing that furnishes the ultimate checks on the theories of physical science, and now also deprived of the systematic use of reason to challenge fundamental assumptions, it is almost impossible to see how contemporary philosophy and social science can ever change the fundamental paradigms in which they have been gripped for most of this century. Even if one were in total agreement with the fundamental drift of the social sciences in this century, the absence of fundamental questioning—the reduction of every discipline to narrow niggling in the journals—would be cause for grave doubts about the soundness of the social sciences.

But if one believes, as the present author does, that the fundamental paradigms of modern, twentieth-century philosophy and the social sciences have been grievously flawed and fallacious from the very beginning, including the aping of the physical sciences, then one is justified in a call for a radical and fundamental reconstruction of all these disciplines, and the opening up of the current specialized bureaucracies in the social sciences to a total critique of their assumptions and procedures.

Of all the social sciences, economics has suffered the most from this degenerative process. For economics is erroneously considered the most "scientific" of the disciplines. Philosophers still read Plato or Kant for insights into truth; political theorists still read Aristotle and Machiavelli for the same reason. But no economist reads Adam Smith or James Mill for the same purpose any longer. History of economic thought, once required in most graduate departments, is now a rapidly dying discipline, reserved for antiquarians alone. Graduate students are locked into the most recent journal articles, the reading of economists published before the 1960s is considered a dilettantish waste of time, and any challenging of fundamental assumptions behind current theories is severely discouraged. If there is any mention of older economists at all, it is only in a few perfunctory brush strokes to limn the precursors of the current Great Men in the field. The result is not only that economics is locked into a tragically wrong path, but also that the truths furnished by the great economists of the past have been collectively *forgotten* by the profession, lost in a form of Orwellian "memory hole."

Of all the tragedies wrought by this collective amnesia in economics, the greatest loss to the world is the eclipse of the "Austrian School." Founded in the 1870s and 1880s, and still barely alive, the Austrian School has had to suffer far more neglect than the other schools of economics for a variety of powerful reasons. First, of course, it was founded a century ago, which in the current scientistic age, is in itself suspicious. Second, the Austrian School has from the beginning been self-consciously *philosophic* rather than "scientistic," far more concerned with methodology and epistemology than other modern economists, the Austrians early arrived at a principled opposition to the use of mathematics or of statistical "testing" in economic theory. By doing so, they set themselves in opposition to all the positivistic, natural-science-imitating trends of this century. Third, it meant, furthermore, that Austrians continued to write fundamental treatises while other economists were setting their sights on narrow, mathematically-oriented articles. And, by stressing the individual and his choices, both methodologically and politically, the

Austrians were setting themselves against the holism and statism of this century as well.

These three radical divergences from current trends were enough to propel the Austrians into undeserved oblivion. But there was another important factor, which at first might seem banal: the language barrier. It is notorious in the scholarly world that, "language tests" to the contrary notwithstanding, no American or English economists or social scientists can *really* read a foreign language. Hence, the acceptance of foreign-based economics must depend on the vagaries of translation. Of the great founders of the Austrian School, Carl Menger's work of the 1870s and 1880s remained untranslated into English until the 1950s; Menger's student Eugen von Böhm-Bawerk fared much better, but even his completed work was not translated until the late 1950s. Böhm-Bawerk's great student, Ludwig von Mises, the founder and head of the "neo-Austrian" school, has fared almost as badly as Menger. His classic *Theory of Money and Credit*, published in 1912, which applied Austrian economics to the problems of money and banking, and which contained the seeds of a radically new (and still largely unknown) theory of business cycles, was highly influential on the continent of Europe, but remained untranslated until 1934. By that time Mises's work was to be quickly buried in England and the United States by the fervor of the "Keynesian Revolution," which was at opposite poles from Mises's theory. Mises's book of 1928, *Geldwertstabilisierung und Konjunkturpolilik*, which predicted the Great Depression on the basis of his developed business cycle theory, remains untranslated to this day. Mises's monumental systematic treatise, *Nationalökonomie*, integrating economic theory on the grounds of a sound basic epistemology, was overlooked also from its being published in 1940, in the midst of war-torn Europe. Again its English translation as

Human Action (1949) came at a time when economics had set
its methodological and political face in a radically different
direction, and therefore, Mises's work, as in the case of other
challenges to fundamental paradigms in science, was not
refuted or criticized but simply ignored.

Thus, while Ludwig von Mises was acknowledged as one
of Europe's most eminent economists in the 1920s and 30s, the
language barrier shut off any recognition of Mises in the Anglo-
American world until the mid-1930s; then, just as his business
cycle theory was beginning to achieve reknown as an explanation for the Great Depression, Mises's overdue recognition
was lost in the hoopla of the Keynesian Revolution. A
refugee deprived of his academic or social base in Europe,
Mises immigrated to the United States at the mercy of his
new-found environment. But while, in the climate of the day,
the leftist and socialist refugees from Europe were cultivated,
feted, and given prestigious academic posts, a different fate
was meted out to a man who embodied a methodological and
political individualism that was anathema to American academia. Indeed, the fact that a man of Mises's eminence was not
offered a single regular academic post, and that he was never
able to teach in a prestigious graduate department in this
country, is one of the most shameful blots on the none too
illustrious history of American higher education. The fact
that Mises himself was able to preserve his great energy, his
remarkable productivity, and his unfailing gentleness and
good humor in the face of this shabby treatment is simply
one more tribute to the qualities of this remarkable man
whom we now honor on his ninetieth birthday.

Agreed then that Ludwig von Mises's writings are the
embodiment of a courageous and eminent man hewing to his
discipline and to his vision unheeding of shabby maltreat-
ment. Apart from this, what substantive truths do they have

to offer an American in 1971? Do they present truths not found elsewhere and, therefore, do they offer intrinsic interest beyond the historical record of a fascinating personal struggle? The answer—which obviously cannot be documented in the compass of this article—is simply and startlingly this: that Ludwig von Mises offers to us nothing less than the complete and developed *correct paradigm* of a science that has gone tragically astray over the last half-century. Mises's work presents us with the correct and radically divergent alternative to the flaws, errors, and fallacies which a growing number of students are sensing in present-day economic orthodoxy. Many students *feel* that there is something very wrong with contemporary economics, and often their criticisms are trenchant, but they are ignorant of any theoretical alternative. And, as Thomas Kuhn has shown, a paradigm, however faulty, will not be discarded until it can be replaced by a competing theory. Or, in the vernacular, "You can't beat something with nothing," and "nothing" is all that many present-day critics of economic science can offer. But the work of Ludwig von Mises furnishes that "something"; it furnishes an economics grounded not on the aping of physical science, but on the very nature of man and of individual choice. And it furnishes that economics in a systematic, integrated form that is admirably equipped to serve as a correct paradigmatic alternative to the veritable *crisis situation*—in theory and public policy—that modern economics has been bringing down upon us. It is not exaggeration to say that Ludwig von Mises is the way out of the methodological and political dilemmas that have been piling up in the modern world. But what is needed now is a host of "Austrians" who can spread the word of the existence of this neglected path.

Briefly, Mises's economic system—as set forth particularly in his *Human Action*—grounds economics squarely upon the axiom of action: on an analysis of the primordial truth that individual men exist and act, that is, make purposive choices among alternatives. Upon this simple and evident axiom of action, Ludwig von Mises deduces the entire systematic edifice of economic theory, an edifice that is as true as the basic axiom and the fundamental laws of logic. The entire theory is the working out of methodological individualism in economics, the nature and consequences of the choices and exchanges of individuals. Mises's uncompromising devotion to the free market, his opposition to every form of statism, stems from his analysis of the nature and consequences of individuals acting freely on the one hand, as against governmental coercive interference or planning on the other. For, basing himself on the action axiom, Mises is able to show the happy consequences of freedom and the free market in social efficiency, prosperity, and development: as against the disastrous consequences of government intervention in poverty, war, social chaos, and retrogression. This political consequence alone, of course, makes the methodology as well as the conclusions of Misesian economics anathema to modern social science.

As Mises puts it:

> Princes and democratic majorities are drunk with power. They must reluctantly admit that they are subject to the laws of nature. But they reject the very notion of economic law. Are they not the supreme legislators? . . . In fact, economic history is a long record of government policies that failed because they were designed with a bold disregard for the laws of economics.
>
> It is impossible to understand the history of economic thought if one does not pay attention to the fact that economics as such is a challenge to the conceit of those in power. An economist can never be a favorite of autocrats and demagogues. With them he is always the mischief-maker. . . .
>
> In the face of all this frenzied agitation it is expedient to establish the fact that the starting point of all praxeological and economic reasoning, the category of human action, is

> proof against any criticisms and objections. . . . From the unshakable foundation of the category of human action praxeology and economics proceed step by step by means of discursive reasoning. Precisely defining assumptions and conditions, they construct a system of concepts and draw all the inferences implied by logically unassailable ratiocination.[5]

And again:

> The laws of the universe about which physics, biology, and praxeology [essentially economics] provide knowledge are independent of the human will, they are primary ontological facts rigidly restricting man's power to act. . . .
>
> Only the insane venture to disregard physical and biological laws. But it is quite common to disdain economic laws. Rulers do not like to admit that their power is restricted by any laws other than those of physics and biology. They never ascribe their failures and frustrations to the violation of economic law.[6]

A notable feature of Mises's analysis of "interventionism"—of government intervention in the economy—is that it is fundamentally what could now be called "ecological," for it

---

[5]Ludwig von Mises, *Human Action* (Auburn, Ala.: Mises Institute, 1998), p. 67.

[6]Ibid., pp. 755–56. As Mises indicates, the revolt against economics as the harbinger of a free-market economy is as old as the classical economists whom Mises acknowledges as his forebears. It is no accident, for example, that George Fitzhugh, the foremost Southern apologist for slavery and one of America's first sociologists, brusquely attacked classical economics as "the science of free society," while upholding socialism as "the science of slavery." See George Fitzhugh in C. Vann Woodward, *Cannibals All!* (Cambridge, Mass.: Harvard University Press, 1960), p. xviii; and Joseph Dorfman, *The Economic Mind in American Civilization* (New York: Viking Press, 1946), vol. 2, p. 929. On the statist and anti-individualist bias embedded deep in the foundations of sociology, see Leon Bramson, *The Political Context of Sociology* (Princeton, N.J.: Princeton University Press, 1961), esp. pp. 11–17.

shows that an act of intervention generates unintended consequences and difficulties, which then present the government with the alternative: either more intervention to "solve" these problems, or repeal of the whole interventionist structure. In short, Mises shows that the market economy is a finely constructed, interrelated web; and coercive intervention at various points of the structure will create unforeseen troubles elsewhere. The logic of intervention, then, is cumulative; and so a mixed economy is unstable—always tending either toward full-scale socialism or back to a free-market economy. The American farm-price support program, as well as the New York City rent-control program, are almost textbook cases of the consequences and pitfalls of intervention. Indeed, the American economy has virtually reached the point where the crippling taxation, the continuing inflation, the grave inefficiencies and breakdowns in such areas as urban life, transportation, education, telephone, and postal service, the restrictions and shattering strikes of labor unions, the accelerating growth of welfare dependency, all have brought about the full-scale crisis of interventionism that Mises has long foreseen. The instability of the interventionist welfare-state system is now making fully clear the fundamental choice that confronts us between socialism on the one hand and free-market capitalism on the other.

Perhaps the most important single contribution of Mises to the economics of intervention is also the one most grievously neglected in the present day: his analysis of money and business cycle. We are living in an age when even those economists supposedly most devoted to the free market are willing and eager to see the state monopolize and direct the issuance of money. Yet Mises has shown that:

1. There is never any social or economic benefit
    to be conferred by an increase in the supply of
    money;

2. The government's intervention into the monetary system is invariably inflationary;

3. Therefore, government should be separated from the monetary system, just as the free market requires that government not intervene in any other sphere of the economy.

Here Mises emphasizes that there is only one way to ensure this freedom and separation: to have a money that is also a useful *commodity*, one whose production is, like other commodities, subject to the supply-and-demand forces of the market. In short, that commodity money—which in practice means the full gold standard—shall replace the fiat issue of paper money by the government and its controlled banking system.[7]

Mises's brilliant theory of the business cycle is the only such theory to be integrated with the economists' general analysis of the pricing system and of capital and interest. Mises shows that the business cycle phenomenon, the recurring alternations of boom and bust with which we have become all too familiar, cannot occur in a free and unhampered market. Neither is the business cycle a mysterious series of random events to be checked and counteracted by an ever-vigilant central government. On the contrary, the business cycle is *generated* by government; specifically, by bank credit expansion promoted and fueled by governmental expansion of bank reserves. The present-day "monetarists" have emphasized that this credit expansion process inflates the money supply and, therefore, the price level; but they have totally neglected the crucial Misesian insight that an

---

[7]Thus, see Ludwig von Mises, *The Theory of Money and Credit* (Irvington-on-Hudson, N.Y.: Foundation for Economic Education, 1971).

even more damaging consequence is distortion of the whole system of prices and production. Specifically, expansion of bank money causes an artificial lowering of the rate of interest, and an artificial and uneconomic overinvestment in capital goods: machinery, plant, industrial raw materials, construction projects. As long as the inflationary expansion of money and bank credit continues, the unsoundness of this process is masked, and the economy can ride on the well-known euphoria of the boom; but when the bank credit expansion finally stops, as stop it must if we are to avoid a runaway inflation, then the day of reckoning will have arrived. For without the anodyne of continuing inflation of money, the distortions and misallocations of production, the overinvestment in uneconomic capital projects and the excessively high prices and wages in those capital goods industries become evident and obvious. It is then that the inevitable recession sets in; the recession being the reaction by which the market economy readjusts itself, liquidates the unsound investments, and realigns the prices and outputs of the economy so as to eliminate the unsound consequences of the boom. The recovery arrives when the readjustment has been completed.

It is clear that the policy prescriptions stemming from the Misesian theory of the business cycle are the diametric opposite of the "post-Keynesian" policies of modern orthodox economics. If there is an inflation, the Misesian prescription is, simply, for the government to *stop* inflating the money supply. When the inevitable recession occurs, in contrast to the modern view that the government should rush in to expand the money supply (the monetarists) or to engage in deficit spending (the Keynesians), the Austrians assert that the government should keep its hands off the economic system—should, in this case, allow the painful but necessary adjustment process of the recession to work itself out as quickly as possible. At best, generating another inflation to end the recession will simply set the stage for another, and deeper, recession later on; at worst, the inflation will simply delay the adjustment process and thereby prolong the recession indefinitely, as happened tragically in the 1930s. Thus, while current orthodoxy maintains that the business cycle is caused by mysterious processes within the market economy and must be counteracted by an active government policy, the Mises theory shows that business cycles are generated by the inflationary policies of government, and that, once under way, the best thing that government can do is to leave the economy alone. In short, the Austrian doctrine is the only *consistent* espousal of laissez-faire; for, in contrast to other "free-market" schools in economics, Mises and the Austrians would apply laissez-faire to the "macro" as well as the "micro" areas of the economy.

If interventionism is invariably calamitous and self-defeating, what of the third alternative: socialism? Here Ludwig von Mises is acknowledged to have made his best-known contribution to economic science: his demonstration, over fifty years ago, that socialist central planning was irrational, since socialism could not engage in that "economic calculation" of prices indispensable to any modern, industrialized economy. Only a true market, based on private ownership of the means of production and on the exchange of such property titles, can establish such genuine market prices, prices which serve to allocate productive resources—land, labor, and capital—to those areas and fields which will most efficiently satisfy the demands of consumers. But Mises showed that, even if the government were willing to forget consumer desires, it could not even allocate efficiently for its *own* ends without a market economy to set prices and costs. Mises was hailed even by Socialists for being the first to raise the whole problem of rational calculation of prices in a socialist economy; but Socialists and other economists erroneously assumed that Oskar Lange and others had satisfactorily solved this calculation problem in their writings of the 1930s. Actually, Mises had anticipated the Lange "solutions" and had refuted them in his original article.[8]

It is highly ironic that, no sooner had the economics profession settled contentedly into the notion that Mises's charge had been refuted, when the Communist countries of Eastern Europe began to find, pragmatically and much against their will, that socialist planning was indeed unsatisfactory, especially as their economies were becoming industrialized. Beginning with Yugoslavia's breakaway from state planning in 1952, the countries of Eastern Europe have been heading with astonishing rapidity away from socialist planning and toward free markets, a price-system, profit-and-loss tests for enterprises, etc. Yugoslavia has been particularly determined in its cumulative shift toward a free market, and away even from State control of investments—the last government stronghold in a socialistic economy. It is unfortunate but not surprising that, neither in the East nor in the West, has Ludwig von Mises's name been brought up as the prophet of the collapse of central planning.[9]

---

[8]Mises's classic article was translated as "Economic Calculation in the Socialist Commonwealth," in F.A. Hayek, ed., *Collectivist Economic Planning* (London: George Routledge and Sons, 1935), pp. 87–130. Mises's and other articles by Lange and Hayek are reprinted in Morris Bornstein, ed., *Comparative Economic Systems* (Homewood, Ill.: Richard D. Irwin, 1969). An excellent discussion and critique of the whole controversy may be found in Trygve J.B. Hoff, *Economic Calculation in the Socialist Society* (London: William Hodge, 1949).

[9]On Yugoslavia, see Rudolf Bicanic, "Economics of Socialism in a Developed Country," in Bornstein, *Comparative Economic Systems*, pp. 222–35: on

If it is becoming increasingly evident that the socialist economies are collapsing in the East, and, on the other hand, that interventionism is falling apart in the West, then the outlook is becoming increasingly favorable for both East and West to turn before very long to the free market and the free society. But what should never be forgotten is that these events are a confirmation and a vindication of the stature of Ludwig von Mises and of the importance of his contribution and his role. For Mises, almost single-handedly, has offered us the correct paradigm for economic theory, for social science, and for the economy itself, and it is high time that this paradigm be embraced, in all of its parts.

There is no more fitting conclusion to a tribute to Ludwig von Mises than the moving last sentences of his greatest achievement, *Human Action*:

> The body of economic knowledge is an essential element in the structure of human civilization; it is the foundation upon which modern industrialism and all the moral, intellectual, technological, and therapeutical achievements of the last centuries have been built. It rests with men whether they will make the proper use of the rich treasure with which this knowledge provides them or whether they will leave it unused. But if they fail to take the best advantage of it and disregard its teachings and warnings, they will not annul economics; they will stamp out society and the human race.[10]

Thanks in no small measure to the life and work of Ludwig von Mises, we can realistically hope and expect that

---

the other countries of Eastern Europe, see Michael Gamarnikow, *Economic Reforms in Eastern Europe* (Detroit, Mich.: Wayne State University Press, 1968).

[10]Mises, *Human Action*, p. 881.

mankind will choose the path of life, liberty, and progress, and will at last turn decisively away from death and despotism.

15
WHY BE LIBERTARIAN?

W hy be libertarian, anyway? By this we mean: what's the point of the whole thing? Why engage in a deep and lifelong commitment to the principle and the goal of individual liberty? For such a commitment, in our largely unfree world, means inevitably a radical disagreement with, and alienation from, the *status quo*, an alienation which equally inevitably imposes many sacrifices in money and prestige. When life is short and the moment of victory far in the future, why go through all this?

Incredibly, we have found among the increasing number of libertarians in this country many people who come to a libertarian commitment from one or another extremely narrow and personal points of view. Many are irresistibly attracted to liberty as an intellectual system or as an aesthetic goal; but liberty remains for them a purely intellectual parlor game, totally divorced from what they consider the "real" activities of their daily lives. Others are motivated to remain libertarians solely from their anticipation of their own personal financial profit. Realizing that a free market would provide far greater opportunities for able, independent men to reap entrepreneurial profits, they become and remain libertarians solely to find larger opportunities for business profit. While it is true that opportunities for profit will be far

greater and more widespread in a free market and a free society, placing one's *primary* emphasis on this motivation for
being a libertarian can only be considered grotesque. For in
the often tortuous, difficult and gruelling path that must be
trod before liberty can be achieved, the libertarian's opportunities for personal profit will far more often be negative than
abundant.

The consequence of the narrow and myopic vision of both
the gamester and the would-be profitmaker is that neither
group has the slightest interest in the work of building a libertarian movement. And yet it is only through building such
a movement that liberty may ultimately be achieved. Ideas,
and especially radical ideas, do not advance in the world in
and by themselves, as it were in a vacuum; they can only be
advanced by *people* and, therefore, the development and
advancement of such people—and therefore of a "movement"—becomes a prime task for the Libertarian who is
really serious about advancing his goals.

Turning from these men of narrow vision, we must also
see that utilitarianism—the common ground of free-market
economists—is unsatisfactory for developing a flourishing
libertarian movement. While it is true and valuable to know
that a free market would bring far greater abundance and a
healthier economy to everyone, rich and poor alike, a critical
problem is whether this knowledge is enough to bring many
people to a lifelong dedication to liberty. In short, how many
people will man the barricades and endure the many sacrifices that a consistent devotion to liberty entails, merely so
that umpteen percent more people will have better bathtubs?
Will they not rather set up for an easy life and forget the
umpteen percent bathtubs? Ultimately, then, utilitarian economics, while indispensable in the developed structure of libertarian thought and action, is almost as unsatisfactory a basic

groundwork for the movement as those opportunists who simply seek a short-range profit.

It is our view that a flourishing libertarian movement, a lifelong dedication to liberty, can only be grounded on a passion for justice. Here must be the mainspring of our drive, the armor that will sustain us in all the storms ahead, not the search for a quick buck, the playing of intellectual games or the cool calculation of general economic gains. And, to have a passion for justice, one must have a *theory* of what justice and injustice are—in short, a set of ethical principles of justice and injustice which cannot be provided by utilitarian economics. It is because we see the world reeking with injustices piled one on another to the very heavens that we are impelled to do all that we can to seek a world in which these and other injustices will be eradicated. Other traditional radical goals—such as the "abolition of poverty"—are, in contrast to this one, truly utopian, for man, simply by exerting his will, cannot abolish poverty. Poverty can only be abolished through the operation of certain economic factors—notably the investment of savings in capital—which can only operate by transforming nature over a long period of time. In short, man's will is here severely limited by the workings of—to use an old-fashioned but still valid term—natural law. But *injustices* are deeds that are inflicted by one set of men on another; they are precisely the actions of men, and, hence, they and their elimination are subject to man's instantaneous will.

Let us take an example: England's centuries-long occupation and brutal oppression of the Irish people. Now if, in 1900, we had looked at the state of Ireland, and we had considered the poverty of the Irish people, we would have had to say: poverty could be improved by the English getting out and removing their land monopolies, but the ultimate elimination of poverty in Ireland, under the best of conditions, would take time and be subject to the workings of economic law. But the goal of ending English oppression—that could have been done by the instantaneous action of men's will: by the English simply deciding to pull out of the country. The fact that of course such decisions do not take place instantaneously is not the point; the point is that the very failure is an injustice that has been decided upon and imposed by the perpetrators of injustice—in this case, the English government. In the field of justice, man's will is all; men can move mountains, if only men so decide. A passion for instantaneous justice—in short, a radical passion—is therefore not utopian, as would be a desire for the instant elimination of poverty or the instant transformation of everyone into a concert pianist. For instant justice *could* be achieved if enough people so willed.

A true passion for justice, then, must be radical—in short, it must at least wish to attain its goals radically and instantaneously. Leonard E. Read, founding president of the Foundation for Economic Education, expressed this radical spirit very aptly when he wrote a pamphlet, *I'd Push the Button*. The problem was what to do about the network of price and wage controls then being imposed on the economy by the Office of Price Administration. Most economic Liberals were timidly or "realistically" advocating one or another form of gradual or staggered decontrols; at that point, Mr. Read took an unequivocal and radical stand on principle: "if there were a button on this rostrum," he began his address, "the pressing of which would release all wage and price controls instantaneously, I would put my finger on it and push!"[1] The true test, then, of the radical spirit, is the button-pushing test: if we could push the button for instantaneous abolition of

---

[1]Leonard E. Read, *I'd Push the Button* (New York: Joseph D. McGuire, 1946), p. 3.

unjust invasions of liberty, would we do it? If we would not do it, we could scarcely call ourselves Libertarians, and most of us would only do it if primarily guided by a passion for justice.

The genuine Libertarian, then, is, in all senses of the word, an "abolitionist"; he would, if he could, abolish instantaneously all invasions of liberty, whether it be, in the original coining of the term, slavery, or whether it be the manifold other instances of State oppression. He would, in the words of another libertarian in a similar connection, "blister my thumb pushing that button!" The libertarian must perforce be a "button-pusher" and an "abolitionist." Powered by justice, he cannot be moved by amoral utilitarian pleas that justice not come about until the criminals are "compensated." Thus, when in the early nineteenth century, the great abolitionist movement arose, voices of moderation promptly appeared counselling that it would only be fair to abolish slavery if the slave masters were financially compensated for their loss. In short, after centuries of oppression and exploitation, the slave masters were supposed to be further rewarded by a handsome sum muleted by force from the mass of innocent taxpayers! The most apt comment on this proposal was made by the English philosophical radical Benjamin Pearson, who remarked that "he had thought it was the slaves who should have been compensated"; clearly, such compensation could only justly have come from the slaveholders themselves.[2]

Antilibertarians, and antiradicals generally, characteristically make the point that such "abolitionism" is "unrealistic;" by making such a charge they are hopelessly confusing the

---

[2]William D. Grampp, *The Manchester School of Economics* (Stanford, Calif.: Stanford University Press, 1960), p. 59.

desired goal with a strategic estimate of the probable out-
come. In framing principle, it is of the utmost importance not
to mix in strategic estimates with the forging of desired goals.
First, goals must be formulated, which, in this case, would be
the instant abolition of slavery or whatever other statist
oppression we are considering. And we must first frame these
goals without considering the probability of attaining them.
The libertarian goals are "realistic" in the sense that they *could*
be achieved if enough people agreed on their desirability, and
that, if achieved, they would bring about a far better world.
The "realism" of the goal can only be challenged by a critique
of the goal *itself*, not in the problem of how to attain it. Then,
after we have decided on the goal, we face the entirely separate
strategic question of how to attain that goal as rapidly as possible, how to build a movement to attain it, etc. Thus, William
Lloyd Garrison was not being "unrealistic" when, in the
1830s, he raised the glorious standard of immediate emancipa-
tion of the slaves. His goal was the proper one, and his strategic realism came in the fact that he did not expect his goal to
be quickly reached. Or, as Garrison himself distinguished:

> Urge immediate abolition as earnestly as we may, it will,
> alas! be gradual abolition in the end. We have never said
> that slavery would be overthrown by a single blow; that it
> ought to be, we shall always contend.[3]

Actually, in the realm of the strategic, raising the banner
of pure and radical principle is generally the fastest way of
arriving at radical goals. For if the pure goal is never brought
to the fore, there will never be any momentum developed for
driving toward it. Slavery would never have been abolished at
all if the abolitionists had not raised the hue and cry thirty

---

[3]Quoted in William H. and Jane H. Pease, eds., *The Antislavery Argument* (Indianapolis: Robbs-Merrill, 1965), p. xxxv.

years earlier; and, as things came to pass, the abolition was at virtually a single blow rather than gradual or compensated.[4] But above and beyond the requirements of strategy lie the commands of justice. In his famous editorial that launched *The Liberator* at the beginning of 1831, William Lloyd Garrison repented his previous adoption of the doctrine of gradual abolition:

> I seize this opportunity to make a full and unequivocal recantation, and thus publicly to ask pardon of my God, of my country, and of my brethren, the poor slaves, for having uttered a sentiment so full of timidity, injustice and absurdity.

Upon being reproached for the habitual severity and heat of his language, Garrison retorted: "I have need to be all on fire, for I have mountains of ice about me to melt." It is this spirit that must mark the man truly dedicated to the cause of liberty.[5]

---

[4]At the conclusion of a brilliant philosophical critique of the charge of "unrealism" and its confusion of the good and the currently probable, Professor Philbrook declares: "Only one type of serious defense of a policy is open to an economist or anyone else: he must maintain that the policy is good. True 'realism' is the same thing men have always meant by wisdom: to decide the immediate in the light of the ultimate." Clarence Philbrook, "'Realism' in Policy Espousal," *American Economic Review* (December, 1953): 859.

[5]For the quotes from Garrison, see Louis Ruchames, ed., *The Abolitionists* (New York: Capricorn Books, 1964), p. 31, and Fawn M. Brodie, "Who Defends the Abolitionist?" in Martin Duberman, ed., *The Antislavery Vanguard* (Princeton, N.J.: Princeton University Press, 1965), p. 67. The Duberman work is a storehouse of valuable material, including refutations of the common effort by those committed to the status quo to engage in psychological smearing of radicals in general and abolitionists in particular. See especially Martin Duberman, "The Northern Response to Slavery," in ibid., pp. 406–13.

16
FREEDOM, INEQUALITY, PRIMITIVISM, AND THE DIVISION OF LABOR

I.

If men were like ants, there would be no interest in human freedom. If individual men, like ants, were uniform, interchangeable, devoid of specific personality traits of their own, then who would care whether they were free or not? Who, indeed, would care if they lived or died? The glory of the human race is the uniqueness of each individual, the fact that every person, though similar in many ways to others, possesses a completely individuated personality of his own. It is the fact of each person's uniqueness—the fact that no two people can be wholly interchangeable—that makes each and every man irreplaceable and that makes us care whether he lives or dies, whether he is happy or oppressed. And, finally, it is the fact that these unique personalities need freedom for their full development that constitutes one of the major arguments for a free society.

Perhaps a world exists somewhere where intelligent beings are fully formed in some sort of externally determined cages, with no need for internal learning or choices by the individual beings themselves. But man is necessarily in a different situation. Individual human beings are not born or fashioned with fully formed knowledge, values, goals, or personalities; they must each form their own values and goals, develop their personalities, and learn about themselves and the world around them. Every man must have freedom, must have the scope to form, test, and act upon his own choices, for any sort of development of his own personality to take place. He must, in short, be free in order that he may be fully human. In a sense, even the most frozen and totalitarian civilizations and societies have allowed at least a modicum of scope for individual choice and development. Even the most monolithic of despotisms have had to allow at least a bit of "space" for freedom of choice, if only within the interstices of societal rules. The freer the society, of course, the less has been the interference with individual actions, and the greater the scope for the development of each individual. The freer the society, then, the greater will be the variety and the diversity among men, for the more fully developed will be every man's uniquely individual personality. On the other hand, the more despotic the society, the more restrictions on the freedom of the individual, the more uniformity there will be among men and the less the diversity, and the less developed will be the unique personality of each and every man. In a profound sense, then, a despotic society prevents its members from being fully human.[1]

-----

[1]On the interrelations between freedom, diversity, and the development of each individual, see the classic work of Wilhelm von Humboldt, *The Limits of State Action* (Cambridge: Cambridge University Press, 1969). On freedom as necessary for the development of individuality, see also Josiah Warren, *Equitable Commerce* (New York: Burt Franklin, 1965) and Stephen Pearl Andrews, *The Science of Society* (London: C.W. Daniel, 1913).

If freedom is a necessary condition for the full development of the individual, it is by no means the only requirement. Society itself must be sufficiently developed. No one, for example, can become a creative physicist on a desert island or in a primitive society. For, as an economy grows, the range of choice open to the producer and to the consumer proceeds to multiply greatly.[2] Furthermore, only a society with a standard of living considerably higher than subsistence can afford to devote much of its resources to improving knowledge and to developing a myriad of goods and services above the level of brute subsistence. But there is another reason that full development of the creative powers of each individual cannot occur in a primitive or undeveloped society, and that is the necessity for a wide-ranging division of labor.

No one can fully develop his powers in any direction without engaging in *specialization*. The primitive tribesman or peasant, bound to an endless round of different tasks in order to maintain himself, could have no time or resources available to pursue any particular interest to the full. He had no room to specialize, to develop whatever field he was best at or in which he was most interested. Two hundred years ago, Adam Smith pointed out that the developing division of labor is a key to the advance of any economy above the most primitive level. A necessary condition for any sort of developed economy, the division of labor is also requisite to the development of any sort of civilized society. The philosopher, the scientist, the builder, the merchant—none could develop these skills or

---

[2]The economists Bauer and Yamey cogently define economic development as "the widening of the range of alternatives open to people as consumers and as producers." Peter T. Bauer and Basil S. Yamey, *The Economics of Underdeveloped Countries* (Cambridge: Cambridge University Press, 1957), p. 151.

functions if he had had no scope for specialization. Furthermore, no individual who does not live in a society enjoying a wide range of division of labor can possibly employ his powers to the fullest. He cannot concentrate his powers in a field or discipline and advance that discipline and his own mental faculties. Without the opportunity to specialize in whatever he can do best, no person can develop his powers to the full; no man, then, could be fully human.

While a continuing and advancing division of labor is needed for a developed economy and society, the extent of such development at any given time limits the degree of specialization that any given economy can have. There is, therefore, no room for a physicist or a computer engineer on a primitive island; these skills would be premature within the context of that existing economy. As Adam Smith put it, "the division of labor is limited by the extent of the market." Economic and social development is therefore a mutually reinforcing process: the development of the market permits a wider division of labor, which in turn enables a further extension of the market.[3]

If the scope of the market and the extent of the division of labor are mutually reinforcing, so too are the division of labor and the diversity of individual interests and abilities among men. For just as an ever greater division of labor is needed to give full scope to the abilities and powers of each individual, so does the existence of that very division depend upon the innate diversity of men. For there would be no scope at all for a division of labor if every person were uniform and interchangeable. (A further condition of the emergence of a division of labor is the variety of natural resources;

---

[3]See George J. Stigler, "The Division of Labor is Limited by the Extent of the Market," *Journal of Political Economy* (June, 1951): 193.

specific land areas on the earth are also not interchangeable.) Furthermore, it soon became evident in the history of man that the market economy based on a division of labor was profoundly *cooperative*, and that such division enormously multiplied the productivity and hence the wealth of every person participating in the society. The economist Ludwig von Mises put the matter very clearly:

> Historically division of labor originates in two facts of nature: the inequality of human abilities and the variety of the external conditions of human life on the earth. These two facts are really one: the diversity of Nature, which does not repeat itself but creates the universe in infinite, inexhaustible variety. . . .
>
> These two conditions . . . are indeed such as almost to force the division of labor on mankind. Old and young, men and women cooperate by making appropriate use of their various abilities. Here also is the germ of the geographical division of labor; man goes to the hunt and woman to the spring to fetch water. Had the strength and abilities of all individuals and the external conditions of production been everywhere equal the idea of division of labor could never have arisen. . . . No social life could have arisen among men of equal natural capacity in a world which was geographically uniform. . . .
>
> Once labor has been divided, the division itself exercises a differentiating influence. The fact that labor is divided makes possible further cultivation of individual talent and thus cooperation becomes more and more productive. Through cooperation men are able to achieve what would have been beyond them as individuals. . . .
>
> The greater productivity of work under the division of labor is a unifying influence. It leads men to regard each other as comrades in a joint struggle for welfare, rather than as competitors in a struggle for existence.[4]

Freedom, then, is needed for the development of the individual, and such development also depends upon the extent

---

[4]Ludwig von Mises, *Socialism: An Economic and Sociological Analysis* (New Haven, Conn.: Yale University Press, 1951), pp. 292–95.

of the division of labor and the height of the standard of living. The developed economy makes room for, and encourages, an enormously greater specialization and flowering of the powers of the individual than can a primitive economy, and the greater the degree of such development, the greater the scope for each individual.

If freedom and the growth of the market are each important for the development of each individual and, therefore, to the flowering of diversity and individual differences, then so is there a causal connection between freedom and economic growth. For it is precisely freedom, the absence or limitation of interpersonal restrictions or interference, that sets the stage for economic growth and hence of the market economy and the developed division of labor. The Industrial Revolution and the corollary and consequent economic growth of the West were a product of its relative freedom for enterprise, for invention and innovation, for mobility and the advancement of labor. Compared to societies in other times and places, eighteenth- and nineteenth-century Western Europe and the United States were marked by a far greater social and economic freedom—a freedom to move, invest, work, and produce—secure from much harassment and interference by government. Compared to the role of government elsewhere, its role in these centuries in the West was remarkably minimal.[5]

By allowing full scope for investment, mobility, the division of labor, creativity, and entrepreneurship, the free economy

---

[5]Historians have been reminding us in recent decades that neither in England nor in the United States did government confine itself strictly to the ideal of laissez-faire. True enough; but we must compare this era to the role of government in earlier—and later—days to see the significance of the difference. Thus, cf. Karl Wittfogel, *Oriental Despotism* (New Haven, Conn.: Yale University Press, 1957).

thereby creates the conditions for rapid economic development. It is freedom and the free market, as Adam Smith well pointed out, that develop the "wealth of nations." Thus, freedom leads to economic development, and both of these conditions in turn multiply individual development and the unfolding of the powers of the individual man. In two crucial ways, then, freedom is the root; only the free man can be fully individuated and, therefore, can be fully human.

If freedom leads to a widening division of labor, and the full scope of individual development, it leads also to a growing population. For just as the division of labor is limited by the extent of the market, so is total population limited by total production. One of the striking facts about the Industrial Revolution has been not only a great rise in the standard of living for everyone, but also the viability of such ample living standards for an enormously larger population. The land area of North America was able to support only a million or so Indians five hundred years ago, and that at a barely subsistence level. Even if we wished to eliminate the division of labor, we could not do so without literally wiping out the vast majority of the current world population.

II.

We conclude that freedom and its concomitant, the widening division of labor, are vital for the flowering of each individual, as well as the literal survival of the vast bulk of the world's population. It must give us great concern, then, that over the past two centuries mighty social movements have sprung up which have been dedicated, at their heart, to the stamping out of all human differences, of all individuality.

It has become apparent in recent years, for example, that the heart of the complex social philosophy of Marxism does not lie, as it seemed to in the 1930s and 1940s, in Marxian economic doctrines: in the labor theory of value, in the familiar proposal for socialist state ownership of the means of production, and in the central planning of the economy and society. The economic theories and programs of Marxism are, to use a Marxian term, merely the elaborate "super-structure" erected on the inner core of Marxian aspiration. Consequently, many Marxists have, in recent decades, been willing to abandon the labor theory of value and even centralized socialist planning, as the Marxian economic theory has been increasingly abandoned and the practice of socialist planning shown to be unworkable. Similarly, the Marxists of the "New Left" in the United States and abroad have been willing to jettison socialist economic theory and practice. What they have *not* been willing to abandon is the philosophic heart of the Marxian ideal—not socialism or socialist planning, concerned anyway with what is supposed to be a temporary "stage" of development, but *communism* itself. It is the communist ideal, the ultimate goal of Marxism, that excites the contemporary Marxist, that engages his most fervent passions. The New Left Marxist has no use for Soviet Russia because the Soviets have clearly relegated the communist ideal to the remotest possible future. The New Leftist admires Che Guevara, Fidel Castro, Mao Tse-Tung not simply because of their role as revolutionaries and guerrilla leaders, but more because of their repeated attempts to leap into communism as rapidly as possible.[6]

Karl Marx was vague and cloudy in describing the communist ideal, let alone the specific path for attaining it. But

----

[6]The New Left, for example, ignored and scorned Marshall Tito despite his equally prominent role as Marxian revolutionary, guerrilla leader, and rebel against Soviet Russian dictation. The reason, as will be seen further below, is because Tito pioneered in shifting from Marxism toward an individualistic philosophy and a market economy.

one essential feature is the eradication of the division of labor. Contrary to current belief, Marx's now popular concept of "alienation" had little to do with a psychological sense of apartness or discontent. The heart of the concept was the individual's alienation from the product of labor. A worker, for example, works in a steel mill. Obviously, he himself will consume little or none of the steel he produces; he earns the value of his product in the shape of a money-commodity, and then he happily uses that money to buy whatever he chooses from the products of other people. Thus, A produces steel, B eggs, C shoes, etc., and then each exchanges them for products of the others through the use of money. To Marx this phenomenon of the market and the division of labor was a radical evil, for it meant that no one consumed any of *his own* product. The steelworker thus became "alienated" from his steel, the shoemaker from his shoes, etc.

The proper response to this "problem," it seems to me, is: So what? Why should anyone care about this sort of alienation? Surely the farmer, shoemaker, and steelworker are very happy to sell their product and exchange it for whatever products they desire; deprive them of this alienation and they would be most unhappy, as well as dying from starvation. For if the farmer were not allowed to produce more wheat or eggs than he himself consumes, or the shoemaker more shoes than he can wear, or the steelworker more steel than he can use, it is clear that the great bulk of the population would rapidly starve and the rest be reduced to a primitive subsistence, with life "nasty, brutish, and short."[7] But to Marx this

---

[7]It is difficult, of course, to see how intangible services could be produced at all without "alienation." How can a teacher teach, for example, if he is not allowed to "alienate" his teaching services by providing them to his students?

condition was the evil result of individualism and capitalism and had to be eradicated.

Furthermore, Marx was completely ignorant of the fact that each participant in the division of labor cooperates through the market economy, exchanging for each other's products and increasing the productivity and living standards of everyone. To Marx, any *differences* between men and, therefore, any specialization in the division of labor, is a "contradiction," and the communist goal is to replace that contradiction with harmony among all. This means that to the Marxist any individual differences, any diversity among men, are contradictions to be stamped out and replaced by the uniformity of the anthill. Friedrich Engels maintained that the emergence of the division of labor shattered the alleged classless harmony and uniformity of primitive society, and was responsible for the cleavage of society into separate and conflicting classes. Hence, for Marx and Engels, the division of labor must be eradicated in order to abolish class conflict and to usher in the ideal harmony of the "classless society," the society of total uniformity.[8]

Thus, Marx foresees his communist ideal only "after the enslaving subordination of individuals under division of labor, and therewith also the antithesis between mental and physical labor, has vanished."[9] To Marx the ideal communist society is one where, as Professor Gray puts it, "everyone must do everything." According to Marx in *The German Ideology*:

---

[8]Thus, see Alexander Gray, *The Socialist Tradition* (London: Longmans, Green, 1947), pp. 306, 328.

[9]Karl Marx, *Critique of the Gotha Programme* (New York: International Publishers, 1938), p. 10.

> In communist society, where nobody has one exclusive
> sphere of activity but each can become accomplished in any
> branch he wishes, society regulates the general production
> and thus makes it possible for me to do one thing today and
> another tomorrow, to hunt in the morning, fish in the after-
> noon, rear cattle in the evening, criticize after dinner, just
> as I have a mind, without ever becoming hunter, fisherman,
> shepherd, or critic.[10]

And the Marxist, August Bebel, consistently applied this
dilettantish notion to the role of women:

> At one moment a practical worker in some industry she is
> in the next hour educator, teacher, nurse; in the third part
> of the day she exercises some art or cultivates a science; and
> in the fourth part she fulfills some administrative func-
> tion.[11]

The concept of the *commune* in socialist thought takes on its
central importance precisely as a means of eradicating individual differences. It is not just that the commune owns all the
means of production among its members. Crucial to the
communal ideal is that every man takes on every function,
either all at once or in rapid rotation. Obviously, the commune has to subsist on no more than a primitive level, with
only a few common tasks, for this ideal to be achieved. Hence
the New Left commune, where every person is supposed to
take turns equally at every task; again, specialization is eradicated, and no one can develop his powers to the full. Hence
the current admiration for Cuba, which has attempted to
stress "moral" rather than economic incentives in production,

---

[10]Quoted in Gray, *The Socialist Tradition*, p. 328. Gray amusingly adds:
"A short weekend on a farm might have convinced Marx that the cattle
themselves might have some objection to being reared in this casual man -
ner, in the evening."

[11]August Bebel, in *Women and Socialism*, Meta L. Stern, trans. (New
York, 1910); quoted in Mises, *Socialism*, p. 190 n.2.

and which has established communes on the Isle of Pines. Hence the admiration for Mao, who has attempted to establish uniform urban and rural communes, and who recently sent several million students into permanent exile into the frontier agricultural areas, in order to eliminate the "contradiction between intellectual and physical labor."[12] Indeed, at the heart of the split between Russia and China is Russia's virtual abandonment of the communist ideal in the face of China's "fundamentalist" devotion to the original creed. The shared devotion to the commune also accounts for the similarities between the New Left, the Utopian socialists of the nineteenth century,[13] and the communist anarchists, a wing of anarchism that has always shared the communal ideal with the Marxists.[14]

The Communist would deny that his ideal society would suppress the personality of every man. On the contrary, freed from the confines of the division of labor, each person would fully develop all of his powers in every direction. Every man would be fully rounded in all spheres of life and work. As Engels put it in his *Anti-Dühring*, communism would give

---

[12]A recent news report disclosed that China has now softened its assault on intellectual labor. The policy of interchanging students and workers seems to have worked badly, and it has been found that "a lack of teachers and of technical training has hampered industrial development and production in recent years." Furthermore, "workers appear often to have been not tempered but softened by their exposure to a more sedentary life as many students, rather than finding life on the farm rewarding, fled China or killed themselves." Lee Lescase, "China Softens Attitude on Profs. School Policy," *The Washington Post* (July 23, 1970): A12.

[13]On the Utopian socialists, see Mises, *Socialism*, p. 168.

[14]It is probable that Mao's particular devotion to the communist ideal was influenced by his having been an anarchist before becoming a Marxist.

"each individual the opportunity to develop and exercise all his faculties, physical and mental, in all directions."[15] And Lenin wrote in 1920 of the "abolition of the division of labor among people . . . the education, schooling, and training of people with *an all-round development* and an all-round training, people *able* to do everything. Communism is marching and must march toward this goal, and *will reach it.*"[16]

This absurd ideal—of the man "able to do everything"—is only viable if (a) everyone does everything very badly, or (b) there are only a very few things to do, or (c) everyone is miraculously transformed into a superman. Professor Mises aptly notes that the ideal communist man is the dilettante, the man who knows a little of everything and does nothing well. For how can he develop *any* of his powers and faculties if he is prevented from developing any one of them to any sustained extent? As Mises says of Bebel's *Utopia*,

> Art and science are relegated to leisure hours. In this way, thinks Bebel, the society of the future "will possess scientists and artists of all kinds in countless numbers." These, according to their several inclinations, will pursue their studies and their arts in their spare time. . . . All mental work he regards as mere dilettantism. . . . But nevertheless we must inquire whether under these conditions the mind would be able to create that freedom without which it cannot exist.
>
> Obviously all artistic and scientific work which demands time, travel, technical education, and great material expenditure, would be quite out of the question.[17]

---

[15] Quoted in Gray, *The Socialist Tradition*, p. 328.

[16] Italics are Lenin's. V.I. Lenin, *Left-Wing Communism: An Infantile Disorder* (New York: International Publishers, 1940), p. 34.

[17] Mises, *Socialism*, p. 190.

Every person's time and energy on the earth are necessarily limited; hence, in order to develop *any* of his faculties to the full, he must specialize and concentrate on some rather than others. As Gray writes,

> That each individual should have the opportunity of developing *all* his faculties, physical and mental, in all directions, is a dream which will cheer the vision only of the simple-minded, oblivious of the restrictions imposed by the narrow limits of human life. For life is a series of acts of choice, and each choice is at the same time a renunciation. . . .
>
> Even the inhabitant of Engels's future fairyland will have to decide sooner or later whether he wishes to be Archbishop of Canterbury or First Sea Lord, whether he should seek to excel as a violinist or as a pugilist, whether he should elect to know all about Chinese literature or about the hidden pages in the life of the mackerel.[18]

Of course, one way to resolve this dilemma is to fantasize that the New Communist Man will be a superman. The Marxist, Karl Kautsky, asserted that in the future society "a new type of man will arise . . . a superman . . . an exalted man." Leon Trotsky prophesied that under communism:

> man will become incomparably stronger, wiser, finer. His body more harmonious, his movements more rhythmical, his voice more musical. . . . The human average will rise to the level of an Aristotle, a Goethe, a Marx. Above these other heights new peaks will arise.[19]

In recent years, communists have intensified their efforts to end the division of labor and reduce all individuals to uniformity. Fidel Castro's attempts to "build communism" in the Isle of Pines, and Mao Tse-Tung's Cultural Revolution, have been echoed in miniature by the American New Left in numerous attempts to form hippie communes and to create

---

[18]Gray, *The Socialist Tradition*, p. 328.

[19]Mises, *Socialism*, p. 164.

organizational "collectives" in which everyone does everything without benefit of specialization.[20] In contrast, Yugoslavia has been the quiet despair of the communist movement by moving rapidly in the opposite direction— toward ever-increasing freedom, individuality, and free-market operations—and has proved influential in leading the other "communist" countries of Eastern Europe (notably, Hungary and Czechoslovakia) in the same direction.[21]

III.

One way of gauging the extent of "harmonious" development of all of the individual's powers in the absence of

---

[20]Thus, one of the major criticisms of the New Left journal, *The Guardian*, by its rebellious split-off, *The Liberated Guardian*, was that the former functioned in the same way as any "bourgeois" staff, etc. The latter is run by a "collective" in which, assertedly, everyone does every task without specialization. The same criticism, along with the same solution, was applied by the women's caucus which confiscated the New Left weekly, *Rat*. Some of the "women's liberation" groups have been so extreme in the drive to extirpate individuality as to refuse to identify the names of individual members, writers, or spokesmen.

[21]Thus, a shock to orthodox communists throughout the world was the 1958 Program of the League of Communists of Yugoslavia, which declared that the individual's "personal interest . . . is the moving force of our social development. . . . The objectivity of the category of personal interest lies in the fact that [Yugoslav] socialism . . . cannot subject the personal happiness of man to any ulterior 'goals' or 'higher aims,' for the highest aim of socialism is the personal happiness of man." From *Kommunist* (Belgrade), August 8, 1963. Quoted in R.V. Burks, "Yugoslavia: Has Tito Gone Bourgeois?" *East Europe* (August, 1965): 2–14. Also see T. Peter Svennevig, "The Ideology of the Yugoslav Heretics," *Social Research* (Spring, 1960): 39–48. For attacks by orthodox communists, see Shih Tung-Hsiang, "The Degeneration of the Yugoslav Economy Owned by the Whole People," *Peking Review* (June 12, 1964): 11–16; and "Peaceful Transition from Socialism to Capitalism?" *Monthly Review* (March, 1964): 569–90.

specialization is to consider what actually happened during primitive or preindustrial eras. And, indeed, many socialists and other opponents of the Industrial Revolution exalt the primitive and preindustrial periods as a golden age of harmony, community, and social belonging—a peaceful and happy society destroyed by the development of individualism, the Industrial Revolution, and the market economy. In their exaltation of the primitive and the preindustrial, the socialists were perfectly anticipated by the reactionaries of the Romantic movement, those men who longed to roll back the tide of progress, individualism, and industry, and return to the supposed golden age of the preindustrial era. The New Left, in particular, also emphasizes a condemnation of technology and the division of labor, as well as a desire to "return to the earth" and an exaltation of the commune and the "tribe." As John W. Aldridge perceptively points out, the current New Left virtually constitutes a generational tribe that exhibits all the characteristics of a uniform and interchangeable herd, with little or no individuality among its members.[22]

Similarly, the early-nineteenth-century German reactionary, Adam Müller, denounced the:

> vicious tendency to divide labor in all branches of private industry. . . . [The] division of labor in large cities or industrial or mining provinces cuts up man, the completely free man, into wheels, rollers, spokes, shafts, etc., forces on him an utterly one-sided scope in the already one-sided field of the provisioning of one single want.[23]

---

[22]John W. Aldridge, *In the Country of the Young* (New York: Harper and Row, 1970).

[23]Quoted in Mises, *Socialism*, p. 304.

The leading French conservatives of the early nineteenth century, Louis de Bonald and Joseph Marie de Maistre, who idealized the feudal order, denounced the disruption by individualism of the preexisting social order and social cohesion.[24] The contemporary French reactionary, Jacques Ellul, in *The Technological Society*, a book much in favor on the New Left, condemns "our dehumanized factories, our unsatisfied senses . . . our estrangement from nature." In the Middle Ages, in contrast, claims Ellul, "Man sought open spaces . . . the possibility of moving about . . . of not constantly colliding with other people."[25] In the meanwhile, on the socialist side, the economic historian Karl Polanyi's influential *The Great Transformation* makes this thesis of the disruption of a previous social harmony by individualism, the market economy, and the division of labor the central theme of the book.

For its part, the worship of the primitive is a logical extension of the worship of the preindustrial. This worship by modern sophisticated intellectuals ranges from Rousseau's "noble savage" and the lionizing of that creature by the Romantic movement, all the way to the adoration of the Black Panthers by white intellectuals.[26] Whatever other pathology the worship of the primitive reflects, a basic part of it is a deep-seated hatred of individual diversity. Obviously, the more primitive and the less civilized a society, the less

---

[24]On the strong influence of these reactionary thinkers on the anti-individualism of nineteenth-century Marxists and socialists, see in particular Leon Bramson, *The Political Context of Sociology* (Princeton, N.J.: Princeton University Press, 1961), pp. 12–16 and passim.

[25]See the critique of Ellul in Charles Silberman, *The Myths of Automation* (New York: Harper and Row, 1966), pp. 104–05.

[26]Thus, see the perceptively satiric article by Tom Wolfe, "Radical Chic: That Party at Lenny's," *New York* (June 8, 1970).

diverse and individuated it can be.[27] Also part of this primitivism reflects a hatred for the intellect and its works, since the flowering of reason and intellection leads to diversity and inequality of individual achievement.

For the individual to advance and develop, reason and the intellect must be *active*, it must embody the individual's mind working upon and transforming the materials of reality. From the time of Aristotle, the classical philosophy presented man as only fulfilling himself, his nature, and his personality through purposive action upon the world. It is from such rational and purposive action that the works of civilization have developed. In contrast, the Romantic movement has always exalted the passivity of the child who, necessarily ignorant and immature, only reacts passively to his environment rather than acts to change it. This tendency to exalt passivity and the young, and to denigrate intellect, has reached its present embodiment in the New Left, which worships both youth *per se* and a passive attitude of ignorant and purposeless spontaneity. The passivity of the New Left, its wish to live simply and in "harmony" with "the earth" and the alleged rhythms of nature, harks back completely to the Rousseauist Romantic movement. Like the Romantic movement, it is a conscious rejection of civilization and differentiated men on behalf of the primitive, the ignorant, the herd-like "tribe."[28]

------

[27]This worship of the primitive permeates Polanyi's book, which at one point seriously applies the term "noble savage" to the Kaffirs of South Africa. Karl Polanyi, *The Great Transformation* (Boston, Mass.: Beacon Press, 1957), p. 157.

[28]Both the passive and the tribal aspects of New Left culture were embodied in its ideal of the "Woodstock Nation," in which hundreds of thousands of herd-like, undifferentiated youth wallowed passively in the mud listening to their tribal ritual music.

If reason, purpose, and action are to be spurned, then what replaces them in the Romantic pantheon are unanalyzed, spontaneous "feelings." And since the range of feelings is relatively small compared to intellectual achievements, and in any case is not objectively known to another person, the emphasis on feelings is another way to iron out diversity and inequality among individuals.

Irving Babbitt, a keen critic of Romanticism, wrote about the Romantic movement:

> The whole movement is filled with the praise of ignorance and of those who still enjoy its inappreciable advantages— the savage, the peasant and above all the child. The Rousseauist may indeed be said to have discovered the poetry of childhood . . . but at what would seem at times a rather heavy sacrifice of rationality. Rather than consent to have the bloom taken off things by analysis one should, as Coleridge tells us, sink back to the devout state of childlike wonder. However, to grow ethically is not to sink back but to struggle painfully forward. To affirm the contrary is to proclaim one's inability to mature. . . . [The Romantic] is ready to assert that what comes to the child spontaneously is superior to the deliberate moral effort of the mature man. The speeches of all the sages are, according to Maeterlinck, outweighed by the unconscious wisdom of the passing child.[29]

Another perceptive critique of Romanticism and primitivism was written by Ludwig von Mises. He notes that "the whole tribe of romantics" have denounced specialization and the division of labor. "For them the man of the past who developed his powers 'harmoniously' is the ideal: an ideal

---

[29]Irving Babbitt, *Rousseau and Romanticism* (New York: Meridian Books, 1955), pp. 53–54. The New Left's emphasis on passivity, primitivism, the irrational, and the dissolution of individuality may account for the current popularity of Taoist and Buddhist philosophy. See ibid., pp. 297ff.

which alas no longer inspires our degenerate age. They rec-
ommend retrogression in the division of labor" with the
socialists surpassing their fellow Romantics in this regard.[30]
But are primitives or preindustrial men privileged to develop
themselves freely and harmoniously? Mises answers:

> It is futile to look for the harmoniously developed man at
> the outset of economic evolution. The almost self-sufficient
> economic subject as we know him in the solitary peasant of
> remote valleys shows none of that noble, harmonious devel-
> opment of body, mind, and feeling which the romantics
> ascribe to him. Civilization is a product of leisure and the
> peace of mind that only the division of labor can make possi-
> ble. Nothing is more false than to assume that man first
> appeared in history with an independent individuality and
> that only during the evolution [of society] . . . did he lose . . .
> his spiritual independence. All history, evidence and obser-
> vation of the lives of primitive peoples is directly contrary
> to this view. Primitive man lacks all individuality in our
> sense. Two South Sea Islanders resemble each other far
> more closely than two twentieth-century Londoners. Per-
> sonality was not bestowed upon man at the outset. It has
> been acquired in the course of evolution of society.[31]

Or we may note Charles Silberman's critique of Jacques
Ellul's rhapsodies on the "traditional rhythms of life and
nature" lived by preindustrial man, as compared to "dehumanized factories . . . our estrangement from nature." Silberman asks:

> But with what shall we contrast this dehumanized world?
> The beautiful, harmonious life being lived by, say, the Chi-
> nese or Vietnamese peasant woman, who works in the fields
> close to nature, for twelve hours a day—roughly the condi-
> tions under which the great bulk of women (and men) have
> worked . . . through all of human history? For this is the
> condition that Ellul idealizes.

---

[30]Mises, *Socialism*, p. 304.

[31]Ibid., p. 305.

And, as for Ellul's paean to the Middle Ages as being mobile, spacious, and uncrowded:

> This would have been startling news to the medieval peasant, who lived with his wife and children, other relatives, and probably animals as well in a one-room thatched cottage. And even for the nobility, was there really more possibility of "moving about" in the Middle Ages, when travel was by foot or hoof, than today, when steelworkers spend sabbaticals in Europe?[32]

The savage is supposed not only to be "noble" but also supremely happy. From the Rousseauans to what Erich Fromm has called "the infantile Paradise" of Norman O. Brown and Herbert Marcuse, the Romantics have extolled the happiness yielded by the spontaneous and the childlike. To Aristotle and the classic philosophers, happiness was *acting* in accordance with man's unique and rational nature. To Marcuse, any purposive, rational action is by definition "repressive," to which he contrasts the "liberated" state of spontaneous play. Aside from the universal destitution that the proposed abolition of work would bring, the result would be a profound *un*happiness, for no individual would be able to fulfill himself, his individuality, or his rational faculties. Diversity and individuality would largely disappear, for in a world of "polymorphous" play everyone would be virtually alike.

If we consider the supposed happiness of primitive man, we must also consider that his life was, in the famous phrase of Hobbes, "nasty, brutish, and short." There were few medical aids against disease; there were none against famine, for in a world cut off from interregional markets and barely above subsistence any check to the local food supply will decimate the population. Fulfilling the dreams of Romantics, the

---

[32]Silberman, *The Myths of Automation*, pp. 104–05.

primitive tribe is a passive creature of its given environment and has no means for acting to overcome and transform it. Hence, when the local food supply within an area is depleted, the "happy-go-lucky" tribe dies *en masse*.

Furthermore, we must realize that the primitive faces a world which he cannot understand, since he has not engaged in much of a rational, scientific inquiry into its workings. *We* know what a thunderstorm is, and therefore take rational measures against it; but the savage does not know, and therefore surmises that the God of Thunder is displeased with him and must be propitiated with sacrifices and votive offerings. Since the savage has only a limited concept of a world knit together by natural law (a concept which employs reason and science), he believes that the world is governed by a host of capricious spirits and demons, each of which can only be propitiated by ritual or magic, and by a priest-craft of witch doctors who specialize in their propitiation.[33] The renaissance of astrology and similar mystic creeds on the New Left marks a reversion to such primitive forms of magic. So fearful is the savage, so bound is he by irrational taboo and by the custom of his tribe, that he cannot develop his individuality.

If tribal custom crippled and repressed the development of each individual, then so too did the various caste systems and

---

[33]Neither is the magic used by primitive tribes any evidence of superior, "idealistic," as opposed to this worldly, "materialistic," ends. On the contrary, the magic rites were unsound and erroneous means by which the tribes hoped to attain such materialistic ends as a good harvest, rainfall, etc. Thus, the Cargo Cult of New Guinea, on observing Europeans obtaining food from overseas by sending away scraps of paper, imitated the Europeans by writing ritualistic phrases on slips of paper and sending them out to sea, after which they waited for cargoes from overseas. Cf. Ludwig von Mises, *Epistemological Problems of Economics* (Princeton,N.J.: D. Van Nostrand, 1960), pp. 62–66, 102–05.

networks of restriction and coercion in preindustrial societies that forced everyone to follow the hereditary footsteps of his father's occupation. Each child knew from birth that he was doomed to tread where his ancestors had gone before him, regardless of ability or inclination to the contrary. The "social harmony," the "sense of belonging," supplied by mercantilism, by the guilds, or by the caste system, provided such contentment that its members left the throes of the system when given an opportunity. Given the freedom to choose, the tribesmen abandon the bosom of their tribe to come to the freer, "atomistic" cities looking for jobs and opportunity. It is curious, in fact, that those Romantics who yearn to restore the mythical golden age of caste and status refuse to allow each individual the freedom to choose between market on the one hand, or caste and tribal commune on the other. Invariably, the new golden age has to be imposed by coercion.

Is it, indeed, a coincidence that the natives of undeveloped countries, when given a chance, invariably abandon their "folk culture" on behalf of Western ways, living standards, and "Coca-Colaization?" Within a few years, for example, the people of Japan were delighted to abandon their centuries-old traditional culture and folkways, and turn to the material achievements and market economy of the West. Primitive tribes, too, given a chance, are eager to differentiate and develop a market economy, to shed their stagnant "harmony" and replace their magic by knowledge of discovered law. The eminent anthropologist, Bronislaw Malinowski, pointed out that primitives use magic only to cover those areas of nature of which they are ignorant; in those areas where they have come to understand the natural processes at work, magic is, quite sensibly, not employed.[34]

---

[34]Bronislaw Malinowski, *Magic, Science, Religion, and Other Essays* (New York: Doubleday Anchor Books, 1955), pp. 27–31.

A particularly striking example of the eager development of a pervasive market economy among primitive tribesmen is the largely unheralded case of West Africa.[35] And Bernard Siegel has pointed out that when, as among the Panajachel of Guatemala, a primitive society becomes large and technologically and societally complex, a market economy inevitably accompanies this growth, replete with specialization, competition, cash purchases, demand and supply, prices and costs, etc.[36]

There is thus ample evidence that even primitive tribesmen themselves are not fond of their primitivism and take the earliest opportunity to escape from it; the main stronghold of love for primitivism seems to rest among the decidedly nonprimitive Romantic intellectuals.

Another primitivistic institution that has been hailed by many social scientists is the system of the "extended family," a harmony and status supposedly ruptured by the individualistic "nuclear family" of the modern West. Yet, the extended family system has been responsible for crippling the creative

---

[35]See the inspiring discussion in Peter T. Bauer, *West African Trade* (Cambridge: Cambridge University Press, 1954).

[36]Bernard J. Siegel, "Review of Melville J. Hershkovits, "Economic Anthropology," *American Economic Review* (June, 1953): 402. On Bauer and Yamey, *The Economics of Underdeveloped Countries*, p. 67 n.1. Also see Raymond Firth, *Human Types* (New York: Mentor Books, 1958), p. 122; Sol Tax, *Penny Capitalism: A Guatemalan Indian Economy* (Washington, D.C.: U.S. Government Printing Office, 1953); and Raymond Firth and Basil S. Yamey, eds., *Capital, Saving, and Credit in Peasant Societies* (Chicago, Ill.: Aldine, 1963).

On the responsiveness of African natives to market economic incentives, see (in addition to Bauer, *West African Trade*), Peter Kilby, "African Labour Productivity Reconsidered," *Economic Journal* (June, 1961): 273–91.

and productive individual as well as repressing economic development. Thus, West African development has been impeded by the extended family concept that, if one man prospers, he is duty bound to share this bounty with a host of relatives, thus draining off the reward for his productivity and crippling his incentive to succeed, while encouraging the relatives to live idly on the family dole. And neither do the productive members of the tribe seem very happy about this supposedly harmonious societal bond. Professor Bauer points out that:

> many admit in private discussion that they dread these extensive obligations. . . . The fear of the obligations of the family system is partly responsible for the widespread use of textiles and trinkets as outlets for savings, in preference to more productive forms of investment which are more likely to attract the attention of relatives.

And many Africans distrust banks, "fearing that they may disclose the size of their accounts to members of their families. They, therefore, prefer to keep their savings under the fireplace or buried in the ground."[37]

In fact, the primitive community, far from being happy, harmonious, and idyllic, is much more likely to be ridden by mutual suspicion and envy of the more successful or better-favored, an envy so pervasive as to cripple, by the fear of its presence, all personal or general economic development. The German sociologist Helmut Schoeck, in his important

---

[37]Bauer, *West African Trade*, p. 8. Also see Bauer and Yamey, *The Economics of Underdeveloped Countries*, pp. 64–67. Similarly, Professor S. Herbert Frankel reports on how West Africans habitually wait at entrances of banks to fall upon their relatives to demand money as they leave. Any man who accumulates money must go to great lengths to deceive his relatives on his actual status. Cited in Helmut Schoeck, *Envy: A Theory of Social Behavior* (New York: Harcourt, Brace and World, 1970), pp. 59–60.

work on *Envy*, cites numerous studies of this pervasive crippling effect. Thus the anthropologist Clyde Kluckhohn found among the Navaho the absence of any concept of "personal success" or "personal achievement"; any such success was automatically attributed to exploitation of others, and, therefore, the more prosperous Navaho Indian feels himself under constant social pressure to give his money away. Allan Holmberg found that the Siriono Indian of Bolivia eats alone at night because, if he eats by day, a crowd gathers around him to stare in envious hatred. The result among the Siriono is that, in reaction to this pervasive pressure, no one will voluntarily share food with anybody. Sol Tax found that envy and fear of envy in "a small community where all neighbors watch and where all are neighbors" accounted for the unprogressiveness, the slowness of change toward a productive economy among the Indians of Guatemala. And when a tribe of Pueblo Indians showed the beginnings of specialization and the division of labor, the envy of their fellow tribesmen impelled them to take measures to end this process, including physical destruction of the property of those who seemed in any way better off than their fellows.

Oscar Lewis discovered an extremely pervasive fear of the envy of others in a Mexican Indian village, a fear producing intense secretiveness. Wrote Lewis:

> The man who speaks little, keeps his affairs to himself, and maintains some distance between himself and others has less chance of creating enemies or of being criticized or envied. A man does not generally discuss his plans to buy or sell or take a trip.[38]

---

[38]The works cited are Clyde Kluckhohn, *The Navaho* (Cambridge, Mass.: Harvard University Press, 1946), and *Navaho Witchcraft* (Boston: Beacon Press, 1967); Allan R. Holmberg, *Nomads of the Long Bow: The Siriono of Eastern Bolivia* (Washington, D.C.: U.S. Government Printing

Professor Schoeck comments:

> it is difficult to envisage what it means for the economic and technical development of a community when, almost automatically and as a matter of principle, the future dimension is banned from human intercourse and conversation, when it cannot even be discussed. Ubiquitous envy, fear of it and those who harbor it, cuts off such people from any kind of communal action directed towards the future. . . . All striving, all preparation and planning for the future can be undertaken only by socially fragmented, secretive beings.[39]

Furthermore, in this Mexican village no one will warn or tell anyone else of imminent danger to the other's property; there is no sense of human social solidarity whatsoever.

Among the Indians of Aritama in Colombia, the Reichel-Dolmatoffs reported:

> Every individual lives in constant fear of the magical aggression of others, and the general social atmosphere in the village is one of mutual suspicion, of latent danger, and hidden hostility, which pervades every aspect of life. The most immediate reason for magical aggression is envy. Anything that might be interpreted as a personal advantage over others is envied: good health, economic assets, good physical appearance, popularity, a harmonious family life, a new dress. All these and other aspects imply prestige, and with it power and authority over others. Aggressive magic is, therefore, intended to prevent or to destroy this power and to act as a levelling force.[40]

Office, 1950); Sol Tax, "Changing Consumption in Indian Guatemala," *Economic Development and Cultural Change* (1957); and Oscar Lewis, *Life in a Mexican Village: Tepoztlan Restudied* (Urbana: University of Illinois Press, 1951). See Schoeck, *Envy*, pp. 26–61.

[39]Ibid., p. 50.

[40]From Gerardo and Alicia Reichel-Dolmatoff, *The People of Aritama: The Cultural Personality of a Colombian Mestizo Village* (Chicago: University of Chicago Press, 1961), p. 396. Quoted in Schoeck, *Envy*, pp. 51–52.

The Reichel-Dolmatoffs also noted that if one member of a group in Aritama should work faster or better than his fellows, his place of work is marked with a cross before he arrives the next morning, and his envious colleagues pray to God to make this more able worker slow and tired.

Finally, Watson and Samora found that the major reason for the failure of a group of lower-class Spanish-speaking citizens of a mountain township in southern Colorado to rise into parity with the upper-class Anglo community, was the bitter envy of the Spanish group toward any of their number who managed to rise upward. Anyone who works his way upward is regarded as a man "who has sold himself to the Anglos," "who has climbed on the backs of his people."[41]

The anthropologist Eric Wolf has even coined the term "institutionalized envy" to describe such pervasive institutions, including the practice and fear of black magic in these primitive societies.[42] Schoeck notes:

> *Institutionalized envy* . . . or the ubiquitous fear of it, means that there is little possibility of individual economic advancement and no contact with the outside world through which the community might hope to progress. No one dares to show anything that might lead people to think he was better off. Innovations are unlikely. Agricultural methods remain traditional and primitive, to the detriment of the whole village, because every deviation from previous practice comes up against the limitations set by envy.[43]

---

[41]James B. Watson and Julian Samora, "Subordinate Leadership in a Bicultural Community: An Analysis," *American Sociological Review* 19, no. 4 (August, 1954): 413–21.

[42]Eric R. Wolf, "Types of Latin American Peasantry: A Preliminary Discussion," *American Anthropoligist* 57, no. 3 (June, 1955): 460.

[43]Schoeck, *Envy*, p. 47.

And Schoeck aptly concludes:

> There is nothing to be seen here of the close community which allegedly exists among primitive peoples in pre-afflu-ent times—the poorer, it is held, the greater the sense of community. Sociological theory would have avoided many errors if those phenomena had been properly observed and evaluated a century ago. The myth of a golden age, when social harmony prevailed because each man had about as lit-tle as the next one, the warm and generous community spirit of simple societies, was indeed for the most part just a myth, and social scientists should have known better than to fashion out of it a set of utopian standards with which to criticize their own societies.[44]

In sum, Ludwig von Mises's strictures against Romanti-cism do not seem to be overdrawn:

> Romanticism is man's revolt against reason, as well as against the condition under which nature has compelled him to live. The romantic is a daydreamer; he easily man-ages in imagination to disregard the laws of logic and nature. The thinking and rationally acting man tries to rid himself of the discomfort of unsatisfied wants by economic action and work; he produces in order to improve his posi-tion. The romantic . . . imagines the pleasures of success but he does nothing to achieve them. He does not remove the obstacles; he merely removes them in imagination. . . . He hates work, economy, and reason.
>
> The romantic takes all the gifts of a social civilization for granted and desires, in addition, everything fine and beau-tiful that, as he thinks, distant times and creatures had or have to offer. Surrounded by the comforts of European town life he longs to be an Indian rajah, bedouin, corsair, or troubadour. But he sees only that portion of these people's lives which seems pleasant to him. . . . The perilous nature of their existence, the comparative poverty of their circum-stances, their miseries and their toil—these things his imag-ination tactfully overlooks: all is transfigured by a rosy gleam. Compared with this dream ideal, reality appears arid and shallow. There are obstacles to overcome which do not

---

[44]Ibid., p. 31.

exist in the dream. . . . Here there is work to do, ceaselessly,
assiduously. . . . Here one must plough and sow if one wishes
to reap. The romantic does not choose to admit all this.
Obstinate as a child, he refuses to recognize it. He mocks
and jeers; he despises and loathes the bourgeois.[45]

The Romantic, or primitivist, attitude was also brilliantly
criticized by the Spanish philosopher, Ortega y Gasset:

> it is possible to have peoples who are perennially primitive
> . . . those who have remained in the motionless, frozen twi-
> light, which never progresses towards midday.
>
> This is what happens in the world which is mere Nature.
> But it does not happen in the world of civilization which is
> ours. Civilization is not "just there," it is not self-support-
> ing. It is artificial. . . . If you want to make use of the advan-
> tages of civilization, but are not prepared to concern your-
> self with the upholding of civilization—you are done. In a
> trice you find yourself left without civilization. . . . The
> primitive forest appears in its native state. . . . The jungle is
> always primitive and, vice versa, everything primitive is
> mere jungle.[46]

Ortega adds that the type of man he sees rising to the fore,
the modern "mass-man," "believes that the civilization into
which he was born and which he makes use of, is as spontaneous and self-producing as Nature." But the mass-man, the
herd-man, is also characterized by his desire to stamp out
those individuals who differ from the mass: "The mass . . .
does not wish to share life with those who are not of it. It has
a deadly hatred of all that is not itself."[47]

---

[45]Mises, *Socialism*, pp. 463–64. See also José Ortega y Gasset, *The
Revolt of the Masses* (New York: W.W. Norton, 1932), pp. 63–65.

[46]Ibid., p. 97.

[47]Ibid., pp. 84, 98. For Ortega, the great looming danger is that the
mass-man will increasingly use the State to "crush beneath it any creative
minority which disturbs it—disturbs it in any order of things: in politics,
in ideas, in industry." Ibid., p. 133.

IV.

The Left, of course, does not couch its demands in terms of stamping out diversity; what it seeks to achieve sounds semantically far more pleasant: *equality*. It is in the name of equality that the Left seeks all manner of measures, from progressive taxation to the ultimate stage of communism.

But what, philosophically, *is* "equality"? The term must not be left unanalyzed and accepted at face value. Let us take three entities: A, B, and C. A, B, and C are said to be "equal" to each other (that is, A = B = C) if a particular characteristic is found in which the three entities are uniform or identical. In short, here are three individual men: A, B, and C. Each may be similar in some respects but different in others. If each of them is precisely 5 feet 10 inches in height, they are then *equal* to each other *in height*. It follows from our discussion of the concept of equality that A, B, and C can be *completely* "equal" to each other only if they are identical or uniform in *all* characteristics—in short, if all of them are, like the same size of nut or bolt, completely interchangeable. We see, then, that the ideal of human equality *can only* imply total uniformity and the utter stamping out of individuality.

It is high time, then, for those who cherish freedom, individuality, the division of labor, and economic prosperity and survival, to stop conceding the supposed nobility of the ideal of equality. Too often have "conservatives" conceded the ideal of equality only to cavil at its "impracticality." Philosophically, there can be no divorce between theory and practice. Egalitarian measures do not "work" because they violate the basic nature of man, of what it means for the individual man to be truly human. The call of "equality" is a siren song that can only mean the destruction of all that we cherish as being human.

It is ironic that the term, "equality," brings its favorable connotation to us from a past usage that was radically different. For the concept of equality achieved its widespread popularity during the classical-liberal movements of the eighteenth century, when it meant, *not* uniformity of status or income, but freedom for each and every man, without exception. In short, equality in those days meant the libertarian and individualist concept of full liberty for all persons. Thus, the biochemist Roger Williams correctly points out that the

> "free and equal" phrase in the Declaration of Independence was an unfortunate paraphrase of a better statement contained in the Virginia Bill of Rights . . . "all men are by nature equally free and independent." In other words, men can be equally free without being uniform.[48]

This libertarian credo was formulated with particular cogency by Herbert Spencer in his "Law of Equal Liberty" as the suggested fundamental core of his social philosophy:

> man's happiness can be obtained only by the exercise of his faculties. . . . But the fulfillment of this duty necessarily presupposes freedom of action. Man cannot exercise his faculties without certain scope. He must have liberty to go and to come, to see, to feel, to speak, to work; to get food, raiment, shelter, and to provide for each and all the needs of his nature. . . . To exercise his faculties he must have liberty

---

[48]Roger J. Williams, *Free and Unequal: The Biological Basis of Individual Liberty* (Austin: University of Texas Press, 1953), pp. 4–5. Williams adds:

> Does not our love of liberty, which seems to be inherent in all of us, rest squarely upon our *in*equalities? If at birth we all possessed the same potential tastes . . . would we care about being free to pursue them as we individually desire? . . . It seems to be clear that the idea of freedom arose directly out of this human variability. If we were all alike there would seem to be no reason for wanting freedom; "living my own life" would be an empty, meaningless expression. (pp. 5, 12)

to do all that his faculties actually impel him to do. . . . Therefore, he has a *right* to that liberty. This, however, is not the right of one but all. All are endowed with faculties. All are bound to . . . [exercise] them. All, therefore, must be free to do those things in which the exercise of them consists. That is, all must have rights to liberty of action.

And hence there necessarily arises a limitation. For if men have like claims to that freedom which is needful for the exercise of their faculties, then must the freedom of each be bounded by the similar freedom of all. . . . Wherefore we arrive at the general proposition, that every man may claim the fullest liberty to exercise his faculties compatible with the possession of like liberty by every other man.[49]

Thus, only the specific case of equality of *liberty*—the older view of human equality—is compatible with the basic nature of man. Equality of *condition* would reduce humanity to an anthill existence. Fortunately, the individuated nature of man, allied to the geographical diversity on the earth, makes the ideal of total equality unattainable. But an enormous amount of damage—the crippling of individuality, as well as economic and social destruction—could be generated in the attempt.

Let us turn from equality to the concept of inequality, the condition that exists when every man is *not* identical to every other in all characteristics. It is evident that inequality flows inevitably out of specialization and the division of labor. Therefore, a free economy will lead not only to diversity of occupation, with one man a baker, another an actor, a third a civil engineer, etc., but specific *in*equalities will also emerge in

---

[49]Herbert Spencer, *Social Statics* (London: John Chapman, 1851), pp. 76–78. In the remainder of the book, Spencer spins out the concrete implications of his basic principle. For a critique of the *Law of Equal Liberty*, see Murray N. Rothbard, *Power and Market* (Menlo Park, Calif.: Institute for Humane Studies, 1970), pp. 159–60.

monetary income and in status and scope of control within each occupation. Each person will, in the free-market economy, tend to earn a monetary income equal to the value placed upon his productive contribution in satisfying the desires and demands of the consumers. In economic terminology each man will tend to earn an income equal to his "marginal productivity," to his particular productivity in satisfying consumer demands. Clearly, in a world of developed individual diversity, some men will be more intelligent, others more alert and far-sighted, than the remainder of the population. Still others, meanwhile, will be more interested in those areas reaping greater monetary gain; those who succeed at wildcatting of crude oil will reap greater monetary rewards than those who remain in secretarial jobs.

Many intellectuals are wont to denounce the "unfairness" of the market in granting a far higher monetary income to a movie star than, say, a social worker, in that way rewarding "material" far more than "spiritual" values and treating "better" people unfairly. Without going into the peculiar usage of such terms as "spiritual" and "material," it strikes one that if the social worker's alleged "goodness" indeed resides in her "spirituality," then it is surely inappropriate and inconsistent to demand that she receive more of the "material" amenities (money) *vis à vis* the movie star. In the free society, those who are capable of providing goods and services that the consumers value and are willing to purchase, will receive precisely what the consumers are willing to spend. Those who persist in entering lower-priced occupations, either because they prefer the work or because they are not sufficiently capable in the higher-paid fields, can scarcely complain when they earn a lower salary.

If, then, *in*equality of income is the inevitable corollary of freedom, then so too is inequality of control. In *any* organization, whether it be a business firm, a lodge, or a bridge club, there will always be a minority of people who will rise to the position of leaders and others who will remain as followers in the rank and file. Robert Michels discovered this as one of the great laws of sociology, "The Iron Law of Oligarchy." In every organized activity, no matter the sphere, a small number will become the "oligarchical" leaders and the others will follow.

In the market economy, the leaders, being more productive in satisfying the consumers, will inevitably earn more money than the rank and file. Within other organizations, the difference will only be that of control. But, in either case, ability and interest will select those who rise to the top. The best and most dedicated steel producer will rise to the leadership of the steel corporation; the ablest and most energetic will tend to rise to leadership in the local bridge club; and so on.

This process of ability and dedication finding its own level works best and most smoothly, it is true, in institutions such as business firms in the market economy. For here every firm places itself under the discipline of monetary profits and income earned by selling a suitable product to the consumers. If managers or workers fall down on the job, a loss of profits provides a very rapid signal that something is wrong and that these producers must mend their ways. In nonmarket organizations, where profit does not provide a test of efficiency, it is far easier for other qualities extraneous to the actual activity to play a role in selecting the members of the oligarchy. Thus, a local bridge club may select its leaders, not only for ability and dedication to the activities of the club, but also for extraneous racial or physical characteristics preferred by the membership. This situation is far less likely where monetary losses will be incurred by yielding to such external factors.

We need only look around us at every human activity or organization, large or small, political, economic, philanthropic, or recreational, to see the universality of the Iron Law of Oligarchy. Take a bridge club of fifty members and, regardless of legal formalities, a half-dozen or so will really be running the show. Michels, in fact, discovered the Iron Law by observing the rigid, bureaucratic, oligarchic rule that pervaded the Social Democratic parties in Europe in the late nineteenth century, even though these parties were supposedly dedicated to equality and the abolition of the division of labor.[50] And it is precisely the obviously frozen inequality of income and power, and the rule by oligarchy, that has totally disillusioned the equality-seeking New Left in the Soviet Union. No one lionizes Brezhnev or Kosygin.

It is the egalitarian attempt by the New Left to escape the Iron Law of inequality and oligarchy that accounts for its desperate efforts to end elite leadership within its own organizations. (Certainly there has been no indication of any disappearance of the power elite in oft-heralded Cuba or China.) The early drive toward egalitarianism in the New Left emerged in the concept of "participatory democracy." Instead of the members of an organization electing an elite leadership, so the theory ran, each person would participate equally in all of the organization's decisionmaking. It was, by the way, probably this *sense* of direct and intense participation by each individual that accounted for the heady enthusiasm of the masses in the very early stages of the revolutionary regimes in Soviet Russia and Cuba—an enthusiasm that quickly waned as the inevitable oligarchy began to take control and mass participation to die.

---

[50]Robert Michels, *Political Parties* (Glencoe, Ill.: Free Press, 1949). See also the brilliant work by Gaetano Mosca, *The Ruling Class* (New York: McGraw-Hill, 1939), which focuses on the inevitability of a minority "ruling class" wielding power in government.

While the would-be participatory democrats have made keen criticisms of bureaucratic rule in our society, the concept itself, when applied, runs rapidly against the Iron Law. Thus, anyone who has sat through sessions of any organization engaged in participatory democracy knows the intense boredom and inefficiency that develop rapidly. For if each person must participate equally in all decisions, the time devoted to decision-making must become almost endless, and the processes of the organization become life itself for the participants. This is one of the reasons why many New Left organizations quickly begin to insist that their members live in communes and dedicate their entire lives to the organization—in effect, to merge their lives with the organization. For if they truly live and pursue participatory democracy, they can hardly do anything else. But despite this attempt to salvage the concept, the inevitable gross inefficiency and aggravated boredom ensure that all but the most intensely dedicated will abandon the organization. In short, if it can work at all, participatory democracy can work only in groups so tiny that they are, in effect, the "leaders" shorn of their following.

We conclude that, to succeed, any organization must eventually fall into the hands of specialized "professionals," or a minority of persons dedicated to its tasks and able to carry them out. Oddly enough, it was Lenin who, despite his lip service to the ultimate ideal of egalitarian communism, recognized that a revolution, too, in order to succeed, must be led by a minority, a "vanguard," of dedicated professionals.

It is the intense egalitarian drive of the New Left that accounts, furthermore, for its curious theory of education—a theory that has made such an enormous impact on the contemporary student movement in American universities in recent years. The theory holds that, in contrast to "old-fashioned" concepts of education, the teacher knows *no more* than any of his students. All, then, are "equal" in condition; one is no better in any sense than any other. Since only an imbecile would actually proclaim that the student knows as much about the content of any given discipline as his professor, this claim of equality is sustained by arguing for the abolition of content in the classroom. This content, asserts the New Left, is "irrelevant" to the student and hence not a proper part of the educational process. The only proper subject for the classroom is not a body of truths, not assigned readings or topics, but open-ended, free-floating participatory discussion of the student's feelings, since only his feelings are truly "relevant" to the student. And since the lecture method implies, of course, that the lecturing professor knows more than the students to whom he imparts knowledge, the lecture too must go. Such is the caricature of "education" propounded by the New Left.

One question that this doctrine calls to mind, and one that the New Left has never really answered, of course, is *why* the students should then be in college to begin with. Why couldn't they just as well achieve these open-ended discussions of their feelings at home or at the neighborhood candy store? Indeed, on this educational theory, the school as such has no particular function; it *becomes*, in effect, the local candy store, and it, too, merges with life itself. But then, again, why have a school at all? And why, in fact, should the students pay tuition and the faculty receive a salary for their nonexistent services? If all are truly equal, why is the faculty alone paid?

In any case, the emphasis on feelings rather than rational content in courses again insures an egalitarian school; or rather, the school as such may disappear, but the "courses" would surely be egalitarian, for if only "feelings" are to be discussed, then surely everyone's feelings are approximately "equal" to everyone else's. Allow reason, intellect, and achievement full sway, and the demon of inequality will quickly raise its ugly head.

If, then, the natural inequality of ability and of interest among men must make elites inevitable, the only sensible course is to abandon the chimera of equality and accept the universal necessity of leaders and followers. The task of the Libertarian, the person dedicated to the idea of the free society, is not to inveigh against elites which, like the need for freedom, flow directly from the nature of man. The goal of the Libertarian is rather to establish a free society, a society in which each man is free to find his best level. In such a free society, everyone will be "equal" only in liberty, while diverse and unequal in all other respects. In this society the elites, like everyone else, will be free to rise to their best level. In Jeffersonian terminology, we will discover "natural aristocracies" who will rise to prominence and leadership in every field. The point is to allow the rise of these natural aristocracies, but not the rule of "artificial aristocracies"—those who rule by means of coercion. The artificial aristocrats, the *coercive* oligarchs, are the men who rise to power by invading the liberties of their fellowmen, by denying them their freedom. On the contrary, the natural aristocrats live in freedom and harmony with their fellows, and rise by exercising their individuality and their highest abilities in the service of their fellows, either in an organization or by producing efficiently for the consumers. In fact, the coercive oligarchs invariably rise to power by suppressing the natural elites, along with other men; the two kinds of leadership are antithetical.

Let us take a hypothetical example of a possible case of such conflict between different kinds of elites. A large group of people voluntarily engage in professional football, selling their services to an eager consuming public. Quickly rising to the top is a natural elite of the best—the most able and dedicated—football players, coaches, and organizers of the game. Here we have an example of the rise of a natural elite in a free society. Then, the power elite in control of the government decides in its wisdom that all professional athletics, and especially football, are evil. The government then decrees that pro football is outlawed and orders everyone to take part instead in a local eurythmics club as a mass-participatory substitute. Here the rulers of the government are clearly a coercive oligarchy, an "artificial elite," using force to repress a voluntary or natural elite (as well as the rest of the population).

The libertarian view of freedom, government, individuality, envy, and coercive *versus* natural elites has never been put more concisely or with greater verve than by H.L. Mencken:

> All government, in its essence, is a conspiracy against the superior man: its one permanent object is to oppress him and cripple him. If it be aristocratic in organization, then it seeks to protect the man who is superior only in law against the man who is superior in fact; if it be democratic, then it seeks to protect the man who is inferior in every way against both. One of its primary functions is to regiment men by force, to make them as much alike as possible and as dependent upon one another as possible, to search out and combat originality among men. All it can see in an original idea is potential change, and hence an invasion of its prerogatives. The most dangerous man to any government is the man who is able to think things out for himself, without regard to the prevailing superstitions and taboos.[51]

Similarly, the libertarian writer Albert Jay Nock saw in the political conflicts between Left and Right:

> simply a tussle between two groups of mass-men, one large and poor, the other small and rich. . . . The object of the tussle was the material gains accruing from control of the State's machinery. It is easier to seize wealth (from the

---

[51]H.L. Mencken, *A Mencken Chrestomathy* (New York: Alfred A. Knopf, 1949), p. 145.

producers) than to produce it; and as long as the State makes the seizure of wealth a matter of legalized privilege, so long will the squabble for that privilege go on.[52]

Helmut Schoeck's *Envy* makes a powerful case for the view that the modern egalitarian drive for socialism and similar doctrines is a pandering to envy of the different and the unequal, but the socialist attempt to eliminate envy through egalitarianism can never hope to succeed. For there will always be personal differences, such as looks, ability, health, and good or bad fortune, which no egalitarian program, however rigorous, can stamp out, and on which envy will be able to fasten its concerns.

POSTSCRIPT

In the two decades since this essay was written (1971), the major social trends I analyzed have accelerated, seemingly at an exponential rate. The flight away from socialism and central planning begun in Yugoslavia has stunningly succeeded over the entire "socialist bloc" of Eastern Europe, and there is now at least rhetorical allegiance to the idea of privatization and a free-market economy. More and more, Marxism has become confined to the academics of the United States and Western Europe, comfortably ensconced as parasites upon their capitalist economies. But even among academics, there is almost nothing left of the triumphalist Marxism of the 1930s and 1940s, with their boasts of the economic efficiency and superiority of socialist central planning. Instead, even the most dedicated Marxists now pay lip-service to the necessity of some sort of "market," however restricted by government.

---

[52]Albert Jay Nock, *Memoirs of a Superfluous Man* (New York: Harper, 1943), p. 121.

NEW AREAS OF INEQUALITY AND "OPPRESSION"

But this does not mean that the struggle over egalitarianism is over. Far from it. On the contrary, after the New Left of the late 1960s and early 1970s had been discredited by its bizarre turn to violence, it took the advice of its liberal elders and "joined the system." New Leftists launched a successful Gramscian "long march through the institutions," and by becoming lawyers and academics—particularly in the humanities, philosophy, and the "soft" social sciences—they have managed to acquire hegemony over our culture. Seeing themselves defeated and routed on the strictly economic front (in contrast to the Old Left of the 1930s, Marxian economics and the labor theory of value was never the New Left's strong suit), the Left turned to the allegedly moral high ground of egalitarianism. And, as they did so, they turned increasingly to de-emphasizing old-fashioned economic egalitarianism in favor of stamping out broader aspects of human variety. Older egalitarianism stressed making income or wealth equal; but, as Helmut Schoeck brilliantly realized, the logic of their argument was to stamp out, in the name of "fairness," all instances of human diversity and therefore implicit or explicit superiority of some persons over others. In short, envy of the superiority of others is to be institutionalized, and all possible sources of such envy eradicated.

In his book on *Envy*, Helmut Schoeck analyzed a chilling dystopian novel by the British writer, L.P. Hartley. In his work, *Facial Justice*, published in 1960, Hartley, extrapolating from the attitudes he saw in British life after World War II, opens by noting that after the Third World War, "Justice had made great strides." Economic justice, social justice, and other forms of justice had been achieved, but there were still areas of life to conquer. In particular, facial justice had not yet been attained, since pretty girls had an unfair advantage over ugly ones. Hence, under the direction of the Ministry of Face Equality, all alpha (pretty) girls and all gamma (ugly) girls were forced to undergo operations at the "Equalization (Faces) Centre" so as all to attain beta (pleasantly average) faces.[1]

Coincidentally, in 1961, Kurt Vonnegut published a pithy and even more bitterly satirical short story depicting a comprehensively egalitarian society, even more thoroughgoing than Hartley's. Vonnegut's "Harrison Bergeron" begins:

> The year was 2081, and everybody was finally equal. They weren't only equal before God and the law. They were equal every which way. Nobody was smarter than anybody else. Nobody was better looking than anybody else. Nobody was stronger or quicker than anybody else. All this equality was due to the 211th, 212th, and 213th Amendments to the Constitution, and to the unceasing vigilance of agents of the United States Handicapper General.

The "handicapping" worked partly as follows.

> Hazel had a perfectly average intelligence, which meant she couldn't think about anything except in short bursts. And George, while his intelligence was way above normal, had a little mental handicap radio in his ear. He was required by law to wear it at all times. It was tuned to a government transmitter. Every twenty minutes or so, the transmitter would send out some sharp noise to keep people like George from taking unfair advantage of their brains.[2]

This sort of egalitarian emphasis on noneconomic inequalities has proliferated and intensified in the decades

---

[1]See the discussion in Helmut Schoeck, *Envy: A Theory of Social Behavior* (New York: Harcourt, Brace and World, 1970), pp. 149–55. Schoeck's work was originally published in German in 1966 under the title *Der Neid*, and the English translation was first published in 1969.

[2]Kurt Vonnegut, Jr., "Harrison Bergeron" (1961), in *Welcome to the Monkey House* (New York: Dell, 1970), p. 7.

since these men penned their seemingly exaggerated Orwellian dystopias. In academic and literary circles "Political Correctness" is now enforced with an increasingly iron hand; and the key to being politically correct is never, ever, in any area, to make judgments of difference or superiority. Thus, we find that a Smith College handout from the Office of Student Affairs lists ten different kinds of "oppression" allegedly inflicted by making judgments about people. They include: "heterosexism," defined as "oppression" of those with nonheterosexual orientations, which include "not acknowledging their existence"; and "ableism," defined as oppression of the "differently abled" (known in less enlightened days as "disabled" or "handicapped"), by the "temporarily able." Particularly relevant to our two dystopian writers is "ageism," oppression of the young and the old by youngish and middle-aged adults, and "lookism" (or "looksism"), defined as the "construction of a standard of beauty–attractiveness." "Oppression" is also supposed to consist not only of discriminating in some way against the unattractive, but even in noticing the difference. Perhaps the most chilling recently created category is "logism" or "logo-centric," the tyranny of the knowledgeable and articulate. A set of "feminist scholarship guidelines" sponsored by the state of New Jersey for its college campuses attacks knowledge and scientific inquiry *per se* as a male "rape of nature." It charges: "mind was male. Nature was female, and knowledge was created as an act of aggression—a passive nature had to be interrogated, unclothed, penetrated, and compelled by man to reveal her secrets."[3]

---

[3]John Taylor, "Are You Politically Correct?" *New York* (January 21, 1991): 38. Also see ibid., pp. 32–40; "Taking Offense," *Newsweek* (December 24, 1990): 48–54.

"Oppression" is of course broadly defined so as to indict the very existence of possible superiority—and therefore an occasion for envy—in any realm. The dominant literary theory of deconstructionism fiercely argues that there can be no standards to judge one literary "text" superior to another. At a recent conference, when one political science professor referred correctly to Czeslaw Milosz's book *The Captive Mind* as a "classic," another female professor declared that the very word classic "makes me feel oppressed."[4] The clear implication is that any reference to someone else's superior product may engender resentment and envy in the rank-and-file, and that catering to these "feelings of oppression" must be the central focus of scholarship and criticism.

The whole point of academia and other research institutions has always been an untrammelled search for truth. This ideal has now been challenged and superseded by catering to the "sensitive" feelings of the politically correct. This emphasis on subjective feelings rather than truth is evident in the current furor over the teaching of the distinguished Berkeley anthropologist, Vincent Sarich. Sarich's examination of genetic influences on racial differences in achievement was denounced by a fellow faculty member as "attempting to destroy the self-esteem of black students in the class."[5]

GROUP QUOTAS

Indeed, one radical change since the writing of this essay has been the rapid and accelerating transformation of old-fashioned egalitarianism, which wanted to make every individual

---

[4]*Newsweek* (December 24, 1990): 53.

[5]Paul Selvin, "The Raging Bull of Berkeley," *Science* 251 (January 25, 1991): 369.

equal, into group-egalitarianism on behalf of groups that are officially designated as "oppressed." In employment, positions, and status generally, oppressed groups are supposed to be guaranteed their quotal share of the well-paid or prestigious positions. (No one seems to be agitating for quotal representation in the ranks of ditch diggers.) I first noticed this trend in a paper written one year after the present essay at a symposium on The Nature and Consequences of Egalitarian Ideology. There I reacted strongly to the quotal representation for designated groups insisted upon by the McGovern movement at the 1972 Democratic Convention. These victorious Democrats insisted that groups such as women, youth, blacks, and Chicanos had fallen below their quotal proportion of the population as elected delegates to previous conventions; this had to be rectified by the Democratic Party overriding the choices of their members and insisting upon due quotal representation of these allegedly oppressed groups. I noted the particular idiocy of the claim that youths aged 18–25 had been grievously "underrepresented" in the past, and indulged in what would now be called a "politically inappropriate" *reductio ad absurdum* by suggesting an immediate correction to the heinous and chronic underrepresentation of five-year-old "men and women."[6]

And yet, only two years before that convention, another form of quotal appeal had met with proper scorn and ridicule from Left-liberals. When one of President Nixon's failed Supreme Court nominees was derided as being "mediocre," Senator Roman Hruska (R., Neb.) wondered why the mediocre folk of America did not deserve "representation"

---

[6]Murray Rothbard, "Egalitarianism as a Revolt Against Nature," in *Egalitarianism as a Revolt Against Nature and Other Essays* (chap. 1, present work).

on the highest Court. Liberal critics mockingly charged the senator with engaging in special pleading. The self-same charge, levelled against denouncers of "logism," would drive such critics from public life. But times, and standards of political correctness, have changed.

It is difficult, indeed, to parody or satirize a movement which seems to be a living self-parody, and which can bring about such deplorable results. Thus, two eminent American historians, Bernard Bailyn and Stephan Thernstrom, were literally forced to abandon their course at Harvard on the history of American race relations, because of absurd charges of "racism" levelled by a few students, charges that were treated with utmost seriousness by everyone concerned. Of particular interest here was the charge against Bailyn's course on race relations in the colonial era. The student "grievance" against Bailyn is that he had read from the diary of a southern planter without giving "equal time" to the memoirs of a slave. To the complainants, this practice clearly amounted to a "covert defense of slavery." Bailyn had patiently explained during the offending lecture that no diaries, journals, or letters by slaves in that era had ever been found. But to these students, Bailyn had clearly failed to understand the problem: "Since it was impossible to give equal representation to the slaves, Bailyn ought to have dispensed with the planter's diary altogether."[7]

Spokesmen for group quotas on behalf of the "oppressed" (labelled for public relations purposes with the positive-sounding phrase "affirmative action") generally claim that a quota system is the furthest thing from their minds: that all they want is positive action to increase representation of the

---

[7]Taylor, "Are You Politically Correct?" p. 33.

favored groups. They are either being flagrantly disingenu-
ous or else fail to understand elementary arithmetic. If
Oppressed Group X is to have its "representation" increased
from, say, 8 to 20 percent, then *some* group or combination of
groups is going to have their total representation reduced by
12 percent. The hidden, or sometimes not so hidden, agenda,
of course, is that the quotal declines are supposed to occur in
the ranks of designated Oppressor Groups, who presumably
deserve their fate.

WHO ARE THE "OPPRESSED"?

In this regime of group egalitarianism, it becomes particularly important to take one's place in the ranks of the
oppressed rather than the oppressors. Who, then, are the
oppressed? It is difficult to determine, since new groups of
oppressed are being discovered all the time. One almost
longs for the good old days of classic Marxism, when there
was only one "oppressed class"—the proletariat—and one or
at most a very few classes of oppressors: the capitalists or
bourgeois, plus sometimes the "feudal landlords" or perhaps
the *petit bourgeoisie*. But now, as the ranks of the oppressed
and therefore the groups specially privileged by society and
the State keep multiplying, and the ranks of the oppressors
keep dwindling, the problem of income and wealth egalitarianism reappears and is redoubled. For more and greater vari-
eties of groups are continually being added to the parasitic
burden weighing upon an ever-dwindling supply of oppressors. And since it is obviously worth everyone's while to leave
the ranks of the oppressors and move over to the oppressed,
pressure groups will increasingly succeed in doing so—so
long as this dysfunctional ideology continues to flourish.

Specifically, achieving the label of Officially Oppressed
entitles one to share in an endless flow of benefits—in
money, status, and prestige—from the hapless oppressors,

who are made to feel guilty forevermore, even as they are forced to sustain and expand the endless flow. It is not surprising that attaining oppressed status takes a great deal of pressure and organization. As Joseph Sobran wittily puts it: "it takes a lot of clout to be a victim." Eventually, if trends continue the result must be the twin death of parasite and host alike, and an end to any flourishing economy or civilization.

There are virtually an infinite number of groups or "classes" in society: the class of people named Smith, the class of men over six feet tall, the class of bald people, and so on. Which of these groups may find themselves among the "oppressed"? Who knows? It is easy to invent a new oppressed group. I might come up with a study, for example, demonstrating that the class of people named "Doe" have an average income, wealth, or status lower than that of other names. I could then coin a hypothesis that people named Doe have been discriminated against because their names "John Doe" and "Jane Doe" have been "stereotyped" as associated with faceless anonymity, and presto, we have one more group who is able to leave the burdened ranks of the oppressors and join the happy ranks of the oppressed.

A political theorist friend of mine thought he could coin a satiric Oppressed Group: Short People, Who Suffer From Heightism. I informed him that he was seriously anticipated two decades ago, again demonstrating the impossibility of parodying the current ideology. I noted in an article almost twenty years ago, written shortly after this essay, that Professor Saul D. Feldman, a sociologist at Case-Western Reserve, and himself a distinguished short, had at last brought science to bear on the age-old oppression of the shorts by the talls. Feldman reported that out of recent University of Pittsburgh graduating seniors, those 6 feet 2 inches and taller received an average starting salary 12.4 percent higher than graduates under 6 feet, and that a marketing professor at Eastern Michigan University had quizzed 140 business recruiters about their preferences between two hypothetical, equally qualified applicants for the job of salesman. One of the hypothetical salesmen was to be 6 feet 1 inch, the other 5 feet 5 inches. The recruiters answered as follows: 27 percent expressed the politically correct no preference; 1 percent would hire the short man; and no less than 72 percent would hire the tallie.

In addition to this clear-cut oppression of talls over shorts, Feldman pointed out that women notoriously prefer tall over short men. He might have pointed out, too, that Alan Ladd could only play the romantic lead in movies produced by bigoted Hollywood moguls by standing on a hidden box, and that even the great character actor Sydney Greenstreet was invariably shot upward from a low-placed camera to make him appear much taller than he was. (The Hollywood studio heads were generally short themselves, but were betraying their short comrades by pandering to the pro-tall culture.) Feldman also perceptively pointed to the antishort prejudice that pervades our language: in such phrases as people being "short-sighted, shortchanged, short-circuited, and short in cash." He added that among the two major party candidates for president, the taller is almost invariably elected.[8]

---

[8]Feldman's case would have been strengthened had he written after the 1988 campaign; not only did Bush tower over Dukakis, but Representative Charles Wilson (D., Texas) was able to express the tallist bigotry of his region: "No Greek dwarf can carry East Texas," without calling forth protests and marches by organized short-dom. On the Feldman study, see Arthur J. Snider, "Society Favors Tall Men: Proof,"

I went on in my article to call for a short liberation movement to end short oppression, and asked: where are the short
corporation leaders, the short bankers, the short senators and
presidents?[9,10] I asked for short pride, short institutes, short
history courses, short quotas everywhere, and for shorts to
stop internalizing the age-old propaganda of our tall culture
that shorts are genetically or culturally inferior. (Look at
Napoleon!) Short people, arise! You have nothing to lose but
your elevator shoes. I ended by assuring the tallies that we
were *not* antitall, and that we welcome progressive, guilt-ridden talls as pro-short sympathizers and auxiliaries in our
movement. If my own consciousness had been sufficiently
raised at the time, I would have, of course, added a demand
that the talls compensate the shorts for umpteen thousand
years of tall tyranny.

THE ROMANTICS AND PRIMITIVISM

Turning from the topic of the oppressed, my own view of the
Romantics, certainly jaundiced twenty years ago, is far more
hostile today. For I have learned, from such sources as Leszek
Kolakowski and particularly the great literary critic M.H.
Abrams, of the devotion of the Romantics, Hegelians, and of
Marxism to what might be called "reabsorption theology."

New York *Post* (February 19, 1972). On all of this, see Murray N.
Rothbard, "Short People, Arise!" *The Libertarian Forum* 4 (April, 1972): 8.

[9]It might be instructive to study whether the savage treatment accorded to Senator John Tower in his confirmation hearings for Secretary of
Defense was due to discrmination against his short size.

[10]A possible project for American historians: most of the big business
tycoons of the late-nineteenth century (for example, Jay Gould and John D.
Rockefeller, Sr.) were very short. By what process did the tallies quietly
seize power in the corporate world?

This view stemmed from the third-century Egyptian Platonist, Plotinus, seeping into Christian Platonism, and from then on constituting a heretical and mystical underground in Western thought. Briefly, these thinkers saw Creation not as a wonderfully benevolent overflow of God's goodness, but as an essentially evil act that sundered the blessed pre-creation unity of the collective entities God, Man, and Nature, bringing about tragic and inevitable "alienation" in Man. However, creation, the outgrowth of God's deficiencies, is redeemable in one sense: history is an inevitable "dialectical" process by which pre-creation gives rise to its opposite, the current world. But eventually history is destined to end in a mighty "reabsorption" of these three collective entities, though at a much higher level of development for both God and man. In addition to other problems with this view, the contrast with orthodox Christianity should be clear. Whereas in Christianity, the individual person is made in God's image and the salvation of each individual is of supreme importance, the allegedly benevolent reabsorptionist escape from metaphysical alienation occurs only at the end of history and only for the collective species man, each individual disappearing into the species–organism.[11]

---

[11]See Leszek Kolakowski, *Main Currents of Marxism*, vol. 1, *The Founders* (Oxford: Oxford University Press, 1981), pp. 9–39; idem, *Natural Supernaturalism: Tradition and Revolution in Romantic Literature* (New York: Norton, 1971); M.H. Abrams, "Apocalypse: Theme and Variations" in C.A. Patrides and Joseph Wittreich, eds., *The Apocalypse in English Renaissance Thought and Literature* (Ithaca, N.Y.: Cornell University Press, 1984), pp. 342–68; Ernest L. Tuveson, "The Millenarian Structure of *The Communist Manifesto*," in ibid., pp. 323–41; and Murray N. Rothbard, "Karl Marx: Communist as Religious Eschatologist," *The Review of Austrian Economics* 4 (1990): 123–79.

As for primitivism, later anthropological research has strengthened the view of this essay that primitive tribes, and premodern cultures generally, were marked, not by communism *à la* Engels and Polanyi, but by private property rights, markets, and monetary exchange. The work of the economist Bruce Benson has particularly highlighted this point.[12]

THE DIVISION OF LABOR

I have come to realize, since writing this essay, that I overweighted the contributions and importance of Adam Smith on the division of labor. And to my surprise, I did not sufficiently appreciate the contributions of Ludwig von Mises.

Despite the enormous emphasis on specialization and the division of labor in the *Wealth of Nations*, much of Smith's discussion was misplaced and misleading. In the first place, he placed undue importance on the division of labor *within* a factory (the famous pin-factory example), and scarcely considered the far more important division of labor among various industries and occupations. Second, there is the mischievous contradiction between the discussions in Book 1 and Book 5 in the *Wealth of Nations*. In Book 1, the division of labor is hailed as responsible for civilization as well as economic growth, and is also praised as expanding the alertness and intelligence of the population. But in Book 5 the division

---

[12]Bruce L. Benson, "Enforcement of Private Property Rights in Primitive Societies: Law Without Government," *Journal of Libertarian Studies* 9 (Winter, 1989): 1–26; and *The Enterprise of Law: Justice Without the State* (San Francisco: Pacific Research Institute for Public Policy, 1990), pp. 11–41. Also see Joseph R. Peden, "Property Rights in Celtic Irish Law," *Journal of Libertarian Studies* 1 (1977): 81–95; and David Friedman, "Private Creation and Enforcement of Law: A Historical Case," *Journal of Legal Studies* 8 (March, 1979): 399–415.

of labor is condemned as leading to the intellectual and moral degeneration of the same population, and to the loss of their "intellectual, social, and martial virtues." These complaints about the division of labor as well as similar themes in Smith's close friend Adam Ferguson, strongly influenced the griping about "alienation" in Marx and later socialist writers.[13]

But of greater fundamental importance was Smith's abandonment of the tradition, since Jean Buridan and the Scholastics, that emphasized that two parties always undertook an exchange because each expected to gain from the transaction. In contrast to this emphasis on specialization and exchange as a result of conscious human decision, Smith shifted the focus from mutual benefit to an alleged irrational and innate "propensity to truck, barter, and exchange," as if human beings were lemmings determined by forces external to their own chosen purposes. As Edwin Cannan pointed out long ago, Smith took this tack because he rejected the idea of innate differences in human talents and abilities, differences which would naturally lead people to seek out different specialized occupations.[14] Smith instead took an egalitarian-environmentalist position, still dominant today in neo-classical economics, holding that all men are uniform and equal, and therefore that differences in labor or occupations can only be the *result* rather than a cause of the system of division of labor. Moreover, Smith inaugurated the corollary tradition

---

[13]On Ferguson's influence, see Abrams, *Natural Supernaturalism*, pp. 220–21, 508.

[14]Edwin Cannan, *A History of the Theories of Production and Distribution in English Political Economy from 1776 to 1848* (3rd ed., London: Staples Press, 1917), p. 35.

that differences in wage rates among this uniform population can only reflect differences in the cost of training.[15,16]

In contrast, the recent work of Professor Joseph Salerno has illuminated the profound contributions of Ludwig von Mises's emphasis on the division of labor as the "essence of society" and the "fundamental social phenomenon." For Mises, as I wrote in the essay, the division of labor stems from the diversity and inequality of human beings and of nature. Salerno, in addition, brings out with unparalleled clarity that for Mises the division of labor is a conscious choice of mutual gain and economic development. The process of social evolution therefore becomes "the development of the division of labor," and this allows Mises to refer to the worldwide division of labor as a vital "social organism" or "*oecumene.*" Mises also points out that division of labor is at the heart of biological organisms, and "the fundamental principle of all forms of life." The difference of the "social organism" is that, in contrast to biological organisms, "reason and will are the originating and sustaining form of the organic coalescence."

---

[15]Contrast Smith's egalitarianism with the great early-fifteenth-century Italian Scholastic, San Bernardino of Siena (1380–1444). In his *On Contracts and Usury*, written in 1431–33, Bernardino pointed out that wage inequality on the market is a function of differences of ability and skill as well as training. An architect is paid more than a ditch digger, Bernardino explained, because the former's job requires more intelligence and ability as well as training, so that fewer men will qualify for the task. See Raymond de Roover, *San Bernardino of Siena and Sant' Antonio of Florence, The Two Great Thinkers of the Middle Ages* (Boston: Baker Library, 1967), and Alejandro Chafuen, *Christians for Freedom: Late Scholastic Economics* (San Francisco: Ignatius Press, 1986), pp. 123–31.

[16]Modern neoclassical labor economics fits in this tradition by defining "discrimination" as any wage inequalities greater than differences in the cost of training. Thus, see the standard work by Gary Becker, *The Economics of Discrimination* (Chicago: University of Chicago Press, 1957).

Therefore, for Mises "human society is thus spiritual and teleological," the "product of thought and will." It therefore becomes of the utmost importance for people to understand the significance of maintaining and expanding the *oecumene* that consists of the free market and voluntary human exchanges, and to realize that breaching and crippling that market and *oecumene* can only have disastrous consequences for the human race.[17]

In the standard account, writers and social theorists are supposed to mellow and moderate their views as they get older. (Two glorious exceptions to this rule are such very different libertarian figures as Lysander Spooner and Lord Acton.) Looking back over the two decades since writing this essay, it is clear that my views, on the contrary, have radicalized and polarized even further. As unlikely as it would have seemed twenty years ago, I am even more hostile to socialism, egalitarianism, and Romanticism, far more critical of the British classical and modern neoclassical tradition, and even more appreciative of Mises's great insights than ever before. Indeed, for someone who thought that he had absorbed all of Mises's work many years ago, it is a constant source of surprise how rereading Mises continues to provide a source of fresh insights and of new ways of looking at seemingly trite situations. This phenomenon, in

---

[17]Joseph T. Salerno, "Ludwig von Mises as Social Rationalist," *The Review of Austrian Economics* 4 (1990): 26–54. See also Salerno's critique of Eamonn Butler's uncomprehending reaction to Mises's insights, charging Mises with the "organic fallacy," and "difficulty with English." Ibid., p. 29n. The implicit contrast of Mises's view with Hayek's emphasis on unconscious action and blind adherence to traditional rules is made explicit by Salerno in the latter part of this article dealing with the socialist calculation debate, and in Salerno, "Postscript," in Ludwig von Mises, *Economic Calculation in the Socialist Commonwealth* (Auburn, Ala.: Ludwig von Mises Institute, 1990), pp. 51–71.

which many of us have experience, bears testimony to the remarkable quality and richness of Mises's thought. Although he died almost two decades ago, Ludwig von Mises remains more truly alive than most of our conventionally wise contemporaries.

Index

Prepared by Richard Perry

justice vs body

About the Author

Murray N. Rothbard (1926-1995), the author of 25 books and thousands of articles, was dean of the Austrian School of economics, restorer of the Old Right, and founder of modern libertarianism. The S.J. Hall Distinguished Professor of Economics at the University of Nevada, Las Vegas, he was also Academic Vice President of the Ludwig von Mises Institute.

Made in United States
Orlando, FL
25 September 2024

51954760R00192